The Rest Is Silence

THE LEWIS WALPOLE SERIES IN EIGHTEENTH-CENTURY CULTURE AND HISTORY

The Lewis Walpole Series, published by Yale University Press with the aid of the Annie Burr Lewis Fund, is dedicated to the culture and history of the long eighteenth century (from the Glorious Revolution to the accession of Queen Victoria). It welcomes work in a variety of fields, including literature and history, the visual arts, political philosophy, music, legal history, and the history of science. In addition to original scholarly work, the series publishes new editions and translations of writing from the period, as well as reprints of major books that are currently unavailable. Though the majority of books in the series will probably concentrate on Great Britain and the Continent, the range of our geographical interests is as wide as Horace Walpole's.

The Rest Is Silence

Enlightenment Philosophers Facing Death

JOANNA STALNAKER

Yale UNIVERSITY PRESS

New Haven and London

Published with assistance from the Annie Burr Lewis Fund, and from the foundation established in memory of Amasa Stone Mather of the Class of 1907, Yale College.

Yale University Press books may be purchased in quantity for educational, business, or promotional use. For information, please e-mail sales.press@yale.edu (U.S. office) or sales@yaleup.co.uk (U.K. office).

Set in Minion Pro type by IDS Infotech Ltd.
Printed in the United States of America.

ISBN 978-0-300-18134-0 (hardcover)
Library of Congress Control Number: 2025934545
A catalogue record for this book is available from the British Library.

Authorized Representative in the EU: Easy Access System Europe, Mustamäe tee 50, 10621 Tallinn, Estonia, gpsr.requests@easproject.com

10 9 8 7 6 5 4 3 2 1

In Memoriam

Saskia Hamilton

Patrizia Lombardo

Brigitte Mahuzier

Alain Viala

Phil Watts

Muriel Ida Massett Younger

Yuko

Why retell the stories of those before us? They already spoke them, or held their tongues—fell silent.

—ALL SOULS, *published posthumously by Saskia Hamilton (1967–2023)*

Contents

Preface

Parce que c'était elle, parce que c'était moi
(Because it was she, because it was me)

This book is dedicated to Kate E. Tunstall, and to Marie de Vichy-Chamrond, marquise du Deffand.

My dear friend Kate gave me the title for this book, *The Rest Is Silence* (on loan from Shakespeare, these are Hamlet's last words). She also carried me, along with so many other loving hands, through a long undiagnosed brain fog and ensuing emergency craniotomy, on April 9, 2023, Easter Sunday. I was heavy. She was further burdened by the twin losses of her beloved Alain Viala and her incomparable mother. Still, she held me up. Her title—given to me prior to my operation, when she knew I was terribly unwell but no one knew why—became my mantra in recovery, when sleep eluded me, and I was manic due to post-operative euphoria and steroids taken to reduce the dangerous swelling in my brain. As I write this dedication, I am two weeks post-craniotomy. Yesterday, or the day before, I found a subtitle for this book. So, put together, it is our shared title, from our hive brain. Years earlier, on a walk in Riverside Park beneath centenarian trees, Kate had asked me a question that transformed the book and eventually gave me its argument. When I told her I was writing a book about the deaths of Buffon, Diderot, Rousseau, and Voltaire, she asked me, with her inimitable wit, "Didn't women also die in the eighteenth century?" To Kate, then.

This book is also dedicated to Marie de Vichy-Chamrond, marquise du Deffand, the writer who lies at its center. She was, according to her lifelong correspondent Voltaire, the rightful leader of the modern philosophers (or, as we call them today, Enlightenment *philosophes*). This was despite the fact that she despised them, with the notable exceptions of Voltaire himself and Michel de Montaigne, whom she considered the father of modern philosophy. And it was despite the fact that she rejected Voltaire's title for her, wanting no recognition for her writings or the brilliant philosophical mind he so admired. When asked to contribute the letters Voltaire had addressed to her to a posthumous edition of his correspondence, she refused, writing to Horace Walpole, "I don't want to give those I have from him, I don't want to give any occasion for myself to be spoken of."[1] One of my arguments in this book is that her refusal to be remembered after her death, through the publication of Voltaire's letters or her own, gave her a singularly clear-eyed view of what it meant to die as a nonbeliever. Deffand described ennui, the spiritual malady she feared almost more than death itself, as "a foretaste of nothingness [*un avant-goût du néant*]."[2] She, more than any of her male counterparts, faced the nothingness she believed she would enter upon her death, as a woman who had borne no children (the mortal's means of attaining immortality, according to Plato's Diotima), and had published nothing.

Yet she did bequeath her writings, along with her dog, Tonton, and a snuffbox adorned with the dog's wax portrait, to her beloved Walpole. And he, despite the shame he felt at their unusual, platonic love affair with its twenty-one-year age gap, preserved them and eventually ensured their publication. He also ordered that his own letters to Deffand be destroyed, with the exception of any passages his literary executrix, Mary Berry, deemed necessary for better understanding hers. This, of course, is the inverse of the situation we so often encounter, in which the correspondence of a famous man is preserved, while the letters of his female correspondent are lost or destroyed. Such is the case for the correspondence between another of the philosophers discussed in this book, Denis Diderot, and his lover, Sophie Volland. We can only dream of the brilliant philosophical mind she might have had, just as Diderot could only dream in a letter to her of a postmortem reunion between their dispersed molecules beyond the grave.[3] How did she respond to that famous letter? We will never know. As the sculptor Étienne Maurice Falconet wrote to Diderot in their exchange of letters about posthumous glory, "Women in general, as well as many men, leave nothing to posterity. When they finish, it is *omnino* [completely]."[4] In Deffand's case, it is thanks to her bequest, and to Walpole's efforts to ensure the preservation of her writings, that her voice is not entirely lost to us. Still, Deffand got her wish: she has been largely forgotten, like so many other women who wrote in her day. At the time of writing, her English Google search result, otherwise accurate, inexplicably identifies her as a French television presenter.[5] She is nearly absent from Dena Goodman's classic work of feminist historiography, *The Republic of Letters,* which first put the *salonnières* on the Enlightenment map. My chapters on Deffand could not have been written without Goodman's pathbreaking book. Yet recognition for Deffand's brilliant philosophical mind and consummate literary style is long overdue. Even if she wouldn't have wanted it, this book seeks to restore her to her rightful place of prominence among Enlightenment philosophers, as a *salonnière*-philosopher. Above all, it seeks to cement her status as a great writer. Deffand is a single woman among the many men I discuss, but she occupies the last two, and most important, chapters of this book. In facing death more squarely than any of her male counterparts, I argue, she proved herself the most radical of Enlightenment philosophers.

Forgive me, Madame du Deffand, for disturbing your nothingness. You did not believe you could turn over in your grave, but maybe you weren't entirely sure, and maybe that was what you feared most of all. Ennui, your lifelong nemesis, was your foretaste of nothingness. Post-craniotomy, after nearly losing myself during two years of brain fog, and then being saved by the most humane of surgeons, I have had my brief taste too. Or, as the Montaigne we both love(d) put it, I have shaken death's hand. I count my material soul blessed in that, as in so much more. "Absorbing, mysterious, of infinite richness, this life."[6] *Mrs. Dalloway* came too late for you to read it. And your blindness deprived you of the solace of reading and writing during your sleepless nights, when your secretary, Jean-François Wiart, was not at your bedside. In the last letter you included in a manuscript collection of letters you bequeathed to Walpole, you ended with these words: "Don't worry at all about my health, I don't feel any pain, that is saying a lot. I would so like it to be the same for you and that that wretched gout not come back anymore; if that could be and if I could sleep, I would be happy."[7] May you now rest in the peace of your nothingness. The rest is silence.

A Note on Translations

I regret that for reasons of space I have been unable to provide the original French for most of my quotations, despite my deep attachment to subtleties of language. I have, however, provided the French, followed by an English translation, for all verse quotations, and for a few prose quotations where the syntax or wording seemed especially important. Unless otherwise indicated (notably for Montaigne), all translations are my own.

The Rest Is Silence

Introduction

We think of the Enlightenment as forward-looking. This makes sense intuitively because the Enlightenment shaped the world we live in. Enlightenment philosophy abounds in metaphors and narratives that encourage this view, from John Locke's blank slate to Jean-Jacques Rousseau's story of the passage from the state of nature to civil society. Immanuel Kant was among the first to define Enlightenment in forward-looking terms, as "man's emergence from his self-incurred immaturity."[1] For Kant, Enlightenment was a process that had not yet been fully realized in 1784, when he sent his answer to the question "Was ist Aufklärung?" (What Is Enlightenment?) to a Berlin newspaper. Answering the same question two hundred years later, in "Qu'est-ce que les Lumières?," Michel Foucault did not diverge fundamentally from Kant's progressive understanding of Enlightenment. For him, the ongoing critical project of Enlightenment was a historical and practical study of the limits on human freedom that was oriented toward liberation at some undefined point in the future.[2]

This book does not seek to dislodge such definitions. Nor does it deny that the Enlightenment contributed to the formation of modern political and social ideals, as Jonathan Israel and others have argued.[3] But it turns our habitual perspective on the

1

Enlightenment on its head, by bringing to light a set of works written at the end of the Old Regime and at the end of their authors' lives. These works differ in genre, style, and philosophical outlook. But they all cast a retrospective glance over the intellectual movement their authors participated in, and over the authors' own lives and works. Read collectively, they also convey the idea that ensuring a posthumous legacy is by no means guaranteed. Indeed, I argue that the inventiveness and beauty of these works stem from their authors' efforts to give literary form to the corporeal ephemerality of human existence and the embrace of nothingness that, for them, death entailed. It is not surprising that we should find in last works a preoccupation with writing as a means of reaching posterity. What is surprising is the extent to which Enlightenment writers embraced in their last works the possibility that neither their names nor their writings would survive long beyond the decomposition of their bodies.

If the Enlightenment's embrace of oblivion has long gone unnoticed, it is perhaps because it runs counter to our own faith in the enduring power of Enlightenment ideals. What was distinctive about the Enlightenment, according to Dan Edelstein, was the narrative its participants told about the power of the scientific revolution and their own philosophical movement to transform society, in the present and into the future.[4] The extent to which we still subscribe to that narrative today is a testament to its remarkable persistence. But as we witness a period of full-scale dismantling of Enlightenment ideals—from the rejection of science to the championing of prejudice over reason—we would do well to consider a very different story Enlightenment writers told about themselves. This was the story of their ending. It was the story of lives devoted to projects and writings potentially subject to the same fate as the body. This story has been forgotten in the wake of Carl L. Becker's classic claim that the eighteenth-century philosophers replaced the Christian faith in the afterworld with an equally fervent faith in posterity. Becker had ample evidence for his claim: he had only to quote Diderot, who wrote to Falconet that "posterity for the philosopher is the afterworld of the religious man."[5] But Becker overstated his case, neglecting to mention that the philosophers' faith in posterity was far from a tranquil one. In his last published work, the *Essai sur les règnes de Claude et de Néron* (*Essay on the Reigns of Claudius and Nero*), Diderot came around to Falconet's view of posterity, espousing the indifference he had once sought to refute. In battling Seneca's detractors and his own, he attacked the freshly buried Rousseau, accusing him of "augment[ing] his dust" through the writing of his *Confessions*.[6] Diderot, in contrast, envisaged in his last work the ultimate destruction of his corpus and the erasure of his name from history. And in this he was not alone.

One might be tempted to explain Diderot's end-of-life attitude in terms of his materialist beliefs. For him, to die was simply to change forms, to go from an organized mass to a dispersed collection of molecules. "To be born, to live and to pass is to change forms," says the fictional Jean le Rond d'Alembert in *Le rêve de d'Alembert* (*D'Alembert's Dream*).[7] This belief allowed Diderot to envisage the dissolution of his self, while also imagining the eventual intermingling of his molecules with those of his lover, Sophie Volland, beyond the grave. But writers of varying religious and philosophical persuasions shared Diderot's clear-eyed embrace of the descent into nothingness. Voltaire, generally considered a deist, and Marie de Vichy-Chamrond, marquise du Deffand, a *salonnière* who eschewed religion but was hostile to the materialists, regularly discussed in their remarkable correspondence the nothingness to which they would eventually succumb. In an especially somber disquisition, Deffand wrote that "there is, in considering it justly, but one misfortune in life, which is to be born. There is no state, whatever it may be, that seems to me preferable to nothingness."[8] In response to this, Voltaire quipped with his usual irony, "It is not that nothingness has no good in it; but I think it is impossible to truly love nothingness, for all its good qualities."[9] However flippant this response may seem, Voltaire went on to write a poem in which he addressed the allegorical figure of Nothingness directly, uttering these last words as he plunged into its midst:

> puisqu'en ton sein tout l'univers se plonge
> tien prend mes vers ma personne et mon songe.
> je porte envie au mortel fortuné
> qui t'apartient au moment qu'il est né.[10]

> [since into your breast all the universe plunges
> here take my verses my person and my dream.
> I envy that fortunate mortal
> who belongs to you from the moment he is born.]

These lines could hardly be further from the redemptive faith in posterity Becker attributed to the eighteenth-century philosophers. In his final embrace, the poet gives up not just his person but also his verses, echoing Deffand's wish never to have been born. In a similar vein, Rousseau claims in his *Rêveries du promeneur solitaire* (*Reveries of the Solitary Walker*) to care little for the fate of the pages he is writing. Although he, like Deffand, despised the materialists, he likens his last work to a fragile, material collection of plant fragments pressed into a herbarium, composed for himself alone and subject to the same eventual disintegration as his body.[11]

The lucidity with which these writers viewed their own deaths was part of a broader set of social and cultural changes. Historians have long recognized the eighteenth century as a key turning point in the history of death, as religious authorities battled to maintain their grip over last rites, and philosophers like Voltaire and David Hume sought to wrest their final moments from clerical control.[12] The death of Socrates—memorialized in a tragedy by Voltaire in 1759 and a painting by Jacques-Louis David in 1787—became a model not just for Enlightenment philosophers, but for all those who sought to avoid what Voltaire called the "abominable accoutrements with which they persecute the last moment of our life."[13] Inspired by the Stoics and the Roman poet and philosopher Lucretius, Enlightenment writers mounted a veritable campaign to free their readers from the fear of death.[14] The best-selling naturalist Georges-Louis Leclerc, comte de Buffon, and the radical materialist Paul-Henri Thiry, baron d'Holbach, were key players in this effort, each identifying the fear of death as yet another prejudice to be eradicated by the rational philosopher.[15] These male philosophers were especially concerned with rescuing women from the fear of death. D'Holbach's materialism was said to be inspired in part by his grief at his first wife's death and the spiritual misery she suffered on her deathbed, and his treatise on the fear of death, *Lettres à Eugénie,* was addressed to a woman.[16]

Philosophy evidently did not cure all women from the fear of death. For some, it may even have exacerbated it. Two of the most famous salon hostesses of the period, Deffand and Suzanne Curchod Necker, wife of the finance minister Jacques Necker and mother of the acclaimed writer Germaine de Staël, shared a morbidly obsessive fear of death.[17] But this fear did not prevent them from facing death more squarely than any of the male philosophers they hosted in their salons. With her relentless questioning and her stark view of nothingness, Deffand pushed Voltaire to confront the implications of death in a materialist framework. Necker's case was different, because unlike many of the philosophers in her salon, she maintained a staunch Protestant faith in the immortality of the human soul. Nonetheless, she was deeply marked by the work of her close friend Buffon and took his precept of paying close attention to the physical realities of death to lengths he never could have imagined. When she attended him at his deathbed, she not only cared for the needs of his body, but painstakingly documented the physical symptoms of his agony in the language of a naturalist. She also devoted herself to the care of the dead and dying in her role as administrator of the Hospice de Charité. Her pamphlet from 1790, *Des inhumations précipitées* (*On Premature Burials*), outlined the elaborate protocols she established to ensure her patients would not be buried prematurely, which included tending to corpses until they reached the state of putrefaction. Most famously, she left macabre directives for the preservation of her and her husband's corpses, which were to be embalmed in liquid and eventually reunited in a joint tomb. According to her daughter, Necker possessed a singular ability "to conceive of the entire idea of death in the midst of life."[18]

While extreme, Necker's obsession with death and premature burial was by no means an isolated phenomenon.[19] It reflected broader social and cultural trends that have been amply documented by historians of death over the past fifty years. More recently, Thomas W. Laqueur has offered a compelling counternarrative to the "narratives of disappearance, disenchantment, loss and secularization" he attributes to earlier historians of death.[20] For him, the decline in traditional death rituals at the end of the eighteenth century did not mean that the dead had lost their prestige. On the contrary, his *Work of the Dead* tells "a story of the ways in which the presence of the dead enchants our purportedly disenchanted world, a reinvention of enchantment in more democratic forms."[21] For all our modern unbelief, we still cannot subscribe to the Cynic philosopher Diogenes's claim that the dead body is nothing of significance. So we have invented new symbolic systems to reenchant the dead in the modern era. Laqueur also differs from earlier historians of death in setting aside his initial project of writing "a history of death as a historical project of the inner life."[22] Rather than addressing attitudes toward death, he focuses on the historical and cultural work that the dead—by which he means dead bodies—have done and continue to do for the living in modern times. This monumental contribution to the history of death has informed my much smaller-scale discussion of how individual philosophers faced death at the end of the Old Regime. But the questions I ask are somewhat different from those posed by Laqueur and earlier social and cultural historians of death. What interests me is a particular set of writings—chosen in part for their literary qualities—that give literary form to the Enlightenment understanding of death as a corporeal experience and an embrace of oblivion. As a literary scholar, I treat these writings not primarily as exemplars of broader social and cultural trends, but as works of individual expression that use the formal resources of language to grapple with the end of life and the end of an era. I discuss a diverse range of material, from Buffon's writings on minerals to Deffand's correspondence. Not all of it fits within a traditional understanding of literature or rises to the level of a masterpiece like Rousseau's *Rêveries du promeneur solitaire*. But we must take a broad view of literature if we wish to remain true to the way eighteenth-century writers saw their own literary landscape. Rousseau expressed the views of many of his contemporaries when he wrote that Buffon was "the most beautiful plume of his century; and I don't doubt at all that posterity will judge it so."[23] We must also take a broad view of literature if we wish, as I do, to recover the lost voices of women writers who were much admired in their own time but have been largely forgotten in ours. Many of them, like Deffand, wrote only letters and other occasional forms of writing such as salon portraits. In giving pride of place to Deffand's correspondence in a book about philosophy, I am indebted to Dena Goodman's insight that we should focus "on writing rather than authorship, and on the writing that women who write do, rather than on women writers."[24] It is also my conviction that despite the diversity of sources discussed in this book, only a sustained practice of literary criticism, of the kind described by Jonathan Kramnick in *Criticism and Truth*, can do justice to the artistry with which these writers cast a last glance over their lives and era.[25] Deffand was not just a *salonnière*-philosopher: she was also a great writer, and she deserves to be recognized as such.

At the same time, this book is intended to have broader implications for our understanding of the Enlightenment, in two respects. First, it offers an unusual perspective on the Enlightenment, one that looks backward rather than forward, from the vantage point of a moment in history when few, if any, of the future political and social gains now ascribed to eighteenth-century philosophy could be perceived with any clarity. It is important to the conception of the book that the authors I discuss all died at the tail end of the Old Regime (from Hume in 1776 to Buffon in 1788), but before the French Revolution. This means that their "sense of an ending," to borrow Frank Kermode's phrase, cannot be explained as a response to the dramatic political and social revolutions that transformed their world beyond recognition.[26] It is tempting to imagine how different their last works might have been had they died just a decade or so later. But in a certain sense, it is precisely their blindness to the future that lay just around the corner that makes their last writings so precious to us. We cannot assess the legacy of the Enlightenment without taking the French Revolution, and all the revolutions it inspired, into account. Whether we defend or attack the Enlightenment, it is always in terms of its relationship to our modern world; as Dorinda Outram puts it, "No other historical period has been depicted with such intensity in relation to our own."[27] To read the last works of the Enlightenment philosophers is to turn that perspective on its head, to be reminded of something that is too often overlooked: that they were by no means complacent about their legacy. On the contrary, they shared an acute sense that human progress is often subject to reversal, if not outright destruction. This was not just the view of an iconoclast like Rousseau, whose negative view of human history has led some to categorize him as a Counter-Enlightenment figure.[28] It was shared by Diderot, who in the preface to the eighth volume of the *Encyclopédie* meditated ruefully on the possible future destruction of everything the encyclopedists held dear. Of course, Diderot brandished the *Encyclopédie* itself as a bulwark against the potential toppling of cities and the return of ignorance and shadows. But even this was presented in the conditional: "If even a single complete copy of this work is preserved, all will not be lost."[29] For all those today who continue to ascribe naive metanarratives of human progress to the Enlightenment, this is a bracing reminder that Enlightenment writers placed just as much emphasis on the decline, destruction, and loss of human civilization as they did on its progress. And it is also a reminder, especially unsettling in our own times, that Enlightenment writers were eminently aware that nothing guaranteed the perpetuation of their legacy. This does not make that legacy any less precious. But it does underscore its fragility and suggest that new modes of reading and interpretation may be in order if we are to renew our understanding and appreciation of the Enlightenment.

Second, this book makes the argument for a literary approach to the Enlightenment as the necessary complement to historical and philosophical approaches (not that these are

mutually exclusive). In the end, death is first and foremost a
corporeal experience, as both Buffon and Diderot emphasized
in their reflections on the physiology of death. In the context
of eighteenth-century materialism, it is not surprising that so
much attention was paid to the material processes of death.
What my book documents, however, is the extent to which
Enlightenment writers invented at the end of their lives new
forms of writing to embody the fragility of the human body
and its eventual dissolution. This is most obvious in the case of
Rousseau, who presented his *Rêveries du promeneur solitaire*
both as a series of walks taken by a body in decline, and as a
collection of dead, severed plant fragments. It is impossible, in
my view, to grasp the philosophical meaning of such a work
without attending to its form and the metaphors Rousseau
elaborated to describe his body and his work. The same can be
said of all the works I discuss in this book. But the case for a
formal, literary approach to the Enlightenment, in conjunction
with historical and philosophical approaches, is not limited to
works concerned with the decline and death of the body. One
of the most distinctive features of Enlightenment philosophy,
more generally, is its attention to the resources of language and
dialogue. To define the Enlightenment in terms of "an abstract
package of basic values," as Israel has done, is to ignore one of
its most precious lessons: that philosophical ideas are forged in
dialogue and embodied in concrete forms, and that we must
attend closely to those forms—the philosophical dialogue, the
letter, the reverie, the collection of fragments—if we are to grasp
the ideas themselves.[30]

As Laqueur and others have shown, the deaths of two of
the philosophers discussed in this book—David Hume in 1776
and Voltaire in 1778—became flashpoints in the struggles surrounding last rites at the end of the Enlightenment.[31] Both men
knew that their final moments would be watched closely for

any signs of fear or any last-minute recusals of their philosophical beliefs. And both sought to shape the debates they
knew would follow close on the heels of their deaths. After
being diagnosed with intestinal cancer, Hume affirmed his
equanimity in the face of death in a brief self-portrait, *My Own
Life*, written just before he died. Voltaire did the same in his
1772 poem "Épître à Horace" ("Epistle to Horace"), although
unlike Hume he ended up recovering from his illness. In the
poem, he depicts himself on his deathbed, and calls upon his
doctor, Théodore Tronchin, to bear witness to his impassivity
in the face of death:

> Aussi, lorsque mon pouls inégal et pressé
> Faisait peur à Tronchin près de mon lit placé,
> Quand la vieille Atropos aux humains si sévère
> Approchait ses ciseaux de ma trame légère,
> Il a vu de quel air je prenais mon congé.
> Il sait si mon esprit, mon cœur était changé.[32]

> [So, when my pulse, irregular and racing,
> Put fear in Tronchin by my bedside,
> When the old Atropos to humans so severe
> Approached her scissors to my slender weft
> He saw with what air I took my leave.
> He knows if my mind, my heart was changed.]

Six years after this poem was written, Voltaire traveled from his
exile in Ferney to Paris for the last time, for the production of
his tragedy, *Irène*. It was there that he died, and most likely there
that he wrote another gorgeous and little-known poem, "Adieux
à la vie" ("Farewell to Life"). Both *My Own Life* and "Adieux à
la vie" are suffused with their authors' awareness of their impending deaths. These works embody what Edward Said, following Theodor Adorno, called late style in his own poignant

last work.[33] They are not unlike the modern American poems Helen Vendler beautifully explicates in her moving *Last Looks, Last Books*. There is, however, a specificity to the last works written at the end of the Enlightenment. The philosophers I discuss all faced the question of how to die an enlightened, philosophical death, worthy of Socrates. They also faced a question that lay beyond the scope of Socrates's non-writing life: how to write philosophically in the face of death.

This question brings me to a writer whose presence looms large in the pages of this book. More than any other work, Michel de Montaigne's *Essais* shaped the way Enlightenment writers thought about the relationship between writing and death. Montaigne's decision to retire from public life, in 1571 at the age of thirty-eight, and to surround himself with books and quotations in his solitary tower, has been seen in part as a response to the death of his beloved friend, Étienne de la Boétie. It was of this friend that he famously wrote, "*Parce que c'était lui, parce que c'était moi*" (Because it was he, because it was I).[34] The *Essais* were also centrally concerned with Montaigne's own death: in his opening address, "Au Lecteur" ("To the Reader"), he offered his book as a source of solace to his family and friends who, he predicted, would soon lose him. In a certain sense, his self-portrait, always in movement to keep pace with the restlessness of his mind, was meant to keep him alive for his loved ones and eventually for all his readers. At the same time, over the two decades Montaigne spent writing and revising his essays, they also became for him a means of "practicing" for death, of "trying it out to some extent."[35] As he so vividly put it in describing his experience of kidney stones in his last essay, "De l'expérience," "If you do not embrace death, at least you shake hands with it once a month."[36]

Montaigne's influence is perhaps most apparent in the case of Deffand, who found in the *Essais* a model for her skep-

tical and anti-systematic approach to philosophy. Her admiration for Montaigne is all the more striking in that she despised
most modern philosophers, with the notable exception of
Voltaire. In response to a letter from the latter she especially
admired, and after reading a philosophical tale that expressed
her own wish never to have been born, she wrote to Voltaire:
"Do you know the desire [your letter] gave me, along with your
Parable of the Brahmin? It is to throw into the fire all those
immense volumes of philosophy, except Montaigne who is
the father of them all; but in my opinion, he produced stupid
and boring children."[37] Voltaire shared Deffand's admiration
for Montaigne's Pyrrhonism, although he was more critical of
his style.[38] Deffand had a harder sell with Walpole. In one of his
few surviving letters to her, he lambasted Montaigne for his
pedantry, his disorderly writing style, and his futile obsession
with learning how to die: "I am reading Montaigne's *Essays,* and
find them even more boring than Bath;—it's truly pedantic
drivel, a rhapsody of disjointed commonplaces—he and his
Seneca kill themselves learning how to die—the thing in the
world one can be most sure to do without having learned how."[39]
Deffand must have found this last criticism especially jarring,
given her own obsession with learning how to die. She responded with a full-throated defense of Montaigne's style and
approach to philosophy:

> I am quite sure that you will get used to Montaigne;
> one finds in him everything one has ever thought,
> and no style is more energetic: he teaches nothing,
> because he decides nothing; it is the opposite of
> dogmatism: he is vain, but aren't all men? and those
> that appear modest, aren't they doubly vain? The *I*
> and the *me* are in each line, but what knowledge
> can one have, if it isn't the *I* and the *me?* Come now,

come now, my tutor, this is the only good philosopher, and only good metaphysician there has ever
been. They are rhapsodies, if you like, and perpetual contradictions; but he doesn't establish any system; he seeks and observes and remains in doubt:
he is useful for nothing, I admit that, but he detaches one from all opinions and destroys the pre-
sumption of knowledge.[40]

This defense of Montaigne gives us a precious window onto
Deffand's preferred approach to philosophy: skeptical, intro-
spective, and anti-systematic, written in an energetic style and
embracing contradiction and doubt. It also reflects her disdain
for the philosophers of her day, whose style she abhorred and
whose dogmatism and claims to knowledge she found presump-
tuous. Paradoxically, Deffand's view of philosophy closely resembles that of the late Rousseau, despite her antipathy for him.
Both placed self-knowledge at the heart of philosophy and
criticized modern philosophers in the same terms. Rousseau
came closest to Deffand's preferred approach in his *Rêveries du
promeneur solitaire,* not coincidentally the work in which he
also acknowledged his debt to Montaigne.

As Michel Beaujour has shown with particular brilliance,
both the *Essais* and the *Rêveries* are works of self-portraiture.[41]
In his programmatic first promenade, Rousseau lays out his
anti-systematic approach to describing the singular situation
of his soul at the end of his life. In doing so, he likens his project
to that of Montaigne:

Such a singular situation surely deserves to be examined and described, and it is to this study that I
devote my last moments of leisure. To do so suc-
cessfully one would have to proceed with order and

method: but I am incapable of this task, and in fact
it would divert me from my goal, which is to record
the modifications of my soul and their succession.
I will perform on myself in a certain sense the operations that physicists perform on the air to know
its daily state. I will apply the barometer to my soul,
and these well-directed and long-repeated operations will furnish me with results just as certain as
theirs. But I don't extend my enterprise that far. I
will content myself with keeping a register of the
operations, without seeking to reduce them into a
system. My project is the same as Montaigne's, but
with a goal quite contrary to his: he wrote his essays
only for others, and I write my reveries only for
myself.[42]

Rousseau's project "to record the modifications of [his] soul
and their succession" is indeed close to that of Montaigne, who
famously describes his self-portrait as one that changes with
each passing moment: "I don't paint the being, I paint the passage: not a passage from one age to another, or as the people
say, from seven years to seven years, but from day to day, from
minute to minute."[43] But Rousseau is careful to point out a key
distinction between the two works: as the solitary walker, detached from all other men, he writes for himself alone. In this
he is quite unlike Montaigne, who offers his book to his family
and friends as a substitution for his living body after his death.

Rousseau also embraces Montaigne's view of philosophy
as a means of preparing for death, observing in his third promenade that "The study of an Old Man, if there is still one remaining to him, is solely to learn how to die."[44] In this he takes his
cue from the essay "De l'exercitation" ("Of Practice"), in which
Montaigne describes his near-death experience after falling

from a horse. Montaigne opens this essay by claiming that death
is the one experience we *cannot* practice for: "as for death, we
can try it out only once: we are all apprentices when it comes
to it." But he then quickly reverses course: "It seems to me,
however, that there is a certain way of familiarizing ourselves
with death and trying it out [*l'essayer*] to some extent."[45] Montaigne's use of the verb *essayer* here connects the act of practicing for death with the literary genre of the essay he is said to
have invented. To describe a near-death experience, as Montaigne does in this same essay, is to try out or test one's death,
and perhaps also to document it before the fact. This was
something Montaigne had done for his friend La Boétie and
aspired to do for himself.

It is therefore significant that Rousseau chooses, in his
second promenade, to rewrite Montaigne's famous description
of his horseback-riding accident. In Rousseau's case, he finds
himself knocked over by a charging Great Dane during a botanical expedition on the outskirts of Paris. In one of the most
often quoted passages from the *Rêveries,* he describes himself
awakening to nature and existence as if for the first time, di-
vorced from any individual sense of self:

> Night was advancing. I perceived the sky, a few stars,
> and a little greenery. This first sensation was a deli-
> cious moment. I only sensed myself through that as
> of yet. I was being born in that moment to life, and
> it seemed to me that I filled with my weightless ex-
> istence all the objects I perceived. Entirely in the
> present moment I remembered nothing; I had no
> distinct notion of myself as an individual, not the
> least idea of what had just happened to me; I didn't
> know who I was nor where I was; I didn't feel any
> pain, nor fear, nor worry. I saw my blood flow as

> I would have seen a stream flow, without even
> imagining that this blood belonged to me in any
> way.[46]

The loss of self Rousseau describes here appears as a communion with nature and with the body (the flowing blood), experienced as a part of nature prior to self-consciousness. But the
reference to Montaigne complicates this picture, inscribing the
description and even the experience itself into a self-conscious
literary tradition. This suggests that Rousseau's debt to Montaigne is not limited to self-portraiture or philosophy as a means
of preparing for death. More crucially, it involves the cultivation
of a form and style of writing as closely aligned with the body
and its mortality as possible. Pierre Manent's analysis of Montaigne is illuminating in this regard: "Cowardly or courageous,
no action gives us knowledge of death. Death occurs in the body
and every action occurs in the soul. If to philosophize is to learn
how to die, that does not consist in detaching the soul from the
body as Plato believed, but in making it come into the body in
order to learn to know the encroachment of death there."[47]
Montaigne's effort to bring the soul into the body, as it were, is
exemplified by his characteristically corporeal writing style. In
"De Democritus et Heraclitus," he describes the mental processes underpinning his essays as if they were physical, even
sensual acts: "Of a hundred members and faces that each thing
has, I take one, sometimes only to lick it, sometimes to brush
the surface, sometimes to pinch it to the bone. I give it a stab,
not as wide but as deep as I know how. And most often I like to
take them from some unaccustomed point of view."[48] In emulat-
ing Montaigne, Rousseau invents his own distinctive approach
to corporeal writing, inscribing mortality into the very form of
his work: in addition to designating each chapter as a walk
taken by a body in decline, he compares the detached pages of

his work (referred to as *feuilles,* both pages and leaves) to the fragile, dead plant fragments he collected in his herbaria.[49]

Montaigne also serves as a model for Diderot's last published work, the *Essai sur les règnes de Claude et de Néron.* As Jerome Schwartz observes, "It is as if Diderot, toward the end of his career, at last recognized the importance of Montaigne's influence on his work and set out deliberately to write an essay *à la Montaigne* which remains nevertheless very much *à la Diderot.*"[50] Although much of the work is devoted to defending Seneca (and Diderot himself) from their detractors, it also offers a stirring defense of Montaigne. Significantly, the passage Diderot chooses to illustrate Montaigne's eloquence is one in which the author of the *Essais* depicts himself plunging headlong into death:

> Montaigne is rich in expressions; he is energetic; he is philosophical; he is a great painter and a great colorist. In a hundred places he displays the full force of his eloquence; he is whatever he wants to be. He has as much taste as was possible in his time and suitable to his subject; it is he who said of death: "I plunge stupidly with my head down into this speechless abyss which engulfs me and suffocates me in an instant, full of insipidity and indolence. Death, which is nothing but a quarter hour of suffering, without consequence or harm, doesn't deserve any particular precepts." That is not very religious, but it is beautiful. There are thousands of passages in his inimitable work that have the same power.[51]

As it turns out, Diderot's quotation is partly of his own invention. As Schwartz has shown, he combines sentences from two different essays, both written at the end of Montaigne's life, while also accentuating their materialist overtones: "Consciously or unconsciously, Diderot has intensified Montaigne's depiction of death as a momentary reduction to nothingness, heightening what the eighteenth century chose to regard as his atheistic tendencies."[52] In this way, the defense of Montaigne becomes an occasion for Diderot to grapple with his own view of death as a reduction to nothingness, as expressed in the *Essai* and in another work he left unfinished at his death, the *Éléments de physiologie* (*Elements of Physiology*).

If I have given Montaigne pride of place in this book, it is in part because he served as a model for several of the writers I discuss. But it is also because he conceived of the *Essais* as a last work, written in the face of death. In his opening address to the reader, written in 1580, he predicts that his family and friends will soon lose him, and offers his book as a source of solace and remembrance: "I have dedicated it to the private convenience of my relatives and friends, so that when they have lost me (as soon they must), they may recover here some features of my habits and temperament, and by this means keep the knowledge they have had of me more complete and alive."[53] As it turned out, Montaigne continued working on the *Essais* for another twelve years, until his death in 1592. During this period, his personal and philosophical attitude toward death changed quite a bit. In his earliest essays, he sought in the Stoicist tradition to cultivate "the habit of having death continually present, not merely in my imagination, but in my mouth."[54] But by the end of his life he had come to see philosophical injunctions to keep death constantly in mind as unnecessary and even harmful:

> We trouble our life by concern about death, and death by concern about life. One torments us, the other frightens us. It is not against death that we

prepare ourselves; that is too momentary a thing.
A quarter hour of suffering, without consequence,
without harm, does not deserve any particular precepts. To tell the truth, we prepare ourselves against
the preparations for death. Philosophy orders us to
have death ever before our eyes, to foresee and consider it before the time comes, and afterward gives
us the rules and precautions to provide against our
being wounded by this foresight and this thought.
That is what those doctors do who make us ill so that
they have something on which to employ their drugs
and their art.[55]

As he approached the end of his own life, Montaigne came to
see death as "the end, but not therefore the goal, of life."[56] Nonetheless, he did not renounce his earlier project of documenting
his death in writing: "I have chosen the time when my life, which
I have to portray, lies all before my eyes; what is left is more
related to death. And even of my death, if I should find it gar-
rulous, as others do, I would willingly give an account to the
public on my way out."[57] Thus Montaigne set for himself the
ultimate test of his capacity as a writer: if death was nothing
more than a quarter hour of suffering, without consequence,
and if to die was to plunge stupidly into an abyss of nothingness,
how could that experience be documented in writing? This was
the test taken up by Montaigne's eighteenth-century descen-
dants in their own last works. But far from finding death gar-
rulous on their way out, they invented new forms of literature
to convey the nothingness and silence that would soon be theirs.

PROLOGUE

Hume's Life

H ume wrote *My Own Life* in April 1776, just four months
before his death. It was to be his last work, and he
conceived of it as such. The "disorder in [his] bowels"
that had plagued him since the previous spring had advanced
to such a degree that he "now reckon[ed] upon a speedy dissolution."[1] Indeed, he referred to the brief work (fourteen
pages in the first edition) in his concluding sentence as a "funeral oration of myself."[2] This oration he intended to "prefix"
the edition of his collected works that was then being prepared
by his publisher, William Strahan.[3] In the event, the work was
published separately in 1777, along with a brief preface by
Strahan and a letter to him by Hume's friend Adam Smith,
recounting Hume's last months of life and his continuing cheer-
fulness in the face of death.

I open this book with Hume's *My Own Life* because it
perfectly embodies the genre of last works and casts an enigmatic light over the question I argue was facing Hume and his
contemporaries: how to write philosophically in the face of
death. Because Hume was much concerned at the end of his

life with ensuring the posthumous publication of his potentially inflammatory *Dialogues Concerning Natural Religion,* and
because he wrote *My Own Life* to preface his collected works,
his self-portrait has generally been seen as part of a broader
effort on his part to shape and preserve his legacy.[4] As Annette
C. Baier puts it, "Hume hoped to be remembered as a great
writer, a distinguished citizen in 'the republic of letters.' *My Own
Life* includes only what serves that end."[5] In keeping with this
idea, there are several indications in the text that Hume's equanimity in the face of death is attributable at least in part to his
confidence that after many years of disappointing public reception of his works, his literary reputation would, after his death,
"[break] out at last with additional lustre."[6] Yet I will suggest
here that for all appearances to the contrary, the very idea of
securing a lasting legacy through writing is cast into doubt in
My Own Life, in a way consistent with the skeptical orientation
of Hume's philosophy and the problems of personal identity he
grappled with in *A Treatise of Human Nature.*

Hume's title, *My Own Life,* seems straightforward enough. But
it is somewhat strange in its insistence on ownership, a quality
erased by the standard French translation as *Ma vie* rather than
Ma propre vie.[7] The title points from the very outset to the
enigmatic nature of the text and some of its key questions: what
is a life? And in what sense do we have ownership over our lives,
especially at the moment we are preparing to give them up?
With respect to the first question, Hume was perfectly clear: *My
Own Life* would not be the history of his life (and certainly not
the history of his inner life), but rather "the History of my writings."[8] Still, the title remains. Does this mean that in Hume's
eyes, as he approached death, his life amounted to little more
than his writings? As Liz Stanley has observed, *My Own Life*

presents a curiously external, circumstantial view of Hume's life, one consistent with his reflections on personal identity in *A Treatise of Human Nature* and its appendix.[9] In the *Treatise,* Hume observes that what he calls *himself* is nothing more than a discontinuous set of perceptions. To illustrate his point, he evokes both the interruption of those perceptions in sleep, when he "may truly be said not to exist," and their eventual cessation upon his death: "And were all my perceptions remov'd by death, and cou'd I neither think, nor feel, nor see, nor love, nor hate after the dissolution of my body, I shou'd be entirely annihilated, nor do I conceive what is farther requisite to make me a perfect non-entity."[10] *My Own Life* gestures toward this eventual annihilation of Hume's self, by substituting his life with his writings as the last surviving traces of his inner perceptions.

My Own Life thus appears to be a classic statement of literary immortality: Hume will live on in his writings after his death.[11] As Baier expresses it, "It was his provocative writings that he depended on for any afterlife, and they are lasting well."[12] But just as Hume questions in his *Treatise* the extent to which we can really be said to possess a self, given the interruption and eventual annihilation of our inner perceptions, so does he question in *My Own Life* the extent to which we have ownership over our lives, and especially our writings. This is in part a function of the publishers being the "Proprietors" of Hume's works, as he put it in a letter to Smith instructing him to send *My Own Life* to Strahan.[13] More importantly, it is a function of the vagaries of literary reception, something Hume emphasizes pointedly throughout *My Own Life*. His first work, *A Treatise of Human Nature*, "fell *dead-born from the press,*" a phrase that suggests both that Hume's works are his progeny, and that a work cannot even be said to exist so long as it does not garner public attention.[14] The power of the public to grant, or deny, the very existence of a work is similarly emphasized in Hume's account of the reception of his favorite work, the second *Enquiry:* "In the same year was published at London, my Enquiry concerning the Principles of Morals; which, in my own opinion (who ought not to judge on that subject), is of all my writings, historical, philosophical, or literary, incomparably the best. It came unnoticed and unobserved into the world."[15] Here, Hume underlines not just the gap between his appraisal of the second *Enquiry* and that of the public, but more importantly the irrelevance of his judgment: it is not for him to express his opinion on the topic, given that the public has not even deigned to notice the work at all.

In the case of the *History of England,* Hume emphasizes his inability to predict the public reception of his work. Whereas he had expected success, the first volume was met first with disapprobation and then with sheer indifference: "I was, I own, sanguine in my expectations of the success of this work. I thought that I was the only historian, that had at once neglected present power, interest, and authority, and the cry of popular prejudices; and as the subject was suited to every capacity, I expected proportional applause. But miserable was my disappointment: I was assailed by one cry of reproach, disapprobation, and even detestation; . . . and after the first ebullitions of [the public's] fury were over, what was still more mortifying, the book seemed to sink into oblivion."[16] Hume's error, in this case, is especially significant because it came at a time when his literary fortunes (and financial situation) had begun to improve. Neither his rising reputation nor the rage provoked among all parties alike by the first volume of the *History of England* were sufficient to rescue the work from the same oblivion into which the dead-born baby of the *Treatise* had earlier fallen. In the case of all three works, the nonexistence of a work unrecognized by the public casts Hume's ownership over his own works, and hence his own life, into doubt.

Hume admits that for all his optimism, he was discouraged by the reception of the first volume of the *History of England.*

And here he sketches out a counterfactual history that suggests his entire literary career and even his name might well have been cast into oblivion had the circumstances been different: "I was, however, I confess, discouraged; and had not the war been at that time breaking out between France and England, I had certainly retired to some provincial town of the former kingdom, have changed my name, and never more have returned to my native country. But as this scheme was not now practicable, and the subsequent volume was considerably advanced, I resolved to pick up courage and to persevere."[17] This counterfactual history underscores Hume's sense that there was nothing inevitable about the perpetuation of his legacy. Even his name might have been changed. The way he writes of his own possible obscurity recalls the way Cleanthes, one of the characters in the *Dialogues Concerning Natural Religion,* speaks of the possible oblivion into which ancient civilization might have fallen had the historical circumstances been only slightly different: "Ancient learning and history seem to have been in great danger of entirely perishing after the inundation of the barbarous nations; and had these convulsions continued a little longer, or been a little more violent, we should not probably have now known what passed in the world a few centuries before us."[18] Like Diderot in his 1765 preface to the eighth volume of the *Encyclopédie,* Hume emphasizes the contingency of all human endeavors, including his own. His life, to the extent that it is reduced to his writings, cannot properly be called his own; it belongs instead to a fickle public and to historical circumstances that might dictate its ultimate survival or destruction.

Yet *My Own Life* also offers a countervailing narrative of Hume's gradually increasing fortune and rising literary reputation. The second volume of the *History of England* was more favorably received than the first, and "not only rose itself, but helped to buoy up its unfortunate brother."[19] Once again we find the metaphor of Hume's works as his progeny (the mortal's form of immortality according to Plato's Diotima). Not all of Hume's literary progeny were to be stillborn or drown in the sea of oblivion. By the age of fifty-seven, he had acquired a comfortable fortune and could entertain the prospect of growing fame: "I returned to Edinburgh in 1768, very opulent (for I possessed a revenue of 1000 l. a year), healthy, and though somewhat stricken in years, with the prospect of enjoying long my ease, and of seeing the increase of my reputation."[20] Yet it is precisely at this high point in the text that Hume introduces his mortality. The illness that would take him to his grave struck at the very moment when he was contemplating the prospect of a long life and rising fame. Not to be discouraged, Hume suggests that posthumous fame offers ample compensation for a life cut short: "I consider, besides, that a man of sixty-five, by dying, cuts off only a few years of infirmities; and though I see many symptoms of my literary reputation's breaking out at last with additional lustre, I knew that I could have but few years to enjoy it. It is difficult to be more detached from life than I am at present."[21] With this statement of detachment, Hume disowns his life, paving the way for his posthumous survival in textual form. What seems to matter most is not whether he will have the occasion to enjoy his literary fame, but simply the fact that it will outlive him. Once again, we seem to have a classic statement of literary immortality. Yet Hume's choice of the word *symptoms* to evoke his increasing fame should give us pause, for it follows directly on his erroneous prognosis about his health. If he was wrong about his physical state, he implies, he might just as well be wrong about his fame. Hence as we reach the end of *My Own Life* and contemplate the end of Hume's life, the survival of his posthumous legacy is cast into doubt.

This explains the enigmatic conclusion to *My Own Life*. In the last paragraph of a work that was to contain "little more than the History of [his] writings," Hume makes no mention of his writings at all. The omission is all the more striking in that it comes at a point when Hume performs his death syntactically by writing himself into the past tense: "To conclude historically with my own character. I am, or rather was (for that is the style I must now use in speaking of myself, which emboldens me the more to speak of my sentiments); I was, I say, a man of mild dispositions, of command of temper, of an open, social, and cheerful humour, capable of attachment, but little susceptible of enmity, and of great moderation in all my passions. Even my love of literary fame, my ruling passion, never soured my temper, notwithstanding my frequent disappointments."[22] Always a consummate stylist, here Hume takes his artful prose to new heights.[23] The truncated opening sentence calls attention to a strange twist in the text: *My Own Life* was never to be a history of Hume's character. The odd truncation encourages us to read *character* in two senses: Hume's temperament, that is, the optimism and good humor evoked throughout the text, and Hume as a character in a literary work.[24] To what extent should we understand *My Own Life* as an attempt to "fix" Hume's character in the latter sense once and for all? How does his ruling passion, his love of literary fame, complicate this picture, given that literary fame is subject to the whims of the public and historical circumstance? We should note here Hume's use of the term *fame* (from the Latin *fama,* which denotes being spoken about by others), as opposed to *glory,* with its religious connotations of everlasting immortality. The possessive emphasis of "my own character," which mirrors the title *My Own Life,* begs the question of who has ownership over Hume's character, and creates a tension between his internal perceptions of his own character and his external depiction of himself as a character.

The doubling of Hume's character in the conclusion to *My Own Life* reflects the "conundrum" of identity he explored elsewhere in his philosophical writings. It is a conundrum Stanley describes as follows: "Intellectually he evacuates 'I' as having any fixed 'principle'; and yet it is 'I' that writes, does this and that, and has continuity; and the writings and the person of 'I' are assailed by others, who also ascribe continuity and fixity to this 'I.'"[25] Hume's concluding paragraph can be read in part as an attempt to "fix" his character once and for all, by stepping outside the frame of his own life. The phrase "I was, I say" creates two different figures of Hume, one who is dead and whose character can be judged definitively in the past tense, and the other who is still alive and still writing (or saying) something in the present. The confusing disjuncture between these two figures is made all the more troubling by Hume's claim that his new style of speaking of himself (in the past tense) has emboldened him to speak more of his sentiments. As readers of the *Treatise,* we know that if Hume has died (as the past tense indicates), his sentiments should already have been annihilated. So of whose sentiments is he speaking and from what vantage point are they being perceived? The subject position of the writer has become an impossible one, lying somehow both outside Hume's life and within it.

Both Stephen Miller and Thomas Laqueur have discussed what Miller calls Hume's "deathbed project," that is, his efforts to orchestrate a death in keeping with his philosophical beliefs.[26] This project was designed to demonstrate to his contemporaries that the death of a nonbeliever was not necessarily a miserable one. It is significant that Hume authorized his friend Adam Smith to further this effort, by supplying an addendum to *My Own Life* that would take the narrative of Hume's life right up until his death.[27] What better way to express the idea that Hume's life (and death) were no longer his own, but were now in the hands of his friend and, eventually, his enemies and the broader public? The addendum, "Letter from Adam Smith, LL.D. to

William Strahan, Esq.," placed great emphasis on Hume's cheer-
fulness and lack of vanity in the face of death. It also recounted
an anecdote that cast the question of Hume's legacy in a humor-
ous light. As Smith tells it, at one of their last meetings, Hume,
having recently read Lucian's *Dialogues of the Dead,* joked about
various excuses he might make to Charon to delay his passage
across the River Styx. He first requests a little more time to "see
how the Public receives the alterations" to the new edition of
his works. When Charon rejects this request, he follows it up
with another: "But I might still urge, 'Have a little patience,
good Charon, I have been endeavouring to open the eyes of the
Public. If I live a few years longer, I may have the satisfaction
of seeing the downfal of some of the prevailing systems of superstition.' But Charon would then lose all temper and de-
cency. 'You loitering rogue, that will not happen these many
hundred years. Do you fancy I will grant you a lease for so long
a term? Get into the boat this instant, you lazy loitering rogue.'"[28]
We might take this anecdote to mean that at the time of his
death, Hume was deeply preoccupied with ensuring that his
works advance the eradication of religious superstition. But we
might also read it in a more satirical light, in keeping with Baier's
claim that with this anecdote, Hume "scoffed at himself and his
own pretensions."[29] It was not just that Hume would not live to
witness the impact his works would have in the distant future:
it was a symptom of human vanity to even entertain the notion
that they would survive that long.

     In authorizing Smith to write an addendum to *My Own
Life,* Hume put his life, and death, into the hands of others. For
Smith, Hume's death reflected his true character, as someone
who "approach[ed] as nearly to the idea of a perfectly wise and
virtuous man, as perhaps the nature of human frailty will permit."[30] For Samuel Johnson, on the contrary, it was merely a
symptom of Hume's vanity. The debate over Hume's death raged

for several decades after he died. What is striking about the conclusion to *My Own Life* is the way it sets the stage for this debate. In his last sentence, Hume writes: "I cannot say there is no vanity in making this funeral oration of myself, but I hope it is not a misplaced one; and this is a matter of fact which is easily cleared and ascertained."[31] Whereas Hume had earlier stepped outside of his own life in order to judge his character from without in the past tense, here he invites his contemporaries (and posterity) to be the ultimate judges of the accuracy of his funeral oration. The meaning of his own life—and death—is no longer in his hands. As readers of *My Own Life*, we know how wide the gap so often was between Hume's own judgment and the public reception of his works. In this context, his closing claim that the accuracy of his funeral oration is a "matter of fact which is easily cleared and ascertained" appears highly ironic. Hume knew full well that the public would hold wildly divergent opinions of his character and his funeral oration—as indeed they did—and he also knew that they could easily let *My Own Life* fall into oblivion.

Much attention has been paid to the cultural and philosophical significance of Hume's death for him and his contemporaries. His death even continues to be interrogated today as a model of how to die as a nonbeliever.[32] Yet Hume was not only preoccupied with dying a death in accord with his philosophical beliefs. The stylistic artistry of *My Own Life* shows that he was equally concerned with the problem of how to *write* philosophically in the face of death. *My Own Life* was clearly in part an effort to shape Hume's legacy, in parallel with his requests to Strahan and Smith to ensure the publication of his *Dialogues Concerning Natural Religion* after his death. Yet this does not mean that Hume's last work upheld a redemptive view of literary immortality as a compensation for death. Hume was unflinching in his contemplation of the ultimate annihilation of the self in his *Treatise*. My reading of *My Own Life* suggests that he was no less unflinching in envisaging the possible destruction of his literary and philosophical legacy. By writing himself into the past tense, he made a bold attempt to have the last word on the meaning of his life, to write his own funeral oration. But even as he did so, he demonstrated the impossibility of occupying such a position, of standing both inside and outside his life. His final gesture in the closing sentence of *My Own Life* was to give up the ultimate meaning of his life—and life's works—to his readers. This literary gesture was consistent with his acceptance of Smith's plan to supplement *My Own Life* with his own account of his friend's final months and comportment in the face of death. In the end, Hume left it up to his readers, if readers there were, to judge whether oblivion was to be his ultimate fate, or whether his stillborn babies and drowning brothers were to be resuscitated.

1

Buffon's Stone

When the great naturalist Georges-Louis Leclerc, comte de Buffon, died on April 16, 1788, at the Jardin du Roi he had long presided over, he was at the height of his fame. His dear friend the *salonnière* and writer Suzanne Curchod Necker attended him at his deathbed and wrote a detailed account of his five days of agony. She later reflected in her journals on the strong impression his death had made on her: "The spectacle of the nothingness [*néant*] of M. de Buffon at the moment when he was going to raise his statue on the globe of this world, puts all men back in their true place, and our heart is left desolate and confused by this terrible lesson; but the refuge it seeks from its own reflections, soon raises it above them."[1]

Unlike Buffon, Necker was a fervent believer in the immortality of the human soul, in keeping with her Protestant faith. In the fourteen years of their impassioned friendship (she had sought him out in 1774, when he was sixty-seven and she thirty-seven), she had often attempted to convert him to her beliefs.[2] He alludes to these efforts in an undated letter written

Les illustres français, Louis Georges le Clerc C.te de Buffon.
After Clément Pierre Marillier, print by Nicolas Ponce, 1790–1816,
Paris. (© The Trustees of the British Museum)

in the last three years of his life. Promising to love her from
beyond the grave, "if, as I desire, your opinion is better than
mine," he goes on to explain their opposing views as a function
of her spiritual nature and his material one:

> With what fineness of tact, with what grace you
> give me a lesson in philosophy in your last letter! It
> contains in four pages more than a volume of sub-
> lime morality; each line is an axiom, and exquisite
> sentiment always precedes profound thought; yes,
> divine one, you are all spirit and all soul; the more
> your body weakens, the more your head gathers
> strength; the two substances are quite distinct in

you, whereas in me they are only one; I feel the faculties of my spirit decline with those of my body,
and therein lies the basis of our difference in opinion; the tenderness of my heart is the only thing
that seems to me to grow rather than decline.[3]

Buffon was apparently not impervious to Necker's efforts to
sway him to believe. On his deathbed he kept a small portrait
of her close at hand (which he also bequeathed to her in his
testament), and asked that her husband's work, *De l'importance
des opinions religieuses* (*On the Importance of Religious Opinions*), be read aloud to him. As Necker took care to specify in
her account of Buffon's death, he received the last Catholic
sacraments from his parish priest, who was rushed in from
Montbard for the occasion. Yet in Necker's view, the deathbed
conversion she had hoped for was not fully achieved: "I had
nothing for which to forgive M. de Buffon; I had only to pity
him. If he had doubts, it was to oblige him for once to feel the
limits of his mind, and the ardent wishes of his heart will have
erased, in the eyes of the Supreme Being, the uncertainty of his
weakness. His last letter makes clear his frame of mind, and my
eternal regret is that death stopped him in the middle of a reading, that of the *Religious Opinions,* which would have brought
all his feelings to completion."[4] According to Necker, Buffon
was undergoing a religious conversion under her influence that
was interrupted by his death. She, in contrast, presents herself
as unswayed by Buffon's materialist worldview. Yet her evocation
of "the nothingness of M. de Buffon" and the desolate thoughts
it inspires in her gives us a clue that she may have been more
unsettled by Buffon's death than she cared to admit.

The extent of Buffon's influence on Necker's thinking about
death becomes apparent when one reads her detailed, clinical
description of his final days. She writes as a naturalist would,

adhering to Buffon's founding principle in the *Histoire naturelle* (*Natural History*) that "one must begin by seeing, and seeing a lot."[5] Although she does detail the last rites, her description is surprisingly devoid of the religious sentimentalism so characteristic of deathbed accounts in the period. In his 1860 edition of his great-great-uncle's correspondence, Henri Nadault de Buffon takes one such account (by Buffon's secretary) as an occasion to laud the naturalist's exemplary Christian death: "It was a truly Christian death, a worthy end to a gloriously occupied life. It was, right in the middle of the eighteenth century, and in a time when an unwholesome philosophy took the place of religion, a great example given by the most profound philosopher of the period; it was a great act of firmness and conviction."[6]

Necker, in contrast, focuses mainly on the physical symptoms of her friend's impending death. Like Montaigne, Buffon suffered from the stone, and Necker describes the blockage of urine, the nausea, the desire to vomit, and the bladder pain. With great precision, she also records the number of sweat-soaked shirts, the sensation of suffocation, the rapid panting, and the ice-cold body warmed by hot compresses.[7] Nowhere does she seek to attenuate the physical reality of Buffon's agony or express any fear or disgust in the face of his death. In this she was following a lesson she had learned from Buffon himself, as she recounted it in a letter to the Swiss naturalist and Alpine explorer Horace Bénédict de Saussure: "What we take to be a corpse deserves another look: it is nothing but the prolongation of life in death; and there is, says Buffon, a kind of courage of mind in the ability to envisage, without too much fear, and even with some gentleness, the grandeur of the bodies of the deceased."[8] The view Necker expresses here—that a corpse was the material sign of life subsisting in death—came directly from the *Histoire naturelle,* where Buffon elaborated his theory of

death as the gradual hardening of the bones and fibers throughout an individual's adult life.

After Buffon's death, Necker would take his lessons further
still. Following her decade-long leadership role at the Hospice
de Charité, she published in 1790 a pamphlet on how to care
for the dead and dying to avoid the horror of premature burial.[9]
As historians of death have documented, she was by no means
alone in this preoccupation. Indeed, the risk of premature
burial was the logical corollary of Buffon's gradualist theory of
death. But Necker's lifelong obsession with avoiding premature
burial was an extreme manifestation of a broader cultural trend.
It reached its paroxysm at the end of her life, when she left
elaborate testamentary instructions for the care of her own
corpse and, eventually, that of her husband. Once her death had
been definitively determined (itself an arduous process), she
was to be embalmed in liquid with her face uncovered to preserve her form as she awaited the arrival of her husband's corpse.
We cannot know what Buffon would have thought of these final
directives. But they were symptomatic of the influence his work
exerted over eighteenth-century readers as they sought to understand death within the new philosophical framework of their
time. I devote my opening chapter to the *Histoire naturelle*
because no single work did more to shape attitudes toward death
in Enlightenment France. In what follows, I will range broadly
across the thirty-six volumes of the *Histoire naturelle* to address
the various ways death is treated in this work. In the last part
of the chapter, I will propose a more focused reading of Buffon's
last work, the little-known *Histoire naturelle des minéraux*
(*Natural History of Minerals*). It was here that Buffon offered
his final reflections on his life and practice as a naturalist, and
it was here that his lifetime of thinking about death crystallized
around the motif of the fossil.

Death appears in many different guises across the thirty-six volumes of the *Histoire naturelle,* published between 1749 and 1789. In his chapter on old age and death in the *Histoire naturelle de l'homme (Natural History of Man)*, Buffon outlines his physiological theory of aging and death as the gradual hardening of the bones and fibers. In his chapter on the senses, he conducts a thought experiment in which he imagines a first man awakening to his senses to discover not only pleasure and knowledge but also a painful sense of his own mortality. In his chapter on racial and cultural diversity, he touches on the funeral rites of non-European peoples, taking this ethnographic description as an occasion to deplore the neglect of death and the dead in his own culture. In several different volumes, he provides demographic tables of life expectancy in Paris and the French countryside and analyzes the moral arithmetic to be derived from them. And in his *Histoire naturelle des minéraux,* published at the very end of his life, he turns his discussion of fossils and the history of the earth into a reflection on his own impending death and its implications for his natural philosophical project.

From a modern perspective, these various approaches to the problem of death may seem incongruous. This is due in part to the fact that Buffon's work spans the modern disciplines of cosmology, physiology, anthropology, demography, zoology, and geology. But is also due to the fact that Buffon made no distinction between, on the one hand, theories or facts about death that might today be referred to as scientific and, on the other, philosophical, ethical, or even personal meditations on death. To grasp the coherence of Buffon's view of death thus requires an awareness of what Michel Foucault called the archaeology of the human sciences.[10] But it also requires, as I will argue here, an awareness of the literary dimension of Buffon's project. It is well known that Buffon, a member of the Académie française and author of an influential discourse on literary style, was viewed in the eighteenth century as one of the best prose stylists of his time. In recent years, Buffon's status as a literary writer has once again been consecrated by his entry into the prestigious Pléiade collection and by a renewed attention to his work among literary scholars. Nonetheless, as Stéphane Schmitt observes in his introduction to the Pléiade edition, "Only the literary dimension still remains (scandalously) underestimated."[11] Despite the pioneering work of Jeff Loveland and, more recently, Hanna Roman, the coherence of imaginative tropes across the many volumes of the *Histoire naturelle,* and the complex ways these tropes shaped Buffon's natural philosophy, have still not received the full attention they deserve.[12] The connection between death and fossils that Buffon developed over the course of his life's work is one striking example of the role played by such tropes in his natural philosophy. This trope has a special significance for Buffon's project because at the end of his life, when he had come to view the *Histoire naturelle* as his complete works, it became the basis for a poetics of testamentary writing that retrospectively gave shape to his entire project.

Death surfaces in the earliest volumes of Buffon's work, in a chapter entitled "De la vieillesse et de la mort" ("On Old Age and Death") from the *Histoire naturelle de l'homme,* published in 1749. It is here that Buffon develops his physiological theory of death as a slow process of ossification whereby the bones and fibers, as soon as they are no longer susceptible to growth, become increasingly dense and gradually lose their liquidity and ductility: "The membranes become cartilaginous, the cartilage becomes bony, the bones become more solid, all the fibers harden, the skin dries out, wrinkles form little by little, the hair turns white, the teeth fall out, the face loses its shape, the body becomes stooped, etc."[13] This account of aging and death—with its charming and terrible *etcetera*—was by no means entirely original. Buffon was indebted to René Descartes, who had speculated that the hardening of bodily fibers gradually compromised the nutritive functions necessary to life.[14] Similar views were held by eighteenth-century physicians such as the surgeon Claude-Nicolas Le Cat, who described the process by which the conduits in the nerves, as John McManners puts it, "gradually became encrusted, as it were with stalactites."[15] But Buffon placed particular emphasis on ossification in his version of these views, explaining changes in bone structure through analogy to the formation of tree trunks: "Finally the substance of the bone becomes over time so compact that it can no longer let through the fluids necessary to the kind of circulation that provides nutrition to these parts; from then on the substance of the bone is necessarily altered, just as the wood of an old tree is altered once it has acquired all its solidity; this alteration in the very substance of the bone is one of the first causes that necessitate the deterioration of our bodies."[16] Buffon's emphasis on the role of bones in the processes of aging and death—which underpins the connection between death and fossils he developed later in his career—was quickly picked up by his contemporaries, as evidenced by Louis de Jaucourt's article "Ossification" in Diderot and d'Alembert's *Encyclopédie*.[17]

Buffon's theory of ossification was characteristic of his method as a naturalist in the sense that it was both highly speculative and based in empirical research (in this case, experiments on the hardening of wood conducted by Buffon and Henri-Louis Duhamel du Monceau, combined with the latter's studies of bone development).[18] It also reflected a broad trend, which can be linked to vitalist medicine, toward viewing death as a gradual transition rather than a distinct event with discernible symptoms. As Peter Hanns Reill has observed, "Vitalist physicians expressed strong doubts about the reliability of the traditional 'outward' signs determining death. By the end of the century, it had become an article of medical and educated belief that death was very difficult to differentiate from dying, that great differences existed between the really dead and the apparently dead."[19] This belief sparked widespread cultural anxieties surrounding premature burial (as evidenced by Necker's pamphlet on the topic) and impassioned revolutionary debates about whether guillotine victims could experience pain after being beheaded.[20]

Buffon contributed to this trend by arguing that death did *not* constitute a marked change in the state of a natural being. Rather, it was the final nuance in a long, continuous process by which life gradually took leave of the body: "All the causes of deterioration we have just indicated act continually on our material being and lead it little by little to its dissolution; death, that ever so marked, ever so dreaded change of state is thus in Nature nothing but the final nuance of a preceding state."[21] This view of death informed a philosophical stance with distinctly Lucretian overtones. After refuting the belief that death is accompanied by violent suffering, Buffon concluded, "I have addressed this topic at some length only in order to try to destroy a prejudice so contrary to man's happiness."[22] Although he was specifically referring here to the belief that the physical experience of death was painful, his broader purpose seemed to be to characterize death itself as a prejudice, at least to the extent that it was understood as a dramatic change in the state of a natural being. (It is worth noting that Buffon concerned himself solely with "natural" death resulting from old age and did not address disease or accidental death.) Buffon's physiological theory of death was thus an occasion for him to echo the Lucretian injunction that man look at things as they are and relinquish all fears of death.[23]

The gradualist conception of death also had important epistemological implications. On the one hand, Buffon sought to banish his readers' fear of death by assuring them that most men are not conscious of their final moments. This lack of awareness could stem either from a physical unconsciousness serving as a transition between life and death, or from a moral illusion that masked impending death even in the face of incontrovertible evidence. His empiricism notwithstanding, Buffon characterized the veil of unconsciousness and illusion surrounding death as one of nature's gifts to man: "The majority of men thus die without knowing it, and in the small number of those who retain their awareness up until their last breath, there is perhaps not a single one who doesn't also retain some hope and who doesn't flatter himself by believing in a return to life; Nature has, for the happiness of man, made this sentiment stronger than reason."[24] On the other hand, Buffon's claim that the processes of death were omnipresent in life—that "life is extinguished by successive nuances, and death is nothing but the last term in this series of degrees, the last nuance of life"—meant that humans could begin to perceive death in the midst of life even without experiencing its final stages.[25] Indeed, Buffon's unflinching description of the aging process (which, he claimed, we would be aware of in ourselves "if we observed ourselves better, if we flattered ourselves less, and if in all things others did not always judge us much better than we judge ourselves") was intended in part to cultivate in his readers a personal awareness of death in life.[26]

Buffon was of course not alone in upholding the philosophical or moral imperative to gain an understanding of death in life. Montaigne's essay "Que philosopher c'est apprendre à mourir" ("That to Philosophize Is to Learn to Die") captures a conception of philosophy that can be traced to Socrates and that manifested itself in different ways in the spiritual exercises of Epicureanism and Stoicism.[27] In a similar way, Christian practices of meditation and prayer revolved around the Pauline

notion of "dying daily" and the belief that, as McManners puts
it, "the most important act of a lifetime is the act of dying, and
a Christian's chief duty is to prepare himself for death."[28] In
Buffon's time, this belief was disseminated in a vast body of
devotional literature on preparing for death, the central message
of which was captured in the title of one famous handbook,
Pensez-y bien (*Think on It Carefully*). What was particular to
Buffon, in this context, was the sensationist orientation he gave
to these traditions. In his famous fable of the first man awakening to nature and his senses, from the chapter "Des sens en
général" ("On the Senses in General"), Buffon gives poetic
expression to the idea that the exercise of the senses is inseparable from man's awareness of death. Like Étienne Bonnot de
Condillac's statue (but predating it by a few years), Buffon's first
man acquires each of his senses in turn, an experience that
culminates in his discovery of a sixth sense combining sexual
pleasure with self-awareness.[29] But with the exercise of each
sense, he also becomes increasingly aware of the limits of his
own existence. When forced by the brilliance of the sun to close
his eyes, he instinctively experiences the ensuing darkness as a
loss of self: "At that moment of darkness I believed I had lost
almost my entire being."[30] Upon awakening from a deep sleep
after tasting his first fruit, he becomes consciously aware for
the first time of the finitude of his existence: "This annihilation
[*anéantissement*] I had just experienced gave me a certain feeling of fear and made me sense that I would not always exist."[31]
Finally, after meeting "a second half of [himself]" and experiencing the sixth sense of sexual pleasure (with the implicit
promise of reproduction), he undergoes a symbolic death in
the last sentence of the fable, as night falls and recalls his initial
slumber: "At that moment the daylight star extinguished its
torch at the end of its course; I barely noticed that I was losing
my sense of sight; I existed too fully to fear ceasing to be, and

it was in vain that the darkness I found myself in reminded me of my original sleep."[32] Although one might conclude with Michel Delon that "the fatality of death disappears with the pleasure of love's union, and implicit promise of posterity," the overall structure of the fable, in which the discovery of each sense brings both pleasure and a heightened awareness of death, logically leads the reader to expect that the man's first night will be followed by a painful new understanding of his fate.[33] In this way, Buffon's fable of the first man implicitly links enlightenment (understood here as the exercise of the senses and the attendant acquisition of knowledge of nature) to self-awareness and more specifically to the awareness of death.

In light of this association between enlightenment and death, it is not surprising that Buffon attacked his own ostensibly enlightened culture for what he viewed as its willful dissemblance of death. His remarks on the topic support the conclusions of social and cultural historians, notably Philippe Ariès, who have argued that the eighteenth century attenuated or neglected traditional funeral rites in an effort to put death at a distance.[34] Dismayed by this neglect of death and the dead in his own culture, Buffon looked to the mortuary rituals of peoples across the globe to provide alternative models:

> We will speak elsewhere about the customs of different peoples with respect to funerals, burial, embalming, etc. The majority even of savages pay more attention to these final moments than we do; they regard as their principal duty what for us is only a ceremony; they respect their dead, they dress them, they speak to them, they recite their accomplishments, praise their virtues, and we who pride ourselves on our sensitivity, we are not even human, we flee from them, we abandon them, we

don't want to see them, we have neither the courage
nor the will to speak of them, we avoid even finding
ourselves in places that may remind us of them; we
are thus either too indifferent or too weak.[35]

For Buffon, our attitude toward death is an important part of
what makes us human. In their avoidance of death, the civilized
Europeans are "not even human," in marked contrast to the
so-called savages whose rituals denote both their awareness of
death and their courageous response to it. Europeans' lack of
humanity reveals a lack of sensitivity, a term best understood
in the context of the rich philosophical tradition, dating back
to Aristotle, which ascribed self-awareness to the workings of
the five senses in conjunction with a sixth, inner sense prior to
the development of rational thought. As Daniel Heller-Roazen
has shown, this tradition, which was interrupted and partially
obscured by Descartes's *cogito,* ascribed sensitivity and a cor-
responding self-awareness to both humans and animals, quite
removed from human cognition and reason.[36] Within this
context, to be sensitive (*sensible,* in French) was not just to
mourn the dead, it was also to cultivate the kind of sensorial
self-awareness that connected human beings to other living
creatures and to the broader natural world. This was indeed the
special sensitivity of Buffon's first man.

Buffon's interest in the death rites of non-European peoples was also part of a broader anthropological conversation
about the treatment of the dead in various cultures, ancient and
modern.[37] This is reflected in the *Encyclopédie* articles under
the rubric "Funerals," which detail the funeral rites of various
cultures. Although these ethnographic descriptions highlight-
ed the diversity of mortuary rituals, they were also an occasion
to underline the natural and universal human imperative to
care for the dead: "It seems that nature has everywhere inspired

men to this final duty toward their fellow creatures, who are taken from them in death; & religion, whether true or false, has consecrated this practice."[38] This assertion laid the ground for the related claim, made in the article "Grave, [*Natural right*]," that burial was a natural right that should not be denied even to the worst of criminals.[39]

Buffon's contribution to this conversation was striking in the specific (and unusual) ethnographic example he chose to highlight. Despite his professed admiration for non-European attitudes toward death and his promise to address them in detail, Buffon included only one reference to funeral rites in his chapter on racial and cultural diversity, "Variétés dans l'espèce humaine" ("Varieties in the Human Species"). This isolated ethnographic description—which he borrowed from a travel account rather than from the late seventeenth-century compendium of mortuary rituals that was the basis for the *Encyclopédie* articles—resonated in significant ways with his physiological theory of death:

> They have very unusual customs in certain provinces of the Congo: for example, when someone dies in Loango they place the corpse on a sort of amphitheater, elevated to six feet, in the position of a man who is seated with his hands resting on his knees; they dress the corpse in the most beautiful things they have and then light a fire in front of it and behind it; as it dries out and the fabrics are imbibed, they cover it with other fabrics until it is entirely dried out, after which they carry it into the earth with much pomp.[40]

Although Buffon did not draw any explicit connection between the rites described here and his own physiological theory of death, it seems evident that the Congolese technique of drying out the corpse in preparation for burial mirrors and furthers the natural process of ossification that led to death itself. In light of the continuum Buffon posited between life and death, such rites could be seen as not merely symbolic, but rather as a means of extinguishing any remaining vestiges of life in the corpse and thereby preparing for its integration into the inert realm of minerals. This example thus reflects not only Buffon's critique of the European avoidance of death rituals and his belief that the transition between life and death warranted special care, but also his elaboration of a rich imaginative trope connecting death to ossification and petrification.

Buffon also treated death within the framework of what Lorraine Daston has identified as the theory of classical probability. Here one might conclude with Jacques Roger that "Buffon collaborate[d] in the dissimulation of death" that he criticized elsewhere as inhuman.[41] As Daston has shown, Buffon's statistical studies of human mortality, first published in the *Histoire naturelle de l'homme* and then revised and expanded in the fourth volume of the *Supplément* to the *Histoire naturelle* (1777), were part of a broader rise in probabilistic thinking that "labored over a model of rational decision, action, and belief under conditions of uncertainty."[42] Statistical research on the length of human life was undertaken from the late seventeenth century forward, the most famous example being Sir William Petty's essays on political arithmetic. The main interest of many such works was in political economy and practical questions surrounding annuities and early forms of life insurance.[43] Although Buffon did not exclude such considerations from his discussion, his real interest in the statistics lay in what he called the "moral arithmetic" that could be derived from them.[44] His statistical studies were thus inseparable from his preoccupation with the place of death in Enlightenment culture. Like his ethnographic description of the Congolese rites, they were part of his attempt to elaborate an appropriate (and appropriately human) philosophical attitude toward death within a rationalist and materialist framework.

Buffon observed in the 1777 *Supplément* that his earlier discussion of life expectancy was a part of the *Histoire naturelle de l'homme* that, although crucial, was misunderstood by many of his readers: "Knowledge of the probabilities of the length of life is one of the most interesting things in the Natural History of Man; it can be drawn from the mortality Tables I have published. Several people seemed to me desirous of seeing the result in detail, & the applications for all ages, & I decided to give them here as a supplement, all the more willingly as I noticed that people often make mistakes in reasoning about this matter, & that false inductions were drawn from the reports presented in these Tables."[45] In acknowledging that his mortality tables had been misinterpreted, Buffon may have been alluding to d'Alembert's critique of his approach to calculating moral expectation.[46] But he may also have simply been acknowledging that probability theory was new enough to provoke a certain amount of confusion amongst his broad readership, which included not only members of professional societies and academies but also salon audiences. Such confusion is not surprising when one considers that Buffon's analysis of the tables combined a bold attempt to confront the omnipresence of death in eighteenth-century France with a seemingly incongruous attempt to shield his readers (and perhaps himself) from any personal fear of death.

On one end of the life spectrum, the mortality tables served as a chilling reminder that most infants born in eighteenth-century France would not survive into adulthood. Buffon summarized his findings as follows:

Here are the general truths this Table presents
to us:

A quarter of the human race perishes, as it
were, before seeing the light, since close to a quarter dies in the first eleven months of life, & in this
short space of time many more die below five
months than above.

A third of the human race perishes before
reaching the age of twenty-three months, that is to
say, before acquiring the use of the limbs & most of
the other organs.

Half of the human race perishes before the
age of eight years one month, that is to say, before
the body is developed, & before the soul manifests
itself through reason.

Two-thirds of the human race perishes before
the age of thirty-nine, such that there is hardly a third
of men who can propagate the species, & not even a
third who can achieve a stable state in society.[47]

Above and beyond the brutal facts of infant and child mortality, Buffon's analysis underlined the extent to which enlightenment remained inaccessible to the majority of people born in
eighteenth-century France simply by virtue of their life expectancy: one-quarter never saw the light; one-third never developed the use of their limbs or senses; one-half never acquired
the use of reason; and two-thirds never reproduced or attained
an established position in society.[48] If one considers that one of
the goals of the Enlightenment was, as Diderot put it in the
Encyclopédie, to advance general instruction, this was a sober-
ing reminder that until infant mortality rates and basic living
conditions improved, enlightenment would remain the province
of a privileged minority.[49]

On the other end of the life spectrum, however, Buffon derived a surprisingly reassuring "moral arithmetic" from the very same mortality tables: "We have said that a reason for living is to have lived, & we have demonstrated it with the scale of probabilities for the length of life; this probability is in truth increasingly smaller as the age increases, but when it is complete, that is to say, at eighty years of age, this same probability, decreasing less and less, becomes as it were stationary and fixed. . . . The Philosopher must therefore regard old age as a prejudice, as an idea that is contrary to man's happiness, & that does not trouble that of animals."[50] On the basis of his statistical tables, Buffon observed that human life expectancy ceased to diminish significantly after age eighty, becoming "as it were stationary and fixed." The moral arithmetic he derived from the tables was thus that old age, like the fear of death, was yet another prejudice to be eradicated by the rational philosopher. Buffon was seventy years old when these words were published, and he had suffered a life-threatening illness six years earlier. But he made no reference to his age or his own attitude toward death. With hindsight, there is a curiously personal dimension to his concluding claim that an eighty-year-old man could have a "legitimate hope" of living another three years and seven months: statistics and legitimate hopes notwithstanding, Buffon died at eighty years of age.[51]

The last work Buffon published before his death was the *Histoire naturelle des minéraux,* five volumes and an atlas published between 1783 and 1788. This remains the least known of his works, despite his personal investment in it and the care he devoted to its redaction.[52] Even the eminent Buffonian Jacques Roger expressed little enthusiasm for the work, judging that "with [its] numerous pages of detailed discussions written most often in the most prosaic style, the *Natural History of Minerals* was and remains a dry work."[53] Roger further downplayed the importance of Buffon's last work by concluding his intellectual biography with a discussion of *Des époques de la nature* (*The Epochs of Nature*), a work published in 1778 that he considered the crowning achievement of Buffon's career. Yet as the editors of the Pléiade edition have observed, the critical neglect surrounding the *Histoire naturelle des minéraux* is "unjust," for this work "is no less rich in beautiful texts than the preceding series and . . . it is not lacking in general considerations."[54] To this I would add that the *Histoire naturelle des minéraux* deserves special attention as Buffon's philosophical and literary testament. By the time he wrote the mineral volumes, Buffon had suffered from a life-threatening illness that elicited discussions at Versailles about who should succeed him as director of the Jardin des Plantes. Although he recovered quickly from this illness (which may have been an abscess in the intestines), he began suffering from painful kidney stones shortly thereafter and continued to do so until his death.[55] We thus have reason to believe that Buffon wrote the *Histoire naturelle des minéraux* with an acute sense that his lifelong contribution to natural philosophy would soon be coming to an end. His awareness of his mortality made its presence felt, in subtle but tangible ways, in his last defense of his method as a naturalist, and above all in his discussion of fossils. It was here that the various strands of his lifelong reflection on the place of death in nature and human culture came together, and that the connection between death and fossils found its fullest and most eloquent expression.

Discussions of Buffon's contribution to the earth sciences have tended to focus on the question of whether his conception of the earth was genuinely historical. In his study of early modern geology, Gabriel Gohau acknowledges that Buffon paved the way for a historical study of the earth by envisioning a far longer time span than the six thousand years of early modern Christian doctrine and by positing the irreversibility of the earth's history. Nonetheless, he groups Buffon with other early modern thinkers who dispense with "the earth's archives . . . because their mind judges itself capable of discovering the laws of nature allowing them to deduce the history of the earth."[56] Martin Rudwick comes to a similar conclusion, observing that the *Époques de la nature* "superficially . . . might seem to anticipate modern reconstructions of geohistory. But in fact it was profoundly ahistorical, for it postulated a series of changes that had in effect been programmed into the system from the start, and that could be extended into the future with the same degree of confidence."[57] From the perspective of the history of science, then, the consensus is that Buffon did not significantly contribute to the "reconstruction of geohistory" that would fundamentally transform the earth sciences in the late eighteenth and early nineteenth centuries.[58]

From a literary perspective, however, the historicist trend of Buffon's late work is significant. Unlike the earlier volumes, Buffon's late works on the earth are organized chronologically: *Des époques de la nature* is structured around seven moments in the earth's history (or, as Buffon puts it, "milestones on the eternal road of time"), and the *Histoire naturelle des minéraux* treats minerals in the order of their probable formation in the earth's crust.[59] As Buffon puts it, "Here, the order of our ideas must be the same as that of the succession of time."[60] In both works, Buffon subscribes to the view, still controversial in his day, that species can become extinct, and to the even more radical view that all life on earth, including human life, would eventually succumb to the progressive and ineluctable cooling of the earth. Whether or not these aspects of Buffon's late work constitute a genuinely historical view of nature, they are important from a literary perspective because they imply a broad shift

from descriptive to narrative modes of writing, in conjunction
with a marked emphasis on endings. What I am suggesting, in
other words, is that at the same time Buffon was attributing an
irreversible history to the earth, he was contemplating the end
of his career as a naturalist and writer and thinking about how
to bring closure to his life's work.

There are several indications that Buffon was preoccupied
with bringing some form of closure to the *Histoire naturelle*.
Toward the end of his life, he began issuing a series of supplementary volumes that included previously unpublished works
from early in his career (the first volume appeared in 1774). As
Schmitt has observed, Buffon "thus deliberately merged his
principal scientific project with the edition of his complete
works."[61] The edition of an author's complete works is closely
linked to the genres of biography and autobiography (and carries an inevitable association with death, since the edition cannot be seen as necessarily complete until the author dies). The
initial impetus for Rousseau's *Confessions,* for example, was his
publisher's request for an autobiography to accompany a projected edition of his works. Buffon's case is different, since the
Histoire naturelle was in important respects a collective work:
he relied on a vast network of traveling correspondents and
collaborated with several naturalists, notably the anatomist
Louis-Jean-Marie Daubenton, whose name appeared alongside
that of Buffon in the original Imprimerie royale edition of the
quadruped volumes. Nonetheless, it seems clear that over the
course of his career, Buffon came increasingly to view his project as coterminous with his name and life as a writer. In 1767,
he authorized an edition of the *Histoire naturelle* that excised
Daubenton's anatomical studies, making himself in effect the
sole author of the abridged work.[62] This gesture was consistent
with the views expressed in his famous *Discours sur le style*
(*Discourse on Style*), where he coined the phrase "style is man

himself" and argued that only well-written works would be preserved for posterity.[63]

Buffon's preoccupation with closure became even more marked in his last work, the *Histoire naturelle des minéraux*. Here, he casts a retrospective glance over his career and offers a final defense of his method as a naturalist. In his chapter "Du fer" ("On Iron"), he predicts (accurately) that his explanations for the formation of metallic mines would be criticized in subsequent generations as "flimsy and purely hypothetical."[64] Yet as he did several times over the course of his career, he defends his recourse to hypotheses and systems in the study of nature: "The goal of the naturalist Philosopher must therefore be to elevate himself high enough to be able to deduce from a single general effect, taken as a cause, all the particular effects; but in order to view Nature from this vast perspective, one must have examined it, studied it, & compared it in all the parts of its great expanse; a certain amount of genius, a lot of study, a little freedom of thought, are three traits without which one will only be able to disfigure Nature rather than representing her."[65] In a certain sense, this is simply a straightforward defense of Buffon's method as a naturalist, which as several scholars have observed combined detailed empiricism with broad-ranging theories of nature.[66] But a subtle shift in emphasis reflects the testamentary orientation of the *Histoire naturelle des minéraux*: here, Buffon justifies his theories as the fruit of a lifetime of careful, empirical research. As a mature naturalist who had reached the end of his career, he believed he had attained the breadth of experience necessary to propose broad-ranging theories and systems.[67]

Buffon's late defense of scientific speculation also took on a new dimension in light of his intimations that his death was approaching. In the chapter "Pétrifications & fossiles," published in the fourth volume of the *Histoire naturelle des minéraux* in

1786, just two years before his death, Buffon alludes to the fact
that he could no longer hope to complete the empirical inves-
tigations that had been one of the hallmarks of his career as a
naturalist.[68] With regret, he concedes that he will have to bequeath the study of fossils to future generations, despite the
fascination they hold for him:

> This work on aged Nature would require more time
> than I have left to live, and I can do no more than
> recommend it to posterity; it [posterity] must seek
> out these ancient titles of nobility of Nature, with
> all the more care that one is further from the time
> of its origin. In gathering and comparing them at-
> tentively, one will find Nature greater and stronger
> in its springtime than it has been in subsequent
> periods: in following its deterioration, one will rec-
> ognize the losses it has suffered and be able to de-
> termine a few more epochs in the succession of
> lives preceding us.[69]

This passage underscores what Benoît de Baere has identified
as the epistemological paradoxes in Buffon's history of the earth:
on the one hand, Buffon granted that his history was provi-
sional and that his followers might discover new epochs and
species in the earth's archives. On the other hand, he assumed
that new empirical evidence would not fundamentally alter the
theoretical underpinnings of his history of the earth.[70] Subsequent generations would invariably discover a history marked
by degeneration and decline, as progressively cooler tempera-
tures adversely affected and gradually destroyed a succession
of species. This was the "environmental determinism" that has
led some historians of science to question whether Buffon's
thought can be seen as genuinely historical.[71]

Nonetheless, Buffon concluded his chapter on fossils and petrification by underscoring the importance of empirical facts in the study of nature and refusing to record his speculations regarding fossils: "I say it again, it is with regret that I leave these interesting objects, these precious monuments of aged Nature, that my own old age does not leave me the time to examine enough to draw the conclusions I discern, but which, being based on mere glimpses, must not find a place in this work where I made it my law to present only truths based on facts. Others will come after me."[72] Here, Buffon envisages his own death, and in the same breath the outer limits of his vast natural historical project. Central to that project was the ability to engage in speculative thinking, to look beyond the confines of his own time-bound existence; as de Baere puts it, "to describe the past, the present and, to a lesser degree, the future of our planet."[73] Equally important, however, was maintaining an awareness of humanity's limited place within the long history of the earth. Human civilizations would rise and fall, and eventually all human life would succumb to the progressive cooling of the earth.[74] On an individual level, even with the most optimistic calculation of life expectancy, human life was but a brief flicker against the backdrop of the long history Buffon boldly attributed to the earth. By inscribing his own mortality into his discussion of minerals, Buffon thus signaled not only the limits of his contribution to the natural sciences but also his acute awareness of his own place within the history of nature.

It was here, too, that these personal reflections converged with Buffon's physiological theory of death as the gradual drying out and hardening of the bones. In explaining petrification to his readers, Buffon situated this mineralogical process on a continuum with the physiological processes of aging and death. Just as death was a gradual process that progressively transformed the body in the midst of life, petrification was a process

in which mineral matter gradually supplanted the living substance of plants and animals: "Often even as the animal or
vegetable substance is being destroyed, the stony matter takes
its place, such that without changing shape, these woods and
these bones find themselves converted into calcareous stone,
marble, rocks, agates, etc."[75] Like the Congolese funeral rites,
the process of petrification thus furthered the natural drying
out and hardening of the flesh and bones, appearing as the final
stage in a long process of mineralization. Moreover, Buffon
viewed this process as nature's means of preserving a memory
of past forms of life, seeming to pay her respects to the dead
just as the Congolese did: "This operation of Nature is the great
means she has used, and continues to use, to preserve forever
the imprints of perishable beings; it is indeed through these
petrifications that we recognize her most ancient productions,
and that we have an idea of those species that are now destroyed,
whose existence preceded that of all currently living or vegetat-
ing beings; these are the only monuments of the first ages of
the world."[76] Thus, in his last work, Buffon's physiological theory of death took on an important new dimension: the processes of aging and death paved the way not for the body's ultimate destruction, but for its preservation as a monument to
be excavated by future generations. Just as the first man developed an awareness of death in the midst of life, the record of
each living being was inscribed into its body long before it
actually died.

Less than ten years after Buffon's death, in year four of the French
Republic (1796 Old Style), Georges Cuvier read a paper that, as
Rudwick observes, "was an occasion of outstanding importance
for the history of paleontology, because for the first time
the world of science was presented with detailed and almost

irrefutable evidence for the reality of extinction."[77] Buffon did not live to witness this sea change in the earth sciences and the ensuing "reconstruction of geohistory in the age of revolution."[78] Nor, of course, did he live to witness the political and social revolution that would transform many of the cultural institutions he had embodied and that would bring his son "Buffonet" to the guillotine.[79] On a certain level, the imaginative connection between death and fossils Buffon developed over the course of his career shared more with the Renaissance view of fossils than with the modern view that was starting to emerge at the end of his life. At a time when the origin of fossils was still very much in doubt, some Renaissance naturalists subscribed to the view that fossils grew within the earth in a way analogous to living organisms. For these naturalists, Rudwick notes, "stones too clearly shared the characteristic of growth, as stalactites and crystals demonstrated. The decay of some minerals likewise suggested an analogy with disease, old age and death."[80] Certainly Buffon did not subscribe to such outmoded views some two hundred years later. Nonetheless, the connections he drew between the physiology of death and the process of petrification bear the mark of those Renaissance analogies.[81] At the same time, Buffon's association between death and fossils has a broader significance beyond its (limited) place in the history of science. It was an imaginative trope that shaped both his natural philosophy and his literary project, making them in an important sense inseparable from each other. Indeed, aging, death, and petrification appear in the *Histoire naturelle des minéraux* as nature's way of writing the record of each living being for preservation in the earth's archives. This idea takes on a special significance in light of Buffon's allusions to his impending death, for he too was writing the record of his life as a naturalist even as he envisioned its end. It is in this sense that I have described the *Histoire naturelle des minéraux* as Buffon's testament, not only because it lends a personal dimension to his natural philosophy, but also because it brings closure to the *Histoire naturelle.*

Buffon died on April 16, 1788, attended by Necker and his household servant Marie Madeleine Blesseau. After his death, an autopsy performed on his body revealed fifty-seven stones in the bladder and left kidney, weighing altogether some eighty-four grams. As was customary at the time, these stones were distributed as keepsakes to a number of Buffon's acquaintances, including the coauthor of the quadruped volumes, Daubenton.[82] This was a strangely fitting way to commemorate the naturalist, encapsulating not only the suffering he had endured from 1771 forward, but also his physiological theory of death and its connection to his late reflections on petrification and fossils. In a similar way, the testamentary poetics developed in Buffon's *Histoire naturelle des minéraux* gave retrospective shape to his entire project, making his contribution to natural philosophy inseparable from his reflection on death and writing. Like the kidney stones, the *Histoire naturelle des minéraux* was a fitting memorial for a writer who had coined the phrase "style is man himself" and who had argued that only well-written works would be preserved for posterity. These volumes were an occasion for Buffon, who by the end of his life had "deliberately merged his principal scientific project with the edition of his complete works," to cast a backward glance over his life's work as a naturalist.[83] They were also an occasion for him to evoke his impending death in a way that brought poetic closure to his work, not only because his life and career were coming to an end, but also because the various strands of his imaginative association between death and fossils were finally coming together. To read the *Histoire naturelle* today is thus not only to unearth past forms of knowledge; it is also to excavate the fossilized remains of Buffon's life as a writer.

2

Diderot's Brain

In the last decade of his life, from the end of his Russian adventure in 1774 until his death in 1784, Denis Diderot was extraordinarily productive. He wrote some of his most radical political texts, critiquing Catherine II of Russia's plan for legislative reform in the *Observations sur le Nakaz* and contributing some fiercely anti-colonialist pages to the Abbé Raynal's *Histoire des deux Indes* (*History of the Two Indies*).[1] He also expended tremendous energy and financial resources preparing two collections of his manuscripts, one to be sent to Russia for Catherine II and the other for the ultimately unrealized publication of his complete works.[2] Amid these activities, and in the face of declining health, Diderot continued to pursue his hugely ambitious *Éléments de physiologie,* a work Kurt Ballstadt has characterized as his "second encyclopedia."[3] Begun in the form of notes taken from 1765 onward on the physiological works of Buffon, Albrecht von Haller, Théophile de Bordeu, Pierre Louis Moreau de Maupertuis, and many others, the goal of this work was, as Ballstadt puts it, "to simply present the sum total of human knowledge that had been acquired up until the

1770s regarding the structure, functions and interrelationships of various parts of the body."[4] This was no small project. Diderot continued working on it until his death, and the diffuse, fragmented form of the work has generally been taken as a sign that he left it unfinished.[5] During the same years, he also published a defense of the ancient Stoic philosopher Seneca in two versions, the *Essai sur Sénèque* in 1778 and the *Essai sur les règnes de Claude et de Néron* in 1782.

On the face of it, the *Éléments de physiologie* and the *Essai sur les règnes de Claude et de Néron* do not appear to have much in common. The former is a not entirely original compendium of the latest advances in the physiological sciences, whereas the latter is a highly personal defense of Seneca that barely conceals Diderot's self-justification as a philosopher.[6] Yet I will argue that these two works, taken together, comprise Diderot's philosophical testament, offering his last word on the problem of death in a materialist framework. Although neither work has been recognized for its literary merit, I will focus on the unusual literary forms Diderot invented in both works. I see these forms as reflective of Diderot's late interpretation of Stoicism and his physiological understanding of death as a disaggregation of sentient molecules. Diderot developed his testamentary poetics in opposition to his "enemy brother," Jean-Jacques Rousseau, who is the object of a virulent posthumous attack in the *Essai*.[7] Although Diderot did not have occasion to read the posthumously published *Confessions,* he accused his former friend of displaying monstrous self-aggrandizement and disregard for others in writing his autobiography. He sought in his own last works, in contrast, to embody his conception of philosophy as a collective enterprise and nature as a continual recycling of living matter. Most strikingly, Diderot renounced in his last works his previous attachment to the rewards of posterity. Whereas in the 1760s he had engaged in a passionate defense of literary and artistic immortality in an exchange of letters with the sculptor Étienne Maurice Falconet, in his last works he displayed little concern for his legacy. His last gesture, on the contrary, was to give up his voice, and his name, to others.

Diderot is believed to have continued working on the *Éléments* right up until his death, but it remains unclear to what extent the final state of the manuscripts reflects the form he intended to give to the work. In a foreword appended to one of the manuscripts, an unidentified editor presents the *Éléments* as the fragments of a project cut short by Diderot's death: "Since death prevented Mr x.x.x. from realizing his project, for which he had only prepared the materials, we thought it was our obligation to gather them into one copy. However incomplete, and despite the lack of order put into them, we believe the public will be pleased to receive these fragments, and that one day someone will take on the work Mr x.x.x. could only sketch out, on the basis of his plans and ideas."[8] Most scholars have taken this account at face value, viewing the *Éléments* as little more than an "undigested" collection of notes marked by its derivative quality.[9] Paolo Quintili has contested this view, arguing that the *Éléments* should be seen as "a work projected and almost completed, which represents the philosopher's spiritual 'testament.'"[10] Yet even those who share Quintili's view have paid little attention to the literary form of the work and its implications for Diderot's late philosophy. One exception is Andrew H. Clark, who delineates the aesthetic and formal implications of the relationship between part and whole in Diderot's theory of physiology. Clark argues that "Diderot extends the idea of the relative autonomy of the *part* and the dynamic *whole* visible in various life forms to the construction, organization, and interpretation of texts and works of art."[11] In keeping with this argument, I will show how the literary form of the *Éléments* embodies Diderot's physiological theory of death. The term *elements,* borrowed from Haller's *Elementa physiologiae corporis humani* (*Elements of Human Physiology*), is especially significant here: it reflects Diderot's conviction that death does not extend to the most basic elements of nature, and informs the fragmented, elemental state in which he left his second encyclopedia.

The *Éléments* deserves its appellation as Diderot's second encyclopedia in two respects: first, it synthesized a lifetime of reading in the medical sciences, begun in the 1740s when the young Diderot took courses in anatomy and undertook a translation of Robert James's *Medical Dictionary.* Second, it aimed to achieve a comprehensive natural history of man based in physiology, psychology, and philosophy.[12] According to Jean Mayer, the first scholar to take Diderot's scientific thought seriously in the 1950s, the *Éléments* realized its ambitions to such an extent that it could claim to rival Buffon's *Histoire naturelle de l'homme.*[13] But unlike Buffon, Diderot was not an experimental scientist and thus relied heavily on a wide range of written sources in composing the *Éléments.* Principal among the authors Diderot quoted, paraphrased, and synthesized were Buffon, the Swiss anatomist and physiologist Albrecht von Haller, and the Montpellier medical doctor Théophile Bordeu, best known as a character in *Le rêve de d'Alembert.* The *Éléments* consists of three parts: a brief opening section on the physiology of plant-animals, animals, and man; a very long middle section on the elements and parts of the human body; and a somewhat shorter concluding section on the workings of the human brain. It is above all the middle section, largely drawn from Haller's writings on the irritability of animal tissues and organs, that has led scholars to characterize the *Éléments* as a derivative work. But I will argue that formal and philosophical meaning can be attributed even to this section, in a way that connects it to the two other, more original parts of the work. My reading underscores three aspects of the *Éléments* that can be roughly mapped onto the three parts of the work: first, Diderot's physiological theory of death, which is outlined in the first section on the nature of life and the organization of its various forms; second, the derivative nature of the second section; and third, Diderot's concept of immense or total memory, which he develops in the third section on the self, consciousness, and memory as phenomena of the brain.

Diderot relied largely on Buffon and Bordeu in developing his physiological theory of death. From Buffon, he took the idea that death is not a singular, catastrophic event, but a gradual process that gets played out in the body over time. He also followed Buffon in describing the process of death as a gradual hardening, or ossification, of the body. From Bordeu, Diderot took a conception of the body as a grouping of organs that work together, but with each possessing its own distinct life force. As Ballstadt puts it, "Bordeu viewed the body as a more-or-less loose assembly of organs, hierarchically arranged, in which each vital organ possessed a certain degree of autonomy. . . . Human life was, for Bordeu, a multi-layered phenomenon. The life of the body as a whole was superimposed onto the lives of the organs themselves, which could be viewed as semi-independent systems in their own right."[14] As Clark has shown, this view of the body can be extended to Diderot's broader conception of nature as "a vital regenerative mass made of autonomous *parts.*"[15] It also informed Diderot's understanding of animal organization, a key concept for eighteenth-century vitalists.[16] As he saw it, the initially fluid animal has sensitivity and life in each of its constituent parts, but lacks "a sensitivity and life common to the mass." As an animal takes on its organized form, "there is established a general and common sensitivity that the organs share diversely."[17] This account of the genesis of animal organization recalls the distinction in *Le rêve de d'Alembert* between a swarm of bees that appears to act as a whole but is in fact merely joined by contiguity (the animal in its initially fluid state) and a swarm of bees that has been fused to form a continuous whole (the animal in its organized state).[18] It should be noted that in *Le rêve de d'Alembert,* the distinction between the two swarms of bees is so slight as to be imperceptible to the human eye.

The fine line between contiguity and continuity also informs Diderot's understanding of death. To the Buffonian conception of death as a process of hardening, Diderot adds the Bordeu-inspired notion that the various parts of the body can harden and lose their sensitivity at different rates, thereby isolating themselves from the whole: "[The sensitivity] appears proportional to the progress of hardening; the harder an organ gets, the less sensitive it is. The more quickly it advances toward hardness, the more quickly it loses its sensitivity and isolates itself from the system."[19] Thus for Diderot, death is not only a gradual process, as it is for Buffon, but also a variegated process in which each part of the body disassociates itself from the whole at its own rhythm. This leads Diderot to posit various levels of life (and death) in any living organism:

> There are certainly two very distinct forms of life, even three.
>> The life of the entire animal.
>> The life of each of its organs.
>> The life of the molecule.[20]

Animal organization is what allows the various organs and molecules of a living being to work together. But in death, the collective life of the animal ceases, even as the life of its various parts persists. In fact, Diderot asserts the relativity of death in quite radical terms, claiming that it does not reach the level of the molecule: "The heart, lungs, spleen, hand, almost all the parts of an animal live for some time separated from the whole. Even the head separated from the body looks and lives. It is only the life of the molecule or its sensitivity that doesn't cease. That is one of its essential qualities. Death stops there."[21] The notion that death does not reach the animal on the level of the molecule is crucial to Diderot's vitalist materialism, because it leaves room for the possibility that the now contiguous (rather than continuous) molecules of an animal's corpse can be re-combined in new forms: "The butterfly is a worm, caterpillar, and butterfly. The mayfly is a chrysalis for four years; the frog starts out as a tadpole. How many metamorphoses escape us! I see some that are rather quick: why wouldn't there be others for which the period would be more distant? Who knows what may become of the insensitive molecules of an animal after its death?"[22] In a similar vein, d'Alembert goes so far as to muse, at the climax of his dream, that to die is merely to change forms: "Alive, I act and react as a whole . . . dead, I act and react as molecules. . . . So I don't die at all. No, without a doubt, I don't die at all in this sense, neither me, nor anything at all. . . . To be born, to live and to pass, is to change forms."[23] In a memorable letter to his lover Sophie Volland, Diderot takes this idea one step further, imagining that the disaggregated molecules of his corpse might one day meld with hers to form a new self, centuries after their deaths:

> Oh my Sophie, there would thus remain for me
> some hope of touching you, feeling you, loving you,
> searching for you, uniting with you, mixing myself
> up in you, when we are no longer! If there were ac-
> cording to our principles a law of affinity, if it were

given to us to form a common being; if I were to
make up a new whole with you in the progression
of centuries; if the dispersed molecules of your lover stirred themselves, moved themselves, searched
for yours scattered in nature. Allow me this chime-
ra. I find it sweet. It would assure me of an eternity
in you and with you.[24]

This fantasy of postmortem procreation might seem more in
keeping with a speculative, poetic work like *Rêve de d'Alembert*
than with the drier, more empirically grounded *Éléments*.[25] But
in fact, Enlightenment vitalists often attempted to find empirical grounding for their theories of reincarnation. To cite just
one example, the Genevan naturalist Charles Bonnet (another
of Diderot's sources) derived his seemingly fantastical theory
of palingenesis from detailed anatomical studies of the elusive
organ of the human soul.[26]

Where Diderot departs from Buffon and Bordeu, however, is in his use of social metaphors to describe the physiological processes of aging and death. Building on the idea that
in life, an animal's various parts work together collectively, he
compares the death of each part to its retreat from the pleasures
and duties of a collective society:

The parts joined to the body appear to die, at least
as a group: with age, the flesh becomes muscular,
the fibers harden, the muscles become tendon-like,
the tendons seem to lose their sensitivity; I say they
seem to, because they might still have sensation
within themselves, without the whole animal being
aware of it. Who can say that there isn't an infinity
of sensations aroused and extinguished there? Little by little the tendon slackens, dries out, hardens,

> ceases to live, at least to live the collective life of
> the entire system; maybe it only isolates itself, cuts
> itself off from the society whose pains and plea-
> sures it no longer shares and to which it no longer
> contributes.[27]

What is lost, when a part secedes from the whole, is not necessarily its individual sensitivity or vitality, but merely its par-
ticipation in the collective life of the body. And just as we may
not perceive the difference between a contiguous and continuous swarm of bees, we may not perceive the continuing sensitivity of organs that have separated themselves from the whole.

These social metaphors take on an added significance
when one considers the encyclopedic, collective dimension of
the *Éléments*. Unlike the *Encyclopédie*, this work was not written by a "Society of Men of Letters." But its derivative nature,
especially in the central section, has always made its status in
Diderot's corpus problematic, fueling arguments that the final
state of the manuscripts cannot possibly represent Diderot's
intentions for the work.[28] For Aram Vartanian, "It is highly
implausible, of course, that Diderot had proposed all along to
give, in the *Eléments de physiologie,* what would have been in
substance merely a compilation—a sort of *cours abrégé* of Haller,
enriched by additions from other specialists, plus an informal
commentary of his own."[29] Yet this assumes that originality is
the overriding value in literary and scientific writing. This
premise must be questioned if we are to take seriously the idea
of the *Éléments* as Diderot's second encyclopedia, and if we are
to take full stock of his social metaphors. Perhaps writing, or
assembling, an original work was not Diderot's primary concern. Or perhaps the originality of the work lies not so much
in its constitution of new scientific knowledge, but in the
elaboration of a *form* that reflects both Diderot's conception of

knowledge as a shared endeavor and his understanding of nature as a constant recycling of vital matter in new forms.

Viewed in this light, the term *elements* takes on a heightened significance, regardless of whether Diderot's age and declining health prevented him from realizing the *Éléments* as he might have intended. The fragmentary, note-like form of the work, with its numerous intriguing aphorisms followed by "to be meditated on" or "to be explained," embodies the motif of elements (or vital molecules) that was the basis for Diderot's materialist vision of life as a continual repurposing of vital matter. This form also reflects Diderot's conviction that knowledge was a collective, encyclopedic enterprise. Just as he believed that the sentient molecules of his body could be recombined after his death to form new selves, he believed that the elements of other physiologists' work that appear in a fragmented form in his *Éléments* could one day be recombined to form new kinds of knowledge in the future. This is not to say that Diderot's role was limited to that of the compiler. As Mayer observes, "He does with his sources what Socrates does with his interlocutors in Plato's dialogues: he takes their refutation from themselves, borrowing from them the facts most likely to overthrow their theories. Moreover, by juxtaposing opposing doctrines, he attains an overall view by virtue of the richness of his documentation."[30] In other words, Diderot plays the role he ascribed to himself as editor of the *Encyclopédie:* the Socratic midwife who helps others give birth to new knowledge. But in the *Éléments,* Diderot does this in a very particular way: he breaks knowledge down into its most basic elements and presents it in fragmentary form so that it can be picked up and incorporated into new bodies of knowledge in the future.

Diderot's social metaphors are also significant in light of his reflections, in the same chapter, on the exclusion of the elderly in society. Unlike Buffon, who discounts old age as a prejudice to be eradicated by the rational philosopher, Diderot presents a disabused view of the burden the elderly represent for the young:

> The child runs toward death with eyes closed: the adult man is stationary. The old man gets there with his back turned. The child doesn't see the term of his life at all; the adult man pretends to doubt one even dies; the old man consoles himself, trembling, with a hope that is renewed each day. It is cruelly impolite to speak of death in the presence of an old man: we honor old age, but we don't love it; even if we only gained with a man's death the end of the unpleasant duties we perform on his behalf, it wouldn't take us long to console ourselves. It is already saying something if we don't secretly rejoice. I was just past sixty-six when I told myself these truths.[31]

As the reference to his own age suggests, this musing may well reflect Diderot's personal experience of aging. But read in light of his physiological theories, it also reflects an implicit analogy between the isolation of an old man from society and the disassociation of an organ from a living, sensitive body. With respect to the dying body, Diderot insists on the fact that we can no longer perceive the sensitivity of an organ after it secedes from the whole; although it may appear dead to us, it may continue to experience sensation apart from the whole. He applies this idea to himself in his last extant letter to Volland, dated September 3, 1774, observing that contrary to his expectations, aging has in no way hardened his heart: "I had thought that the fibers of the heart hardened with age. This is not the case at all. I think my sensitivity may even have increased. Everything touches me, everything affects me, I will be the most remarkably weepy old man you have ever known."[32]

The third and final part of the *Éléments,* on the workings of the brain, is also marked by Diderot's preoccupation with aging and decline at the end of his life. This is the most original part of the work, where he takes on what Ballstadt calls "the 'big issues' of life in general, and of human life in particular."[33] Central among these issues is the self: how it is constituted, and what are its contours as a part, or element, of nature. For Diderot, "memory is constitutive of the self."[34] But he is also interested in the way the brain filters sensory input to create a unified sense of experience. Echoing Buffon, who observed that the seemingly continuous thread of our lives is broken every time we fall asleep, Diderot claims that even a single day is punctuated by multiple "nights" every time we blink: "It seems we spend our days in little days and little nights. First of all, night falls every time we close our eyelids. And doesn't that happen to us all the time? If we don't notice all those little nights, it's because we're not paying attention to them."[35] Diderot insists here on the gap between the illusion of continuous perception created by our brains and the reality of intermittent perceptions. In another compelling analogy, he compares the soul (understood as a material entity in the context of his monist materialism) to a person at a noisy dinner party: "The soul is amidst its sensations like a guest at a tumultuous table who is speaking with the person next to him: he doesn't hear the others."[36] Once again, Diderot emphasizes the way our brains filter out a unified, continuous sense of experience (a single conversation) amidst the cacophony of competing sensations (the tumultuous table). Yet just as the "little nights" remain a part of our experience, whether consciously or not, so do the other conversations at the dinner table remain part of the soul's experience ("The soul is amidst *its* sensations").

Diderot's interest in the unnoticed sensations—the conversations *not* attended to at the dinner table—plays an important role in his chapter on memory. Here he develops an original concept of what he calls immense or total memory. This concept is extraordinarily expansive, consisting of an enormous memory bank of all the sensations—including the unnoticed ones—we have absorbed over the course of our lives. It is fitting that the sentence in which Diderot expresses this idea is one of the most expansive and syntactically complex of his corpus. I will quote it both in the original French and in translation to give a sense of its living, breathing syntax:

> Je suis porté à croire que tout ce que nous avons vu, connu, entendu, aperçu, jusqu'aux arbres d'une longue forêt, que dis-je, jusqu'à la disposition des branches, à la forme des feuilles et à la variété des couleurs, des verts et des lumières; jusqu'à l'aspect des grains de sable du rivage de la mer, aux inégalités de la surface des flots, soit agités par un souffle léger, soit écumeux et soulevés par les vents de la tempête, jusqu'à la multitude des voix humaines, des cris des animaux et des bruits physiques, à la mélodie et à l'harmonie de tous les airs, de toutes les pièces de musique, de tous les concerts que nous avons entendus, tout cela existe en nous à notre insu.[37]

> [I am inclined to believe that everything we have seen, known, heard, noticed, all the way down to the trees of a long forest, what am I saying, to the arrangement of branches, to the form of the leaves and the variety of colors, of greens and lights; down to the aspect of grains of sand on the seashore, to the unevenness of the surface of the waves, whether stirred up by a light breeze, or foaming and whipped up by the winds of a storm, down to the multitude

of human voices, of animal cries and of physical
noises, to the melody and the harmony of all the
airs, of all the pieces of music, of all the concerts
we have heard, all of this exists in us, unbeknownst
to us.]

What makes this single sentence remarkable, in addition to its
sinuous rhythm, is how deeply into the self and nature Diderot's
concept of immense memory reaches. The human brain appears
as an immensely powerful tool for preserving the tiniest details
of nature absorbed over a lifetime of experience. Especially
significant, in my eyes, is the way the encyclopedic reach of
memory breaks down the boundaries between the self and
nature; by extension, it also breaks down the boundaries between individual selves, since each individual brain reaches so
deeply into nature. This reflects the mysterious state of affairs
in *Le rêve de d'Alembert,* where the philosophical dream is
shared by d'Alembert (who dreams it), Mlle de Lespinasse (who
writes it down), and Bordeu (who somehow knows its content
without having spoken to d'Alembert or read Lespinasse's text).
As individual parts, or elements, of nature, the characters in *Le
rêve de d'Alembert* seem to share some sort of collective consciousness or memory. And although Diderot never formulates
this idea explicitly, the *Éléments* begs the question of whether
the most basic elements of a person might preserve some trace
of their immense memory after their death. In this, Diderot was
prescient: recent scientific research has shown that decapitated
tapeworms preserve some form of memory after their heads
have been regenerated.[38] Diderot would not have been surprised
by this finding. In fact, he formulated a similar hypothesis in
his love letter to Volland about reincarnation: "Those who have
loved each other during their lives and who have themselves
buried next to each other are perhaps not as crazy as we think.

Perhaps their ashes press up against each other, are mixed together and reunite. What do I know? Perhaps they haven't lost all sentiment, all memory of their original state."[39] This intuition, formulated in 1759, is consistent with the concept of immense memory Diderot developed at the end of his life, so deeply ingrained in us that it gives unity to a lifetime of experience, and so encyclopedic that it reaches far beyond the contours of a single self.

Diderot even goes so far as to formulate the Proustian idea that immense memory can be recalled to our conscious perception by certain actions: "Immense memory is the connection between everything we have been in a single instant and everything we have been in the following instant, states of being that if linked by an action will remind a man of everything he has sensed throughout his life. I believe all men have this kind of memory. The conclusions are easy to draw."[40] Although Diderot does not draw these conclusions for his readers, the concept of immense memory clearly has important implications for his understanding of the self and its dissolution in death. The unity of the self, for Diderot, lies not in the illusory sense of unity created by the brain's filtering of sensations and memories, but rather in "immense or total memory, [which] is a state of complete unity. Partial memory, state of incomplete unity."[41] He is less interested in conscious memory as the locus of a continuous sense of self than in unconscious memory as a receptacle for the multiple sensations that crowd in on our brain and are constantly being filtered to create continuous perceptions. This idea takes on a heightened significance in old age, when "old men remember the past in forgetting the present."[42] Just as Diderot had insisted on the possible vitality of an apparently deadened organ, he alludes here to the old man's renewed contact with portions of his immense or total memory that had previously been inaccessible to him.

Diderot's conviction that our brains preserve a record of the sum total of our experiences also informs his understanding of the way intellectual endeavors take shape over time. In the allusive style typical of the *Éléments*, he writes: "Intellectual actions interrupted and picked up again after a long interval; phenomenon to be explained."[43] The specific context for this remark concerns thoughts or intentions interrupted by an illness or accident and then picked up again at a later date. But Diderot's broader interest in these kinds of mental phenomena speaks to the long and discontinuous genesis of the *Éléments* and, more generally, to the way intellectual projects can take shape over a long period of time. If our immense memory records everything we have seen, heard, learned, noticed (or presumably read), this might explain why our thought processes are both more discontinuous than we might expect (ideas and projects can be apparently dropped or stalled for long periods of time) and more continuous (unfinished ideas and projects are picked up later in life; forgotten facts or readings can play an unconscious role in the constitution of knowledge). Once again, this idea informs the fragmented, collage-like form of the *Éléments:* it is as if Diderot were seeking to capture the discontinuous form of a lifetime of readings in the physiological sciences. Just as Buffon claimed at the end of his life to have attained a broad, sweeping view of nature in its entirety, Diderot sought to represent, through the form of his last encyclopedic project, his mind as an encyclopedic (but not entirely synthetic) repository for a lifetime of learning about the body.

We can thus see a deep connection between the first and third parts of the *Éléments:* in the first part, Diderot is concerned with what happens to the elements of the body when they isolate themselves from the whole and are restored to their original place in the broader universe of vital matter. In the third part, he is concerned with the relationship between the unified

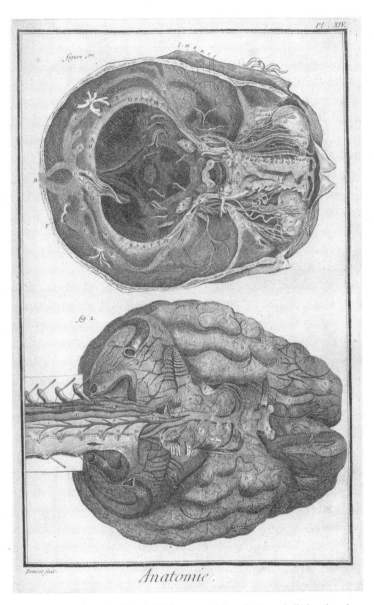

Anatomie plates in Denis Diderot and Jean le Rond d'Alembert's *Encyclopédie,* 1762, Paris. (Courtesy of the ARTFL *Encyclopédie* Project, University of Chicago)

self (constituted by the brain's sensorial filtering) and immense
memory (constituted by the undifferentiated mass of sensations). In the first part, we get a fairly clear sense of what happens
to the elements of the body after death: sentient molecules are
recycled to create new beings. In the third part, however, we get
much less of a sense of what happens to the self, and especially
the brain, after death. This absence is all the more striking in
that the structure of the third part begs that very question: it
begins with chapters on sensations, understanding, and memory (which are constitutive of the self) and ends with chapters
on organs and illnesses (which contribute to its dissolution).
Moreover, the chapter on illnesses is followed by a general conclusion to the work that appears to deviate for the first time
from strictly physiological matters. In bringing this seemingly
unfinished work to a close, Diderot turns to a traditional Stoic
understanding of philosophy as a means of preparing for death.
He evokes two spiritual exercises in preparation for death, the
first of which relies on the imagination, a faculty discussed in
an earlier chapter: "A common fantasy among the living is to
imagine themselves dead, standing alongside their corpses and
following their funeral convoy. It's like a swimmer who sees his
clothing hung up on the shore. You men who are no longer to
be feared, what then will you hear?"[44] This classic Stoic meditation also reflects Diderot's personal anguish at the end of his
life. Would he attain the posthumous glory he had aspired to in
his epistolary exchange with Falconet? As Elena Russo has as-
tutely observed, at the end of his life "Diderot's earlier optimism
vis-à-vis his status in the Republic of Letters and his role as a
public intellectual gave way to a profound identity crisis like the
one that gripped his former friend Jean-Jacques Rousseau in
his final years."[45] Yet with the second spiritual exercise evoked
in the closing pages of the *Éléments*, Diderot seemingly rejects
posterity altogether. Philosophy appears not as a means of at-

taining posthumous glory, but rather as a means of removing oneself from the concerns of everyday life and freeing oneself from the fear of death. In keeping with Montaigne's philosophy, it is a practice of death, a form of self-annihilation: "Another apprenticeship of death is philosophy, a habitual and profound meditation that removes us from everything surrounding us and annihilates us. The fear of death, says the Stoic, is a handle by which the strong man grabs us and takes us where he likes. Break the handle and trick the hand of the strong man."[46] As a practice, philosophy relies on repetition, in keeping with the tradition of spiritual exercises and philosophy as a way of life. Diderot put this repetition into practice on a literary level, recycling his Stoic sentence about the fear of death in several of his late works, including the *Histoire des deux Indes* and the *Essai sur les règnes de Claude et de Néron*.[47] To repeat the same sentence across works that are so different in tone and content suggests that just as living matter is recycled with the death of the individual, the same sentences must be repeatedly recycled as the philosopher faces death. In keeping with this idea, Diderot concludes the *Éléments,* a work generally seen as unfinished, by distilling his entire philosophy into a single principle: "There is only one virtue, justice; only one duty, to make oneself happy; only one corollary, not to overestimate life and not to fear death."[48]

In fact, Diderot's Stoic meditation on the annihilation of the self contains the reverse image of his concept of immense memory. Whereas immense memory unifies a lifetime of sensory experiences, blurring the boundaries between self and nature, and between self and others, the Stoic meditation removes us from nature and obliterates the self as a means of better understanding our true place in nature. Ultimately for Diderot, the philosophical life is one that tracks immense memory through its encyclopedic attempts to understand nature;

but it also sees its own efforts as subject to the eventual annihilation of the self, whereby a lifetime of memories and intellectual pursuits will be restored to their elemental nature, only to
be recombined by new selves at some point in the future. In this
sense, his philosophical testament offers both his last word on
philosophy, and his acknowledgment that his words could
only ever be one combinatory possibility in the infinite and
ever-shifting body of shared human knowledge.

During the same years he was composing the *Éléments*, Diderot
embarked on a new project that, according to his daughter,
Marie-Angélique de Vandeul, destroyed his already weakened
health.[49] This was a life of Seneca, to preface a new translation
of the Stoic philosopher's works commissioned by Diderot's
friend d'Holbach. The translation was part of a broader campaign on the part of d'Holbach's circle to defend materialist
philosophy from its detractors by highlighting its ancient ante-
cedents. The initial translator, N. Lagrange, who was the tutor
of d'Holbach's children, began working on the project in 1768,
two years before the publication of d'Holbach's radical materialist tract, the *Système de la nature*. When Lagrange died an
untimely death in 1775, Diderot's literary executor, Jacques-
André Naigeon, took over. It was to him that Diderot addressed
the opening pages of his work. Thus the *Essai sur Sénèque*,
later republished as the *Essai sur les règnes de Claude et de Néron*,
was from the beginning part of a broader collective endeavor.

At the same time, the *Essai* was also a deeply personal work
and became all the more so in its expanded version. It marked
Diderot's return to publishing after several decades of hiding his
works entirely or making them available only in the limited
manuscript circulation of the *Correspondance littéraire*. First
published less than six months after Rousseau's death in July 1778,

the *Essai* issued a virulent attack on Diderot's former friend and collaborator. It also couched its defense of Seneca in terms that were designed to justify Diderot's own philosophical and political choices. This explains Jean Ehrard's assessment of the *Essai* as "a true intellectual and moral testament."[50] Nonetheless, Diderot's attack on Rousseau has long been seen as an unfortunate and somewhat embarrassing lapse; as his biographer Arthur Wilson put it, "It was entirely gratuitous of Diderot to allude to Rousseau in the *Essai sur Sénèque,* and the fact that he did so proves what an obsession his '*frère ennemi*' had become."[51] In recent years, however, both Russo and Yves Citton have contested this view, demonstrating how integral the attack on Rousseau was to Diderot's ethics and politics.[52] I build on these interpretations to show how Diderot developed his poetics of testamentary writing in opposition to Rousseau's autobiographical project. If we take seriously the idea of the *Essai* as a philosophical and literary testament, the attack on Rousseau appears not gratuitous at all, but deeply grounded in Diderot's late Stoicism and his self-perception as a philosopher. Diderot's tendency, brilliantly analyzed by Jean Starobinski, of integrating "the words of others" into his own voice culminates in the *Essai,* where it becomes part of a broader poetics of self-effacement.[53] At the end of his life, having reached "the age when one lives from day to day," Diderot gave literary form to his Stoicist philosophy, lending his voice to others and preparing to give his body back to the elements.[54]

In the preamble to the *Essai,* addressed to Naigeon, Diderot reflects on the relationship between writing (and reading) and the passage of time, thereby defining the poetics of his last published work:

> Every age writes and reads in its own way; youth
> loves events; old age reflections. An experiment
> I would gladly propose to a man of sixty-five or

sixty-six, who finds my reflections too long or too
frequent, or too foreign to my topic, would be to
take Tacitus, Suetonius, and Seneca with him in his
retreat; to throw casually onto the page the things
that interest him, the ideas they awaken in his
mind, the thoughts he would like to retain from
these authors, the sentiments he feels, having no
other project than to learn without fatigue; and
I am almost sure he would recreate this work just
about as it is, stopping at the places I have stopped,
comparing his century to those of the past, and
drawing from circumstances and characters the
same conjectures as to what is presaged by the present day. I compose nothing, I'm not an author;
I read or discuss; I inquire or respond.[55]

Here Diderot takes his biological determinism to its logical
extreme, denying any personal dimension to the *Essai*. Any
man of his age who mimics the conditions under which the
Essai was written will produce a nearly identical work. Yet
Diderot also makes clear that his claim that each age reads differently is grounded in his personal experience: in his thirties,
he had judged Seneca harshly for accumulating riches under
Nero rather than choosing death in the name of virtue. In his
sixties, he chastises his younger self for making such a harsh
and impetuous judgment, at an age when he was "without
knowledge, without the least experience of life or people, nor
of the dreadful alternatives our treacherous existence draws us
into, nor of the difficulty of walking with a sure step on the
narrow line between good and evil."[56] Even as he draws on
personal experience, Diderot's collective "we" suggests that
every man will eventually become aware of the moral ambi-
guities and ethical compromises inherent to human existence.

The phrase "every age writes and reads in its own way" also reflects Diderot's heightened attention to historical change at the end of his life. He invites his reader to compare his era to that of Seneca, to note the striking similarities between the two, but also to be attentive to historical differences that make it unwise to judge Seneca by the moral standards of a later time. In fact, Diderot suggests that reading the *Essai,* alongside Seneca, Tacitus, and Suetonius, will cultivate historical consciousness in his reader. It will allow the reader to reflect not only on the past, but also on the future that his generation will bequeath to its children.

Diderot's attentiveness to the ages of writing and reading also has implications for his understanding of literary history and style. For him, "There is the style of the century, of the thing itself, of the profession, of the man."[57] The historical nature of literary style explains why a writer like Seneca might fall in and out of favor depending on the era. This insight deserves special emphasis in a work that has itself suffered from a long period of critical neglect. In his influential biography of Diderot, Wilson condemned the *Essai* as a work Diderot "did not have to write and almost surely would have been wiser not to have written."[58] In contrast, the recent surge of interest in the *Essai* suggests that our own historical moment may be more receptive than Wilson's was to the issues of late style and testamentary writing that suffuse the *Essai* and other late works of the Enlightenment.[59]

Even as Diderot emphasizes biological determinism and historical relativism, his reading of Seneca leads him to look beyond the limits of his own body and the historical moment he inhabits. He proposes that all writers imagine themselves writing from the grave: "One only thinks, one only speaks with force from the bottom of the grave: it is there that one must place oneself, it is from there that one must address men. The

man who advised the philosopher to leave a last will and testament had a great and useful idea. I hope for the progress of
science, for the good of the academies and for the interest of the
oppressed, that he will make us wait a long time for his own."[60]
The unnamed man Diderot cites here is his fellow encyclopedist
d'Alembert, who died in 1783, less than two years after the
expanded version of the *Essai* was published. In his 1775 *Éloge
de l'abbé de Saint-Pierre* (*Eulogy of the Abbé de Saint-Pierre*),
d'Alembert invites every man of letters to write "a final will and
testament, in which he would express himself freely on the
works, opinions, and men his conscience would reproach him
for having flattered, and beg his century's forgiveness for having
been sincere only after death."[61] For d'Alembert, such testaments
would serve as an antidote to the mutual flattery common
among men of letters and its pernicious effect on the advance-
ment of taste. Diderot takes the idea of the testament in a more
political direction: for him, it is a means of speaking the truth
to a despotic regime, as he himself spoke to Catherine II of
Russia in his posthumous *Observations sur le Nakaz*.

Diderot did not wait until his death, however, to publish
his vitriolic condemnation of Rousseau. His initially veiled attack in the 1778 edition has generally been seen as a preemptive
strike designed to counter any harmful personal revelations
about him and his circle that the *Confessions* might contain.
The *Essai* has thus been linked to another "shameful" episode
in Diderot's career, when he, Melchior Grimm, and Louise
d'Épinay revised the latter's fictionalized memoirs, the *Histoire
de Madame de Montbrillant* (*Story of Madame de Montbrillant*),
to darken the portrayal of Rousseau.[62] But to discount these
episodes as petty personal lapses is to ignore the depth of Diderot's engagement with Rousseau in the last decades of his life.
As Jean Fabre has observed, "in the last fifteen years of his career,
Diderot's thought and work are only illuminated by a perpetu-

al reference, manifest or hidden, to Rousseau."[63] In this vein, Russo has read the *Essai* alongside *Rousseau juge de Jean-Jacques* (*Rousseau Judge of Jean-Jacques*), arguing that both works "display disarticulation, a split in the authorial persona that nonetheless does not prevent the author's voice from exerting a powerful impact on the reader."[64] Citton has also linked these two works, observing that "both authors became simultaneously and symmetrically aware of the traps and dangers inherent in the public sphere: through their mutual attacks, they both anticipated a certain form of liberalism, and denounced its inability to adequately evaluate the productions of human creativity and intelligence."[65] In both interpretations, Diderot's attack on Rousseau in the *Essai* appears not as an embarrassing lapse, but as integral to the meaning of the *Essai* as a whole.

The attack specifically concerns Rousseau's autobiographical project as Diderot perceived it. Although he had not read the posthumously published *Confessions,* much less *Rousseau juge de Jean-Jacques* or the *Rêveries,* Diderot was categorical in his condemnation: "It must be acknowledged that it is insane, it is horrible, to sacrifice one's friends and one's enemies in dying so they can serve as a funeral procession for one's shadow; to give up gratitude, discretion, loyalty, domestic tranquility to the arrogant passion to have oneself talked about in the future; in short, to drag one's whole century into the grave, to augment one's dust."[66] This passage confirms that there is far more at stake in Diderot's attack on Rousseau than protecting his personal reputation or defending his philosophical circle. What seems to offend Diderot is the very notion of striving to be spoken of in the future. To seek to "augment one's dust" in this way runs counter to the Stoic lesson Diderot takes from Seneca. It reflects the vanity of those who prepare magnificent funereal monuments for themselves rather than leaving that task to the bereaved: "This marble, covering nothing but dust, reveals the veneration of the people, the respect of relatives, the gratitude of friends, or else are the enduring monuments of the vanity of the living and the dead."[67] Diderot's late reading of Seneca, in contrast, has led him to cultivate a heightened awareness of the brevity and insignificance of his own life: "At my age, at an age when one no longer mends one's ways, I have not read Seneca without benefit for myself, for everything surrounding me: it seems to me that I fear men's judgment less, and that I fear my own more; it seems to me that I have less regret for the years that have passed, and that I do not hold the ones that are to follow in such high esteem; it seems to me that I am better able to see existence as a rather insignificant point between a nothingness [*un néant*] that preceded and the term that awaits me."[68] Reading Seneca as his life draws to a close, Diderot sees his existence as a mere point, caught between nothingness and death. This view makes Rousseau's efforts to ensure he will be spoken of after his death, at the expense of his former friends, all the more unnatural and unethical. The question then becomes whether there is any form of testamentary writing that would be consistent with a Stoicist acceptance of life's brevity and insignificance.

One possible answer to this question can be found in Seneca's *On Tranquility of Mind*, when he rejects any form of writing intended for posterity. Instead of writing to be remembered in the future, one should write exclusively for the self and self-study: " 'Where is the need,' I ask, 'to compose something to last for ages? Why not stop trying to prevent posterity being silent about you? You were born to die, and a silent funeral is less bothersome. So if you must fill your time, write something in a simple style for your own use and not for publication: less toil is needed if you study only for the day.' "[69] The kind of writing Seneca advocates here reflects the Stoic practice of soliloquy, in which the wise man judges his own actions at the end of each day as if it were his last. In this way, he prepares himself for a peaceful sleep and, eventually, a peaceful death. It belongs to the tradition of philosophy as a way of life that Pierre Hadot has traced from antiquity into the present, and that Michel Foucault foregrounded in his last lessons at the Collège de France.[70] Paradoxically, it was Rousseau who may have come closest to this Senecan ideal at the end of his life, when he wrote his *Rêveries* as a series of daily walks and reveries recorded for himself alone and in preparation for death.

Diderot, in contrast, rejects what he calls the "monastic spirit" of Stoicism, preferring a philosophy of social engagement to one of solitary retreat. He takes issue with Seneca's advice to one of his contemporaries that he leave his administrative post in favor of self-study and the pursuit of philosophical wisdom: "The philosopher is a worthy man wherever he goes, but more so in the senate than in the school, more so in a tribunal than in a library; and the kinds of occupations you despise are those I honor."[71] In fact, Diderot seems to draw his ethical model more from Seneca's life than from his writings: he admires the Seneca who stayed by Nero's side despite the ethical compromises, while he rejects the Seneca who counsels a retreat from public duties in favor of an illusory Stoic self-sufficiency.

Above all, Diderot admires Seneca's final moments. This is significant because Seneca was denied the opportunity to write his final will and testament. When a centurion sent by Nero refused to give him access to his tablets, he instead offered the image of his life as a final bequest to his friends: "[Seneca], without being troubled, asks for the tablets of his testament. Upon the refusal of the centurion, he turns to his friends and tells them that 'since he was not permitted to reward their good service, there was nonetheless still one bequest remaining to him, and of all those he could make the most precious, the image of his life, the memory of which they would not preserve without being applauded for their love of honest knowledge, and their constancy in friendship.'"[72] This scene of Seneca's final moments, which Diderot takes from Tacitus, sanctions Diderot's preference for Seneca's life over his teachings. Paradoxically, it also provides him with a model of testamentary writing (or non-writing) in which the writer submits to necessity and accepts the effacement of his own voice. This model stands in stark contrast to Rousseau's amplification of his own voice beyond the grave.

The poetics of self-effacement Diderot develops in the *Essai* is exemplified by his choice to devote his last work to a defense of Seneca. As he describes it, he can sometimes be found hiding behind Seneca and at other times shielding him from the attacks of his critics: "Here, presenting the philosopher to the censor and hiding myself behind him; there, taking the opposite role and opening myself to arrows that won't injure Seneca who is hiding behind me."[73] More than mere self-protection, this game of hide-and-seek reflects the ethical principle that we must not judge others without putting ourselves in their place: "A beautiful precept of natural and evangelical morals is to put oneself in the place of the accused: may the most innocent among you cast the first stone at him. We overshoot the severity of laws when we weigh actions without regard for circumstances."[74] This same precept dictates how we should read the *Essai,* by putting ourselves in Diderot's position when he wrote it: "That was the disposition in which I wrote, and that is the disposition in which I hope to be read."[75] Yet in the context of Diderot's biological determinism and historical relativism, this precept begs the question of whether we can ever truly put ourselves in the place of another. Could Diderot have read Seneca more charitably when he was in his thirties? Could Seneca's eighteenth-century critics have imagined the historical and social context that made his ethical choices different from

their own? More generally, can any writer step outside their
body and historical moment to write from the grave?

Diderot's choice to defend Seneca at the end of his life, as
part of a commissioned, collective project, is also symptomatic of his tendency to give his time freely to others rather
than guarding it jealously for himself. In his discussion of *On
the Shortness of Life,* he acknowledges that this tendency of his
may run counter to Seneca's teachings:

> One cannot read this treatise without applying to
> oneself most of the wise reflections spread through-
> out. A man of letters complained of the rapid pas-
> sage of time. One of his friends, witness to his re-
> grets, and knowing how generous he was with his
> own, interrupted him by quoting this passage from
> Seneca: *You complain of the brevity of life, and you
> let your own be stolen from you.* "My life is not sto-
> len from me," responded the philosopher: "I give it
> up; and what better can I do than to give a portion
> of it to him who has enough esteem for me to seek
> this gift?"[76]

As Lucien Nouis has observed, Diderot distances himself here
from Seneca's injunction to reserve time for the self, and rejects
his claim that life only seems short because we do not use our
time wisely.[77] According to him, any man who has tried to
master a single science knows full well that life is too short, and
it was certainly too short for Lagrange, whose translation of
Seneca was interrupted by his untimely death. At other moments in the *Essai,* however, Diderot expresses doubts, and even
shame, at the way he has spent his time. In response to Seneca's
account of the many ways men waste time, he writes: "I did not
read chapter 3 without blushing: it is my story. How fortunate

is he who doesn't come away from it convinced that he has lived only a very small part of his life!"[78] These expressions of self-doubt are all the more significant that Diderot may well have written them with Rousseau in mind: in keeping with the precepts of *On the Shortness of Life*, Rousseau withdrew from the literary scene, rejected many of the constraints of public life, and centered his last works on the self.

Nonetheless, Diderot's lifelong tendency to give his time, and his voice, to others culminates in the *Essai*. This can be seen, most notably, when his defense of Seneca unexpectedly turns into a defense of Montaigne. In order to demonstrate the excellence of Montaigne's oft-maligned style, Diderot quotes a page and a half from Montaigne's essay "Des boiteux" ("Of Cripples"). He justifies this lengthy digression as follows: "A critic will have quite a bit of taste when he senses that of Montaigne; he is condemned to have none at all, if the richness, the warmth, and the life of the following passage escapes him.—'But Seneca's letters?' . . . —I will get back to them when I can. Wherever I feel at ease, I stay, and what I would say is not worth what Montaigne will say."[79] Diderot's renunciation of his own voice in favor of Montaigne's is all the more striking in that "Des boiteux" is not even about Seneca (the passage in question concerns false accounts of miracles and their propagation, a typically Enlightenment theme). In effect, Diderot has quite literally given up one of his pages to Montaigne; as he puts it, "I would gladly give up the best of my pages for that one."[80] This act of self-effacement gestures toward Diderot's eventual silence and encourages us to read his titular *essai* in the sense Montaigne used it: as a practicing or testing out of death in life.

The effacement of Diderot's voice becomes even more pronounced in the last part of his work, when he intersperses extended quotations from Jean-François Marmontel's commentary on the *Essai* with brief comments of his own. After a few dozen pages of this dialogue, in which Marmontel's voice predominates, he concludes: "Of the entire preceding passage, I can only claim the additions."[81] Prior to this clarification, the reader could easily have failed to distinguish between Marmontel's commentary and Diderot's brief additions. These pages thus take Diderot's lifelong tendency to integrate "the words of others" into his writings to an extreme.[82] In this case, there is a veritable melding of voices, as if Diderot were attempting to achieve the effacement of proper names and individuals that he claims the passage of time inevitably brings. He drives this point home with a reference to Antoine Léonard Thomas's epic poem about Peter the Great of Russia, *La Pétréïde:* "What comparison is there between a beautiful line, even if I knew how to write it, and a good action? One only writes the beautiful line to exhort to a good action, which is not done: one only writes the beautiful line to increase one's reputation; and one doesn't realize that at the end of a rather short number of years, and which pass quickly, it will be quite immaterial whether there is on the frontispiece of the *Pétréïde,* Thomas, or another name."[83] This claim is all the more surprising that in his exchange with Falconet in the 1760s, Diderot had referred to the very same work in defending his own attachment to posterity. At the time, he insisted that Thomas, like Diderot himself, wanted to be remembered by posterity: "Here is Thomas who is going to attempt the Tsar Peter, epic poem. . . . He wants in dying to be counted among the seven or eight rare geniuses that nature has produced since the creation of the world. He wants to leave a great name."[84] In the *Essai,* in contrast, Diderot seems to renounce his attachment to leaving a great name, embracing the idea that the names of all writers are inevitably effaced by the passage of time. As we have seen, the preamble to the *Essai* already denies Diderot's individuality by claiming that any man of sixty-five would write the same work. In keeping with this idea, Diderot concludes the *Essai* by inviting his readers to issue their own judgment of Seneca, Diderot, and the *Essai* itself. He even goes so far as to extend this invitation to his censors, whom he attacks elsewhere in the *Essai* for their uncharitable attitude toward Seneca and himself: "If the last one to speak is the one who is right, speak, censors, and be right."[85] In these lines, we can hear an echo of the last words of Rameau's Nephew: "Laughs best who laughs last."[86]

At the end of his life, Diderot's scientific interest in the physiology of death became inextricable from his cultivation of a Stoicist attitude toward his own death. In July 1780, while revising the *Essai* for the expanded version, Diderot wrote to Naigeon: "If you only knew how trivial everything becomes, when one is sixty-eight years old; when one has been living at the expense of others for eight or nine years; and when one can barely promise oneself a few more years, before returning oneself to the elements, to dust."[87] This view of death as giving oneself back to the elements bears the mark of the theory of death outlined in the *Éléments,* with the implication that nature will transform the elemental dust of the body for its own purposes. But it is also informed by Seneca, according to whom the wise man "regards as held on sufferance not only his goods and possessions and status, but even his body, his eyes and hand, and all that makes life more dear, and his very self; and he lives as though he were lent to himself and bound to return the loan on demand without complaint."[88] I would like to suggest, in conclusion, that the effacement of Diderot's voice at the end of the *Essai* gives literary form to the act of giving oneself back to the elements. By the conclusion of the *Essai,* the distinction between Diderot's voice, and those of Seneca, Montaigne, and Marmontel, has become irrelevant. Like his body, the voice and language he used to compose his literary testament were merely on loan to him. Knowing this, and sensing that he would soon join Seneca along with so many of his own generation, he chose to give up his voice as a final bequest to his readers.

According to Diderot's daughter, Marie-Angélique de Vandeul, it was working on the *Essai* and the *Histoire des deux Indes* that sent her father to his grave. In her *Mémoires pour servir à l'histoire de la vie et des ouvrages de M. Diderot* (*Memoirs to Serve the History of the Life and Works of M. Diderot*), she describes his diminished physical state in the last few years of his life: "He began then to complain a lot about his health; he found that his head was worn out; he said he no longer had any ideas; he was always weary; it was hard work for him to dress himself; his teeth didn't bother him, but he removed them gently just as one detaches a pin; he ate less, he went out less; for three or four years he had felt a decline that strangers couldn't see, because he still had the same spark in conversation, the same gaiety and kindness."[89] Even amidst his decline, however, Diderot never stopped seeking to expand his knowledge of the workings of the human body. If we are to believe Vandeul's testimony, when he suffered an apoplexy in February 1784, he immediately stood up, looked at himself in a mirror, and identified the nature of the illness.

In the *Éléments,* Diderot claims, "Taste is the last of the organs to be extinguished: it is therefore not surprising that old men love the pleasures of the table."[90] In the event, he died at the dinner table, after enjoying a last meal. Here is the way Vandeul describes his last moments in her *Mémoires:* "He sat down at the table; ate some soup, some boiled mutton and chicory. He took an apricot; my mother wanted to prevent him from eating this fruit. 'But what in the devil's harm do you think it will cause me?' He ate it, leaned his elbow on the table to eat a few stewed cherries, coughed lightly. My mother asked him a question; since he was silent, she raised her head and looked at him: he was no longer."[91] Like the soul amidst its sensations, Diderot was until his very last moment at a table surrounded by a host of sensations that all entered, in one way or another, into his immense memory. After his death, an autopsy he had ordered was performed, so that the elements of his body could further contribute to the medical knowledge he had pursued throughout his life. According to Vandeul, his head was that of a twenty-year-old man and his heart was two-thirds bigger than normal.[92] In the *Éléments,* Diderot expresses his belief that the molecules of his body will undergo distant metamorphoses and live again in another form. And in the *Essai,* he gives literary form to the act of giving himself over to others, signaling that the unity and separateness of the self are illusions. Not only is the conscious self but a fragment of the immense storehouse of sensations contained in our brains, but our bodies, like our written works, are made up of the living matter of other selves. To die, for Diderot, is thus perhaps to lose the self, but it is also to be restored to the living whole of nature of which any given person is only a tiny part.

3

Rousseau's Flower

Rousseau came to writing relatively late in life. He first gained fame with his *Discours sur les sciences et les arts* (*Discourse on the Sciences and the Arts*) at the age of thirty-eight. But almost as soon as he had established his reputation as a writer, he brought his literary career to a dramatic end: he left Paris, traded his fashionable Parisian garb for the coarser garments of an artisan, and rejected a pension from the king in favor of the onerous and unprofitable trade of copying music.[1] This retreat from the Parisian world of letters and its conventions was the first in a series of endings that would punctuate Rousseau's career as a writer. *Émile,* published in 1762, just before his fiftieth birthday, was for Rousseau the last piece in a philosophical system that first came to him as a vision on his way to visit Diderot at Vincennes in 1749. According to the Frenchman in *Rousseau juge de Jean-Jacques,* the best way to perceive the coherence of that system is to read Rousseau's works in reverse order, "attaching oneself first to *Émile* with which he ended."[2] *Émile* was also Rousseau's last dialogue with materialist philosophers (many of whom were by then his former friends) on matters of faith. His intention in the "Profession de foi du vicaire Savoyard" ("Profession of Faith of the Savoyard Vicar"), as he later described it, was to fix his religious beliefs definitively, so he would never again be compelled to revise them in the face of paralyzing doubts. As Rousseau saw it, *Émile* fulfilled the vision at Vincennes and closed a painful chapter in his life: no longer would the likes of Diderot and d'Holbach unsettle his religious convictions with their corrosive atheist dogma.

But the endings did not end there. With *Rousseau juge de Jean-Jacques,* a work written during a period of intense mental anguish in the last decade of his life, Rousseau made his final attempt, after the aborted self-justification of the *Confessions,* to defend himself against what he perceived as a wide-ranging plot to sully his reputation and falsify his life's works. In the "Histoire du précédent écrit" ("History of the Preceding Text") that brings this tortured work to a close, Rousseau announces his "final resolution" to give in to his destiny and abandon himself and his reputation to his persecutors.[3] So persistent was Rousseau's obsession with the plot against him in these years that we might tend to doubt the finality of this resolution, were it not for the dramatic change in writing (and, apparently, in Rousseau's mental state) that accompanied the transition from *Rousseau juge de Jean-Jacques* to the *Rêveries du promeneur solitaire.* A number of Rousseau's friends and acquaintances commented on the unusual tranquility of his mental state during the period when the *Rêveries* was written. Madeleine-Catherine Delessert, Rousseau's dear friend and addressee of his *Lettres sur la botanique* (*Letters on Botany*), wrote in March 1777: "I have the pleasure of seeing from time to time our Friend Rousseau who enjoys good health and a calm of mind and heart that I had never known in him before."[4] The newfound quietude of the *Rêveries* is all the more remarkable in that Rousseau wrote the first promenade just a few months after completing the "Histoire du précédent écrit," and the prose of the *Rêveries* seems to have been nourished by sentences and phrases from the anguished work that directly preceded it. *Rousseau juge de Jean-Jacques* was also the last work Rousseau wrote with the express intention of being read by others. The *Rêveries*, in contrast, he claims to have written solely for himself, and the unfinished state of the manuscript makes it difficult to ascertain his intentions for this work.

So with Rousseau we have the curious case of a writer who proclaimed a series of last works, but whose actual last work defies easy categorization as a philosophical or literary testament. My first purpose in this chapter is to determine how Rousseau's self-imposed endings should affect our understanding of his philosophical system, in light of Arthur Melzer's claim that one of the principal challenges in interpreting that system is that it must be grasped in its entirety to be adequately understood.[5] My second and primary purpose is to situate the *Rêveries* within, or outside of, Rousseau's philosophical system and to evaluate its status as a philosophical or literary testament. My hesitation between *philosophical* and *literary* here is intentional: attempts to demonstrate the systematic nature of Rousseau's thought have generally relied on Rousseau's own account of his system in *Rousseau juge de Jean-Jacques,* focusing primarily on the first two discourses and *Émile,* and in some cases tracing the implications of that system for Rousseau's political thought in the *Contrat social (Social Contract).*[6] For Melzer, who has given the most complete and convincing of these accounts, "Rousseau's *thought* is indeed exceptionally systematic—but his *writings* are exceptionally unsystematic."[7] The task of Rousseau's interpreters, in this view, is to rescue his thought from the obfuscation caused by his writings. But, as I will argue here, philosophical thought and literary expression are inseparable in the *Rêveries,* where for

the first time Rousseau makes writing integral to his philosophical project. At the same time, the writing of the *Rêveries* is
by design incompatible with any closed, complete system; as
Rousseau observes, "These pages [*ces feuilles,* also *leaves*] will
not properly be anything but a formless journal of my reveries."[8]
It is thus not surprising that philosophical and political readings
of Rousseau's system of thought have paid scant attention to the
Rêveries or have offered only an impoverished account of this
work as an expression of Rousseau's retreat into solitude to recover the primordial sentiment of existence.[9] It is my contention
that only by taking the writing of the *Rêveries* into account can
the full implications of this work for Rousseau's philosophical
thought be understood. The *Rêveries* is Rousseau's true ending,
not just because he continued writing it until a few months
before his death, but above all because its ethics of philosophical
writing casts a new light on everything he wrote before it.

Rousseau was entering his last year of life when he wrote the
third promenade of the *Rêveries du promeneur solitaire*. This
promenade opens with a line from Solon, "I grow old while
continuing to learn," and offers a meditation on the kinds of
learning best suited to old age. But as the promenade draws to
a close, Rousseau sets himself apart from Solon, observing that
his own days of learning are long past: "Thus constrained in the
narrow sphere of my former knowledge, I do not have, like
Solon, the good fortune of being able to learn each day as I grow
older, and I must even preserve myself from the dangerous pride
of wanting to learn what I am henceforth no longer in a state
to know well."[10] At age sixty-five, Rousseau has resolved to
limit himself to knowledge gained earlier in his life. What he
can hope to acquire, if not new knowledge, are the virtues
necessary to his current state. By this he means the virtues

necessary to an old man whose only remaining task is to learn how to die: "The study of an Old Man, if there is still one remaining to him, is solely to learn how to die, and that is precisely what one does least at my age, one thinks of everything but that."[11] In cultivating this study, Rousseau sets himself apart not just from Solon, but above all from modern philosophers, who ignore death and whose philosophy focuses on the universe and the acquisition of "useful knowledge [*lumières utiles*]" rather than on self-knowledge.[12]

Up to this point, there is nothing very unusual about the philosophical position Rousseau stakes out in the third promenade. He rejoins a classical conception of philosophy, espoused by the Stoics, as a means of preparing for death, and echoes the language of Montaigne, who titled one his essays "Que philosopher c'est apprendre à mourir." What is unusual, however, is that Rousseau links this classical conception of philosophy to a highly idiosyncratic philosophical method he developed in writing *Émile*. It becomes clear, over the course of the third promenade, that the narrow sphere of knowledge Rousseau associates with old age can be traced back to the "Profession de foi du vicaire savoyard," a work he wrote at age forty-five, when he was at the height of his powers as a writer (in just a few explosive years, Rousseau wrote *Julie, ou La Nouvelle Héloïse* [*Julie, or the New Heloise*], *Émile,* and the *Contrat social*).[13] It was then that Rousseau developed a philosophical method that proceeded by limiting his sphere of inquiry to the few questions he felt compelled to answer for his personal well-being. The Savoyard Vicar characterizes this method as follows: "The first fruit that I drew from these reflections was to learn to limit my inquiry to what interested me most immediately; to find repose in a profound ignorance about everything else, and to worry myself to the point of doubt only for things that were important to me to know."[14] It was also then that Rousseau perceived himself to be at the height of his intellectual powers and on the brink of a precipitous decline. This perception prompted him to conceive of the "Profession de foi" as a last work, in the sense that he wrote it with the conviction that once completed, he would never again reopen the inquiry pursued therein.

In the third promenade, Rousseau frames the "Profession de foi" as a last work by drawing an explicit connection between the end of his career as a fashionable writer and the definitive resolution of his religious doubts. His external reform (consisting in his departure from Paris, his change of costume, his refusal of a pension, and his new trade as a music copyist) is mirrored by an even more vital internal reform: "I didn't limit my reform to exterior things. I sensed that even that reform required another that would undoubtedly be more painful but more necessary, in my opinions, and having resolved not to do it twice, I undertook to subject my interior to a severe examination that would fix it for the rest of my life as I would like to find it at my death."[15] What is striking here is the finality Rousseau attributes to his internal reform: at age forty-five, he seeks to fix (régler) his inner self such that for the rest of his life it will be as he would like to find it at his death. Such a reform is not unrelated to the spiritual exercises of the Stoics, but it is different in the sense that Rousseau seeks to prepare his inner self for death not on a daily basis through repeated exercises, but once and for all. And despite the echoes of Montaigne throughout the third promenade, the notion of fixing one's inner self in such a definitive way is antithetical to the spirit of the Essais.

Rousseau also frames the "Profession de foi" as a last work by characterizing it as his last dialogue with modern philosophers on matters of faith. When he wrote the "Profession de foi," he had already quit the tumult of society to cultivate the "absolute retreat" necessary for this task, but he had not yet rid himself of the doubts instilled in him by the fashionable philosophers of his day: "I was living then with modern philosophers who hardly resembled the ancients. Instead of lifting my doubts and fixing my irresolutions, they had shaken all the certainties I thought I had on the points it mattered to me most to know: for as ardent missionaries of Atheism and very imperious dogmatists they couldn't stand without anger that on any point whatsoever one dare to think differently from them."[16] This portrait of the materialists and of d'Holbach's coterie in particular mirrors the depiction of modern philosophers in *Rousseau juge de Jean-Jacques,* where Rousseau accuses them of being just as dogmatic as the Jesuits, of cultivating a wholly destructive approach to philosophy, and of having gained a stranglehold on public opinion.[17] In contrast, both ancient philosophy and Rousseau's own approach provide spiritual sustenance by resolving doubts and constructing a core set of beliefs by which to live. Yet the accusation of dogmatism leveled against modern philosophers in the third promenade has a curious ring to it, given the fixity Rousseau ascribes to his own religious beliefs. In fact, the Savoyard Vicar even uses the term *dogma* to refer to the religious principles established in his profession of faith.[18] And Rousseau regularly refers to atheism and his own religious doctrine as two competing "systems," thereby underlining the analogy between them.

In the third promenade, Rousseau justifies the fixity of his system and distinguishes it from that of his contemporaries in two ways. First, he suggests that his is a personal philosophy based in self-knowledge, whereas the modern philosophers focus entirely on the world without in complete ignorance of themselves: "I saw a lot of them who philosophized much more learnedly than I did, but their philosophy was so to speak foreign to them. Wanting to be more learned than others, they studied the universe to know how it was arranged, as they would have studied some machine they would have caught a glimpse of, out of sheer curiosity. They studied human nature to be able to talk about it more learnedly, but not to know themselves; they worked to instruct others, but not to enlighten themselves within."[19] Modern philosophers, like Rousseau before he ended his career as a fashionable man of letters, are motivated by *amour propre* in developing their philosophical knowledge. Their philosophy is outer-directed, both in its attempt to dominate others and in its encyclopedic focus on the world without. In contrast, Rousseau develops an inner-directed approach to philosophy that lends an entirely different character to the fixity of his beliefs: "The tone of dogmatism in these matters belongs only to charlatans; but it is important to have a feeling for oneself, and to choose it with all the maturity of judgment one can put into it."[20]

Second, Rousseau justifies the fixity of his system by situating the "Profession de foi" in a narrative of intellectual decline. If he resolved at age forty-five to settle his religious beliefs once and for all, it was not only because he wanted to bring his dialogue with modern philosophers to a close. It was also because he sensed that he was at the height of his intellectual powers and on the cusp of a dramatic decline. This sense of impending decline lends great urgency to Rousseau's project of combating materialist philosophy and makes it imperative that he never revisit his religious beliefs once they have been established:

> Their philosophy is for others; I would need one for myself. Let us search for it with all my strength while there is still time in order to have a fixed rule of conduct for the rest of my days. Here I am at a mature age, with all the strength of my understanding. Already I am reaching my decline. If I wait any longer, I will no longer have in my late deliberation the use of all my strength; my intellectual faculties will have already lost their activity, I will do less

> well what I can do today at my best: let us seize this
> favorable moment; it is the era of my external re-
> form, let it also be that of my intellectual and moral
> reform. Let us fix once and for all my opinions, my
> principles, and let us be for the rest of my life what
> I will have found I should be after having thought
> carefully about it.[21]

This passage, with its combined sense of urgency and delay,
echoes Saint Augustine's meditations on his coming conversion
in the *Confessions*. Rousseau reinforces the sense of urgency by
using the present tense and the imperative (even though he is
writing this retrospective account some twenty years after the
fact) and by characterizing the current moment as the last possible occasion for him to pursue his inquiry. At the same time,
the repetition of imperative verbs implies a certain resistance
to the reform and a need to push oneself toward it, in a way
analogous to Saint Augustine's words to God, "Grant me chas-
tity and continence, but not yet."[22] The fact that these verbs
(*cherchons, saisissons, fixons, soyons*) are in the first person
plural further implicates the reader in the process of conversion.
What sets Rousseau apart from Saint Augustine, however, is
that the moment of conversion or inner reform is dictated not
by the state of his soul or God's will, but by his sense of an impending intellectual decline. In other words, the "Profession de
foi" will be Rousseau's definitive statement of religious dogma
not because he has attained definitive truths, or even exorcised
all his doubts, but because his intellectual faculties will never
again be as powerful as they are at this moment.

Rousseau thus makes it perfectly clear, in the third promenade, that his gesture of restricting his knowledge in old age
can be traced back to a much earlier moment in his life, when
he first perceived his intellectual faculties to be subject to

decline. He is remarkably candid about the fact that the "Profession de foi" neither addresses all the objections of his fellow philosophers nor resolves all his personal doubts. He even grants that his religious upbringing and personal preferences may have swayed him in reaching his conclusions. But in keeping with his inner-directed approach to philosophy, he concludes that what matters most is that the "Profession de foi" provide him with the only philosophical system suited to his personal well-being: "In any other system I would live without resources and I would die without hope. I will be the most unhappy of creatures. Let us then keep to the only one that suffices to make me happy in spite of fortune and men."[23]

In a certain sense, then, Rousseau's career as a philosopher ends with *Émile,* just as his career as a fashionable writer ends with his external reform. It is not just that he closes off all dialogue with modern philosophers from this point forward, but above all that he initiates the restriction of his knowledge that would culminate in his old age. His repeated use of the term *system* to characterize his religious beliefs, along with his claim that *Émile* marked the completion of his philosophical system, should be understood in this light. As a system, the "Profession de foi" is complete and hermetically sealed, not subject to further amplification or modification. Its completion is justified not by its attainment of ultimate truths, but by the history of mental decline within which Rousseau situates it. How, then, are we to interpret the works composed in the aftermath of that decline, and in particular those that repeat Rousseau's gesture of ending his career as a philosopher and writer?

Rousseau juge de Jean-Jacques (also known as the *Dialogues*) has a curious status in Rousseau's corpus. For nearly two centuries it was neglected (astonishingly, the first English translation did not appear until 1990), or was treated merely as a symptom of Rousseau's clinical paranoia.[24] This critical response is on a certain level understandable: Rousseau's belief that the *philosophes,* in cahoots with the powers that be, had engineered a universal plot against him threatens to consume the entire work and destroy its coherence. And no one (including Rousseau himself) seems to deny that *Rousseau juge de Jean-Jacques* makes for a painful read, with its excessive length, repetitive ramblings, and agonizing display of Rousseau's disturbed mental state. But in recent decades, a number of scholars have rightly observed that this work contains perhaps the most cogent exposition of Rousseau's philosophical system. Others have viewed Rousseau's nightmarish vision of the new world created by modern philosophy—a vision that bears a striking resemblance to Theodor Adorno and Max Horkheimer's critique of Enlightenment—as a precious contribution to our historical understanding of the Enlightenment public sphere.[25] As Roger Masters and Christopher Kelly have observed, Rousseau is careful to emphasize that the plot is not solely or even essentially concerned with him: "Its true object is to destroy the current foundation of society and to provide a new one that would solidify the influence of a faction or sect of individuals sharing the opinions of Grimm, Diderot, and the others. This charge warrants serious attention because it so precisely mirrors these men's understanding of themselves."[26] If we adopt Dan Edelstein's definition of Enlightenment as a new narrative about the transformative effects of philosophy on society, Rousseau's counternarrative becomes crucial to understanding the Enlightenment and Rousseau's relationship to it.[27] *Rousseau juge de Jean-Jacques* thus appears, paradoxically, to offer us Rousseau at his most lucid and at his most deranged.

Rousseau wrote this strange work in the last decade of his life, when he had finally returned to Paris after the long period

of exile and wandering prompted by the proscription of *Émile*
and the *Contrat social*. In England, where he suffered from some
of his most acute bouts of paranoia during his quarrel with
Hume, he had started writing his *Confessions,* in part as a response to scurrilous published attacks on his reputation by
Voltaire and others. Upon arriving in Paris, he held readings of
the *Confessions* at the homes of various acquaintances. It was
when these readings were suppressed by the police (owing to
the intervention of his former friend and benefactress, Louise
d'Épinay) that he undertook *Rousseau juge de Jean-Jacques*. This
was to be, as he framed it, his last attempt to justify himself in
the eyes of a reading public. It was also a work in which Rousseau
grappled openly with his death and the meaning it would hold
for future generations. In the terrifying world of the plot, Jean-
Jacques is at constant risk of being buried alive by his enemies.
The struggle to defend his personal reputation and philosophical system is thus mirrored by a struggle to rescue him from the
death that modern philosophers have planned for him.

As we have seen, Rousseau claimed in the third promenade
that he was never seriously shaken in his religious beliefs after
he wrote *Émile*. The immutable articles of faith laid out in the
"Profession de foi"—which include the existence of a providential deity and the immateriality of the soul—serve as a bulwark
against the ravages of modern philosophy.[28] And yet, *Rousseau
juge de Jean-Jacques* is manifestly haunted by a vision of death
that Rousseau ties to materialist and atheist philosophy. This
can be seen most clearly in the Frenchman's diatribe against
modern philosophy in the third dialogue. Modern philosophers,
by his account, are guilty of many things: they have undermined
the basis of all moral behavior by destroying religion, free will,
and any sense of remorse. They have supplanted the authority
of their enemies, the Jesuits, and have gained control of public
opinion by making themselves the "supreme interpreters" of

nature.[29] But above all, they have destroyed the traditional deathbed ritual of confession, thereby making it impossible for the plot ever to be revealed. "Don't you see," the Frenchman says to Rousseau, "that it's been a long time since we heard anyone talk about restitutions, reparations, reconciliations at the deathbed; that all those who are dying, without repentance, without remorse carry off without terror in their conscience the fortune of others, the lies and fraud they burdened it with during their life?"[30] In the world of modern philosophy, the deathbed is no longer, as it once was, a site for the revelation of truth, but has become the place where the lies and falsifications of the plot triumph definitively. Even if there were a few repentant souls seeking in their final moments to make reparations to Jean-Jacques, their confessions would be buried in eternal secrecy along with their bodies: "Are you unaware that the confessors have been won over, that the doctors are complicit, that all those in league together, spying on each other, force others and are forced to remain true to the plot, and that surrounded, especially at their death, none of them would find to receive their confession at least with respect to J.J. anyone but false guardians who would only take it on in order to bury it in eternal secrecy [?]."[31] This evocation of buried confessions recalls the insistent imagery of Jean-Jacques being buried alive by his enemies, which Jean Starobinski has interpreted in terms of the deep psychic structures of Rousseau's personality and writings.[32] But in the context of Rousseau's dialogue with materialist philosophers (which was to have ended with the "Profession de foi," but which continues in another form in *Rousseau juge de Jean-Jacques*), this imagery takes on a broader meaning.

The philosophical significance of Jean-Jacques's death must be interpreted in light of Rousseau's conviction that the fear of death is not natural to man. If we follow Melzer's interpretation that the basis of Rousseau's philosophy is the natural goodness of man, it becomes crucial that natural man not be divided against himself. This leads Rousseau to insist that the fear of death does not exist in the state of nature.[33] Thus *Rousseau juge de Jean-Jacques* combines the clearest exposition of Rousseau's philosophical system with the most haunting images of his death. If Jean-Jacques is vilified and his writings falsified, it is natural man himself who is destroyed; for as the Frenchman puts it, "Where can the painter and apologist of nature, today so disfigured and maligned, have taken his model, if not from his own heart? He described nature as he felt himself to be."[34] In a similar way, if Jean-Jacques dies the death he fears most— surrounded by enemies who are determined to stifle any revelation of his true self—the socially created fear of death will have triumphed and the living model for natural man will have been deprived of the tranquil death nature intended for him.

Rousseau's preoccupation with achieving a tranquil death for Jean-Jacques can be seen in the closing words of the third and final dialogue. The Frenchman has by this point been convinced of the essential goodness of Jean-Jacques, and the two interlocutors have agreed to join him in a "society that is sincere and without fraud" and to safeguard his works for future generations.[35] But the dialogue, and the work as a whole, ends not with the idea of protecting Jean-Jacques's works or restoring his reputation for posterity, but with the idea of accompanying him at the moment of his death. In fact, the tranquil death the Frenchman imagines for Jean-Jacques appears above all as a consolation for the fact that neither he nor Rousseau has any intention of intervening publicly to salvage Jean-Jacques's reputation: "In conclusion, without making useless efforts on his behalf that could cause great upheaval and the success of which would no longer touch him, let us prepare this consolation for his final hour that his eyes be closed by friendly hands."[36] This final death scene, in its intimacy and simplicity, stands in marked contrast to the famous opening page of the *Confessions* where Rousseau proclaims: "May the trumpet of the last judgment sound when it will; I will come with this book in my hand to present myself before the sovereign judge."[37] By the end of the last dialogue, Jean-Jacques has renounced public reparation and has been virtually dispossessed of his writings, as the two interlocutors plan to accept the precious "deposit" of his remaining papers. This ending paves the way for the Rousseau of the *Rêveries*, who expresses "a profound indifference for the fate of my true writings and the monuments of my innocence that have perhaps already been destroyed forever."[38]

Yet *Rousseau juge de Jean-Jacques* does not end there. The evocation of Jean-Jacques's eyes being closed by loving hands is only an image of closure, the hypothetical projection of a disembodied interlocutor who has come to appear by the end of the third dialogue both as Rousseau himself and as his ideal reader. This image is almost immediately erased by the "Histoire du précédent écrit," an autobiographical postface that depicts in agonizing detail the author Rousseau's frenzied search for an actual reader for his work. As Starobinski has observed, Rousseau's intention to leave the dialogues on the altar of Notre-Dame, bearing the inscription "DEPOSIT LEFT TO PROVIDENCE," is less a call for divine judgment (as in the opening scene of the *Confessions*) than an attempt to reach human readers through divine intervention.[39] Yet Rousseau's anguished efforts to find a receptive reader for *Rousseau juge de Jean-Jacques* are continually frustrated. First, he attempts to attract the attention of the king by leaving his text on the altar; then, he turns to the philosopher Étienne Bonnot de Condillac, who disappoints him by responding to it as a mere work of literature; next, he addresses the Englishman Brooke Boothby, whom he rapidly suspects of belonging to the conspiracy; finally, he resorts to handing out a pamphlet entitled "To Any Frenchman Who Still

Loves Justice and Truth," a gesture that is not surprisingly rejected by passersby on the street. After all these failed attempts,
he settles on what he calls, significantly, "the last use remaining
to me to make of this text."[40] He will keep a single copy in his
possession and offer it to the least suspicious of his acquaintances for their perusal. It is here that Rousseau's rational faculties appear closest to their breaking point, as he folds into a
single sentence both the possibility and impossibility of ever
finding the reader he seeks: "No one will listen to me, experience
forewarns me of that, but it is not impossible that there will be
found one person who listens, and it is henceforth impossible
that men's eyes will be opened to the truth of their own accord."[41]
The logical tension of this sentence, which holds out the possibility for a redemptive reading even as it is definitively with-
held, brings Rousseau close to his final gesture of renouncing
all readers in the *Rêveries*. From the king, to Condillac, to
Boothby, to passersby on the street, to his acquaintances, none
of Rousseau's actual readers has lived up to the ideal society
formed by the two virtual readers in his dialogues. In other
words, none of them has proved worthy of assisting him in his
final moments. By the end of the "Histoire du précédent écrit,"
it has become clear that there will be no loving hands to close
Rousseau's eyes; instead, "they have found the art of making me
suffer a long death by keeping me buried alive."[42]

Rousseau's death as an author is also signaled by his "final
resolution" to give himself up to his enemies: "Giving up is
henceforth my fate, no longer persisting in fighting against it,
letting my persecutors dispose as they wish of their prey, remaining their plaything without any resistance for the rest of
my old and sad days, abandoning to them even the honor of
my name and my reputation in the future, if it pleases the
Heavens that they dispose of it, without being affected by anything no matter what happens; that is my last resolution."[43] This

final resolution imposes yet another definitive ending on Rousseau's life and works. Just as he did with his personal reform, he seeks here to fix his behavior and inner disposition until the time of his death: he will no longer seek public reparation and will in fact abstain from any public action whatsoever. Underlying this resolution is a renunciation of writing as a form of public action directed toward a reading public.[44] Such a renunciation signals the end of Rousseau as an author, if we accept Christopher Kelly's argument that Rousseau's view of authorship was marked by its ethics of public responsibility. Unlike Voltaire, who published under multiple pseudonyms, or Diderot, who left his most radical works unpublished until his death, Rousseau insisted on publishing and signing even his most inflammatory works and incurring the risk of proscription, exile, and punishment.[45] By renouncing his public role as author, Rousseau seems to have renounced authorship itself. How, then, are we to interpret his actual last work, written in the immediate aftermath of this dramatic end to his life as an author?

Rousseau started writing the *Rêveries* just a few months after completing *Rousseau juge de Jean-Jacques*. The dramatic opening sentence—"Here I am, thus, alone on the earth, no longer having any brother, relative, friend, society but my own"—binds the *Rêveries* to the work immediately preceding it through the use of *thus,* or *donc*. Rousseau's solitude is presented as following directly, even logically, from the final resolution announced in the "Histoire du précédent écrit." At the same time, his renunciation of authorship creates an unbridgeable divide between the two works, and indeed between the *Rêveries* and the rest of his corpus. For the first time, Rousseau claims to write for himself alone. In doing so, he abandons the philosophical system he had completed with *Émile* and defended in *Rousseau*

juge de Jean-Jacques. His project of describing the operations
of his soul, unlike the rest of his thought, cannot be reduced to
a system: "I will content myself with keeping a register of the
operations, without seeking to reduce them into a system. My
project is the same as Montaigne's, but with a goal quite contrary to his: he wrote his essays only for others, and I write my
reveries only for myself."[46] By comparing his work to the *Essais,*
Rousseau does more than simply insist on the solipsism of his
last work: he implicitly frames the *Rêveries* as a work written in
preparation for death.[47] But the reference to Montaigne also
throws Rousseau's purpose in writing the *Rêveries* into question.
What he fails to mention (but what every reader of the *Essais*
knows) is that Montaigne claimed to write the *Essais* so that his
loved ones could keep a record of him after his death.[48] If Rousseau is, like Montaigne, writing in the face of death, what can
be the purpose of preserving a record of himself for himself
alone? This question rejoins the broader one of whether the
Rêveries can properly be interpreted as a testament that brings
closure to Rousseau's life and works. I will address this question
with a reading of the tenth and final promenade, using this brief
fragment to recapture the sense of an ending that emanates
from the *Rêveries* as a whole.

The tenth promenade of the *Rêveries* appears to be an
unfinished fragment, unlike the other nine. It breaks off
abruptly amidst an evocation of the few years of happiness
Rousseau spent with his protectress and lover, Madame de
Warens, at their pastoral retreat in Charmettes.[49] It is also by
far the shortest promenade, covering only two pages in the
Pléiade edition, whereas the other promenades range from
seven to sixteen pages. How are we to understand the status of
this fragment as a conclusion to Rousseau's life and works? The
fact that he neatly copied the first seven promenades into a
notebook, as if for publication, while leaving the other three in

a rough state complicates matters.[50] It is entirely possible, and even likely, that Rousseau simply did not have time at the end of his life to complete the last promenade. Based on his dating of the promenade in the opening sentence, he wrote it on April 12, 1778, just a few months before his death on July 2: "Today on the day of Easter blooms it has been exactly fifty years since my first acquaintance with Madame de Warens."[51] In May he left Paris for his final pastoral retreat in Ermenonville. It is significant that before leaving Paris, he gave his friend Paul Moultou copies of *Rousseau juge de Jean-Jacques* and the *Confessions,* among other papers, but did not give him any papers pertaining to the *Rêveries.* In Ermenonville, he spent much of his time botanizing, an activity he predicted in the seventh promenade would soon bring his reveries, and his writing, to a premature end: "The collection of my long dreams has hardly begun, and already I sense that it is coming to an end. Another amusement succeeds it, absorbs me and deprives me even of the time to dream."[52] Thus the tenth promenade may have been left as a fragment simply because an ailing, decrepit Rousseau preferred to spend his last days botanizing rather than writing, or because he died before he got a chance to finish it.

And yet these simple, biographical explanations are unsatisfying given that Rousseau explicitly framed the *Rêveries* as a collection of fragments. In the first promenade, he refers repeatedly to his work as *ces feuilles* (these pages, or leaves) and embraces its lack of any definite form: "These pages [*feuilles*] will be nothing but a formless journal of my reveries."[53] He also calls the *Rêveries* "an appendix to my *Confessions,*" thereby reinforcing the impression of a collection of disjointed material rather than a complete, unified work.[54] Moreover, as suggested by the term *feuilles,* Rousseau develops an implicit analogy between the *Rêveries* and the herbarium in which he gathers a botanical record of his daily walks. Functioning as an

optical chamber (a device that makes flat pictures appear three-
dimensional), the herbarium allows Rousseau to recover the
entire spectacle of nature simply by looking at plant fragments:

> I will never again see those beautiful landscapes,
> forests, lakes, groves, rocks, mountains whose as-
> pect has always touched my heart: but now that I
> can no longer roam this pleasing countryside all I
> have to do is open my herbarium and it soon takes
> me there. The fragments of plants I picked suffice
> to remind me of the magnificent spectacle in its en-
> tirety. This herbarium is for me a journal of plant-
> collecting trips that allows me to recommence
> them with a new charm and creates the effect of an
> optical chamber that would paint them anew in
> front of my eyes.[55]

The effect of the optical chamber provides a model for Rousseau's
writing in the *Rêveries*. One day, he hopes, these pages or leaves
will allow him to revisit his walks and reveries at a time when
he is no longer able to experience them directly: "If in my older
days as I near departure I remain, as I hope, in the same disposition I am now, reading them will remind me of the sweetness
I taste in writing them, and, making time be reborn for me, will
double as it were my existence."[56] Just as the plant fragments
allow Rousseau to recapture the whole spectacle of nature, the
pages of the *Rêveries* will one day recreate the entirety of his
existence, just as its end draws near. The effect is somewhat akin
to Diderot's concept of immense memory and its reactivation.

The motif of the fragment (whether a plant or a page of
writing) is closely tied to the central theme of happiness that
animates the tenth promenade. This can be seen by comparing
the tenth promenade to the sixth book of the *Confessions*, where

the same years of happiness with Madame de Warens are evoked. In the opening page of this book, Rousseau confronts the challenge of recording his brief period of happiness in writing:

> Here begins the brief period of happiness in my life; here come the peaceful but rapid moments that have allowed me to say I have lived. Moments that are precious and so missed, ah, recommence for me your pleasant course; flow more slowly in my memory, if it is possible, than you actually did in your fleeting stream. What shall I do to prolong this touching and simple story as I wish; to say the same things all over again, and in repeating them bore my readers no more than I bored myself in perpetually beginning them anew? If all this were a matter of facts, actions, words, I could describe it and represent it: but how can one say what was neither said, nor done, nor even thought, but tasted, felt, without me even being able to express any other object of my happiness than the sentiment itself?[57]

In this passage, Rousseau comes up against the limits of his project in the *Confessions*. As a narrative comprised of facts, actions, and verbal exchanges, the *Confessions* is fundamentally unsuited to describing a sentiment that expands beyond the minute circumstances of life. Rousseau's desire to prolong his narrative, in order to recover the fleeting moments of his happiness and make them last, poses a problem not just because he might bore his readers, but also because he has no material to fill that longer narrative. In this context, it is significant that Rousseau's second attempt to describe these years, in the tenth promenade, takes the form not of an extended narrative but of a fragment.

Already in the *Confessions,* Rousseau had used a fragment
(not coincidentally in the form of a tiny flower) to overcome
the difficulties inherent in describing his years at Charmettes.
Finding himself unable to compose an extended narrative, he
limits himself to "a single example" to evoke his memories of
those years.[58] This example involves the two occasions on which
he saw a periwinkle flower, first when Madame de Warens in-
troduced him to the flower at Charmettes, and then when he
came across the same flower some thirty years later on a botanical expedition with his friend Pierre Alexandre Du Peyrou:
"While climbing up and looking among the bushes I let out a
cry of joy: *ah, there is the periwinkle;* and it was indeed one. Du
Peyrou noticed my elation, but he didn't know its cause; he will
learn it, I hope, when one day he reads this. My reader can judge
from the impression made by such a small object the one made
by all those related to this period."[59] In the *Confessions,* the tiny
periwinkle must stand in for the unwritten narrative of Rousseau's years of happiness. It is a fragment that connects two
moments in time (before and after Madame de Warens's death)
and reconnects Rousseau to a sentiment that extends far beyond
the limits of those years. It also serves as the sole possible means
of communicating to the reader the vividness of Rousseau's
impressions and memories of Charmettes. The periwinkle thus
gives us a model for understanding the status of the tenth
promenade, as a fragment that connects two moments in time
("Today on the day of Easter blooms it has been exactly fifty
years since my first acquaintance with Madame de Warens")
and allows Rousseau to recapture the lost happiness of those
years.

Both the periwinkle and the tenth promenade link two
moments in time separated by Madame de Warens's death. In
a similar way, another flower links the moments before and
after Rousseau's accident with the Great Dane, which he repre-

sents as a virtual death in the second promenade. Rousseau describes his discovery of this flower, before his accident, as follows (I will quote the French first due to the importance of syntax): "Cette decouverte me réjouit et m'amusa très longtems et finit par celle d'une plante encor plus rare sur tout dans un pays élevé, savoir le *cerastium aquaticum*, que malgré l'accident qui m'arriva le même jour j'ai retrouvé dans un livre que j'avois sur moi et placé dans un herbier"[60] (This discovery delighted and amused me for some time and ended with that of a plant that is even more rare, especially at a high altitude, namely the *cerastium aquaticum*, which despite the accident that befell me the same day I found in a book I had on me and placed in a herbarium"). Rousseau places the *cerastium aquaticum* right in the middle of this sentence, surrounding it by two clauses, one pertaining to the time before his accident and the other after it. He does not tell us in the first clause that he placed the plant in a book, but only recounts (in the past tense) his subsequent discovery of it after the accident. In this way, he conveys the impression of an erasure of memory, a gap between the before and after of his accident. Here we have yet another image of how plant fragments (held within the pages of a book) function. But this time, the flower does not merely allow Rousseau to recapture a lost memory or sentiment, or to bridge the gap of Madame de Warens's death. It allows him to bridge the gap of his own death, which is represented figuratively by his accident with the Great Dane, and which takes on a social reality when the news of the accident sparks rumors of his death across Paris.

In both examples (the periwinkle and the *cerastium aquaticum*), we find plant fragments serving as a channel to connect Rousseau to a broader whole and to bridge the gap between life and death. A similar process gets played out in the tenth promenade, with respect to the passage of time. Rousseau opens the promenade by inscribing his encounter with Madame

Petit herbier pour Mademoiselle Julie Boy-de-la-Tour.
By Jean-Jacques Rousseau, [1772], [Paris]. (Courtesy of
Zentralbibliothek Zürich, Var. 12, page 180)

de Warens in the temporal framework of a century (she was
"born with the century" and their encounter took place "exactly fifty years ago"). He then characterizes their brief years at
Charmettes as a century of happiness: "An isolated house on

the slope of a small valley was our refuge, and it is there that in
the space of four or five years I enjoyed a century of life and a
pure and full happiness that covers with its charm everything
that is dreadful in my current fate."[61] The years at Charmettes
appear here as a brief fragment of time (and happiness) that
somehow extends beyond its actual temporal duration to encompass an entire century. This temporal expansion provides
a model for reading the tenth promenade (a fragment that seems
to encompass Rousseau's entire project in the *Rêveries*) and
illuminates Rousseau's understanding of the brevity of human
existence. His existence may be limited in time, but the tenth
promenade connects it to a larger time span, or perhaps even
to something that lies beyond the constraints of time.

But the tenth promenade also underscores the fragility of
Rousseau's happiness, and by extension of itself as a fragment.
It ends (if we can consider it to have an ending) by evoking the
material constraints that threatened the idyll at Charmettes.
With his last words, Rousseau raises the properly testamentary
question of how he could repay his debts to Madame de Warens
and provide for her in times of need:

> I desired nothing more than the continuation of
> such a sweet state. My only trouble was the fear that
> it would not last long, and this fear born of our fi-
> nancial difficulties was not without foundation. I
> thus thought about giving myself distractions from
> this worry and at the same time resources to pre-
> vent its effect. I thought that a provision of talents
> was the surest resource against destitution, and I
> resolved to spend my leisure putting myself in a
> position, if at all possible, to give back one day to
> the best of women the assistance that I had received
> from her.[62]

The significance of this ending as a conclusion to Rousseau's life and works cannot be overstated. Readers of the *Confessions* (to which Rousseau adds the *Rêveries* as an appendix) will know that Rousseau's desire to provide for Madame de Warens prompted his decision to leave for Paris to make his fortune, a decision that eventually led to him becoming an author. The tenth promenade thus breaks off at the precise moment that separates the two parts of the *Confessions*. In the opening pages of the second part, Rousseau frames these two parts as covering two distinct periods in his life (of thirty years each) situated before and after a dramatic break: "What a different painting I will soon have to develop! The fate that for thirty years favored my penchants, thwarted them for the other thirty, and from this continual opposition between my situation and inclination were born enormous mistakes, extraordinary misfortunes, and all the virtues, except strength, that can honor adversity."[63] Read in light of this passage, the tenth promenade appears to open out onto the *tableau* of Rousseau's unhappiness, at the center of which lie his career as an author and the resulting plot against him. But it stops there, refusing to move to the other side that is the second part of the *Confessions*. In keeping with Rousseau's claim that he wrote the *Rêveries* for himself alone, the tenth promenade stops short of recounting the process by which he became an author.

The conclusion to the tenth promenade is also significant for what it says about writing as a form of social contract. As a solitary walker, Rousseau appears to eschew social obligations of any kind. In the sixth promenade, he explores his natural resistance to the tacit but nonetheless binding social contracts formed by even the smallest acts of charity, which he characterizes as follows: "I know there is a sort of contract and even the most holy one between the benefactor and the beneficiary. It is a sort of society they form with each other, closer than the one that generally binds men together, and if the beneficiary tacitly commits to be grateful, the benefactor commits in the same way to maintain for the other, as long as he doesn't make himself unworthy of it, the same goodwill he has just shown him, and to renew the actions associated with it as many times as he can and is requested of him."[64] By the end of the sixth promenade, Rousseau has come to the radical conclusion that he is by nature ill-suited to civil society, due to his inability to engage in such contractual relationships: "The conclusion I can draw from all these reflections is that I was never really suited to civil society where everything is hindrance, obligation, and duty, and that my independent nature always made me incapable of the subjection necessary for anyone who wants to live in the company of other men."[65] This conclusion (along with Rousseau's claim that he wrote the *Rêveries* for himself alone) has led most critics to read the *Rêveries* as "an escape from his historical thinking." In contesting this view, Bernhard Kuhn acknowledges that to read this work "as vitally engaged with the social and political world is to read Rousseau's final autobiography against its own explicit and repeated declarations to the contrary."[66] And yet, the testamentary question raised at the end of the *Rêveries* suggests that Rousseau continued to be preoccupied with social contracts (as defined in the sixth promenade) right up until the end of his life. This becomes especially apparent if we consider that the closing lines of the tenth promenade mirror an actual testament Rousseau drew up in 1737 (when a laboratory accident threatened him with blindness and made him fear for his life). This document is largely concerned with the assistance Rousseau received from Madame de Warens and his commitment to pay his debts to her.[67] By the time Rousseau revisited the issue in the tenth promenade, he was no longer in a position to assist Madame de Warens in her hour of need: she had died in indigence sixteen years earlier. Rousseau only saw her once after leaving for Paris, and in the *Confessions* he recounts the miserable state in which he found her and his enduring regret that he did not choose to stay with her until her death: "Ah! That was the moment to acquit my debt! I should have left everything to follow her, attach myself to her until her final hour and share her fate whatever it was. I did nothing of the sort. Distracted by another attachment, I felt mine for her loosen, through lack of hope to be able to make it useful to her. I bemoaned her and didn't follow her. Of all the remorse I have felt in my life this is the most acute and the most permanent."[68] My point in quoting these lines is not to reproach Rousseau for not having provided for Madame de Warens at the end of her life. Rather, it is to underscore the testamentary dimension of the closing lines of the tenth promenade. With his last words, Rousseau continued to pose the question of how he could pay his debt to Madame de Warens and by extension to society as a whole. As the solitary walker, it would appear that the only way he could pay those debts at the end of his life was through writing. In keeping with the notion that a plant fragment can reach across the boundary between life and death, Rousseau thus seems to offer the tenth promenade as a final testament to Madame de Warens, one that extends beyond the material constraints of time, money, and even death itself. He may not have paid his actual debts to her, ill-suited as he was to any form of social engagement, but these few pages of happiness seem to have been written as much for her as for himself. The strangeness of Rousseau's writing in the *Rêveries* can thus be explained not only as a function of its solipsism, but as an indication that it was written more for the dead than for the living. Like the *cerasticum aquaticum* that connects two moments separated by Rousseau's virtual death, the fragment of the tenth promenade seems to reach out across the divide between life and death, addressing both Madame de Warens and Rousseau himself after both of their deaths.

Rousseau repeatedly claimed, over the course of his life, that he was bringing his career as a writer to an end. His personal reform was an early manifestation of a tendency that would shape his works, along with his understanding of his philosophical system, from *Émile* to *Rousseau juge de Jean-Jacques* to the *Rêveries*. This tendency must be taken into account if we are to grapple with the oft-repeated question of the coherence of Rousseau's work. Some commentators, like Melzer, have insisted on the systematic nature of his thought, while others have emphasized his contradictions. For Jonathan Israel, Rousseau "was a strange mixture of radical, moderate, and Counter-Enlightenment tendencies and on all sides continually accused of contradicting himself."[69] In response to these conflicting interpretations, it is worth emphasizing Rousseau's tendency to inscribe his works into a history of personal decline. We can see this in the way he frames *Émile* in the third promenade, as a work written in the face of his declining rational powers. This retrospective framing is presented not merely as an autobiographical anecdote, but as essential to understanding the form that Rousseau's system of belief took in the "Profession de foi": the threat of decline dictated a closed system of belief that was to be fixed irrevocably in preparation for his death. Not coincidentally, Rousseau made the broader claim in *Rousseau juge de Jean-Jacques* that *Émile* brought his philosophical system to a close, thereby giving a curious status to his post-system works.

The same tendency manifests itself in the *Rêveries*, where Rousseau observes that the decline in his senses and imagination threatens his ability to experience reveries. But in this case, he goes so far as to suggest that he wrote the *Rêveries* too late in the history of his decline:

> I soon sensed that I had delayed too long in executing this project. My imagination, already less lively,

is no longer inflamed as in past times by the contemplation of an object that enlivens it, I am less
intoxicated by the delirium of reverie; there is now
more reminiscence than creation in what it produces, a tepid listlessness enervates all my faculties,
the vital spirit is extinguished in me by degrees; my
soul no longer projects itself without difficulty
from its expired envelope, and without hope for the
state I aspire to because I feel I have the right to it, I
would no longer exist anymore except through
memories.[70]

Here, the *Rêveries* appears not just as a work written for the
dead, but as a work written after death. Unlike the "Profession
de foi," which was written when Rousseau was still at the height
of his rational powers, the *Rêveries* is written too late in the
history of Rousseau's decline. His life, along with his capacity
for reverie, is already in the process of being extinguished. This
claim is especially striking because it appears early in the second
promenade, before any actual reveries have been described
(since the first promenade is largely programmatic). From the
outset, then, Rousseau's project of describing his reveries is
threatened and perhaps even undermined by his impending
death. This gives a virtual cast to the work, as if it could only
exist as an unrealized project (or dream). Rousseau reinforces
this impression when he suggests that writing and dreaming
are two mutually exclusive activities: "Amidst such riches how
can one keep an accurate record? In wanting to remember so
many sweet reveries, instead of describing them I fell back into
them. It is a state that is brought back by the memory of it, and
one would soon cease to know it, in ceasing altogether to feel
it."[71] Here, the project of the *Rêveries* appears to be caught in a
double bind: either Rousseau will fall back into reveries in at-

tempting to describe them (thereby interrupting his writing), or he will have lost the capacity to experience and thus to know his reveries. What we have here is an impossible project: a work whose very existence is negated by the gradual death of its author.

The virtual nature of writing in the *Rêveries* gives us another way of understanding the incompleteness of the tenth promenade. It is as if Rousseau were staging for us the end of his life as a writer. Unlike all his other endings, this one involves not just a renunciation of his public role as author, but a renunciation of writing itself. The *Rêveries* suggests multiple ways this renunciation might be understood: Rousseau's writing may have been subsumed by botanizing; it may have been interrupted by a reverie prompted by the memories of Charmettes; or it may have been cut short by death. These are all genuine biographical possibilities, but they are also literary possibilities given the way Rousseau inscribes them into his work, tracing the various paths by which his life as a writer could come to an end. The design of Rousseau's last ending—the way it mirrors the gap between the two parts of the *Confessions* and opens out onto testamentary questions that Rousseau could not resolve in his life but kept grappling with in his writing—gives this ending a literary meaning that is inextricable from biographical contingency, but not limited to it.

So what is the ethics of testamentary writing that emerges from the *Rêveries*? In this work, Rousseau for the first time takes the full measure of the endings that punctuate his career as a writer. No longer seeking to make his thought cohere in a system that lies outside the history of his personal decline, he embraces a method of philosophical self-examination that must be practiced on a day-to-day basis and that takes its meaning not just from philosophical thought but also from the concrete forms in which that thought is expressed. These forms—and

most notably the fragment—reflect the fragility of a philosophical discourse that is deeply personal and human in nature,
and that can thus never be abstracted from the personal history of decline or written forms within which it is developed.
Rousseau had already gestured toward this view of philosophical writing in *Rousseau juge de Jean-Jacques,* by juxtaposing his
most cogent defense of his philosophical system with his most
anguished representation of the self that lay at its origins. But
it found its fullest expression in the *Rêveries,* where he looked
back on the ending of his philosophical system in *Émile* and
inscribed it into the same personal history of decline that dictated his final, fragmented ending. The *Rêveries* cannot be
considered a retreat from philosophy any more than it can be
considered a retreat from Rousseau's lifelong social preoccupa-
tions. But this work offers a vision of philosophy that bears the
mark of Rousseau's mortality, as he reaches across the divide of
death that will soon separate him from his readers.

Rousseau died on July 2, 1778, after taking a morning walk in
the park at Ermenonville. An autopsy performed after his death
(in accordance with the dictates of his final will and testament)
concluded that he died of natural causes.[72] Nonetheless, just as
his accident with the Great Dane had sparked false reports of
his death, his actual death almost immediately provoked rumors
of suicide and fabricated accounts of his final moments. As
R. A. Leigh explains it, "Such a man could not simply disappear.
The public wouldn't have allowed it. Could an extraordinary
destiny end in a common death? . . . He lived in a drama and a
certain logic required that he die in the same way."[73] The myth
of suicide was not put to rest for several decades, and some of
Rousseau's most ardent admirers, including Germaine de Staël,
continued to adhere to it in the early nineteenth century. Rous-

seau, of course, would not have been surprised by such fabulation surrounding his death: had he not predicted, in *Rousseau juge de Jean-Jacques,* that in the world of modern philosophy any truth that might be revealed at his deathbed would invariably be stifled?

The accounts of Rousseau's final moments that proliferated in newspapers and periodicals in the months following his death were quickly picked up by popular poets. In the descriptive poem *Les mois* (*The Months*), published in 1779, Jean-Antoine Roucher appears to take up the mantle of the Frenchman and the Rousseau character in *Rousseau juge de Jean-Jacques,* brandishing Jean-Jacques's peaceful death as a proof of his innocence:

> Mais ce qui de Rousseau dira mieux l'innocence,
> C'est la profonde paix qui couronne sa fin:
> Méchant, serait-il mort avec ce front serein?
> Sans trouble, résignant ses jours à la nature:
> «Laissez-moi voir encor cette belle verdure,
> «Dit-il; sur moi jamais un si beau jour n'a lui;
> «Je vois Dieu; je l'entends; ce Dieu m'appelle à lui.»
> Il expire; et trois jours, sur cette cendre éteinte,
> De la gloire du juste a rayonné l'empreinte.[74]

> [But what will best show Rousseau's innocence,
> Is the profound peacefulness that crowns his end:
> If evil, would he have died with this serene brow?
> Untroubled, relinquishing his days to nature:
> "Let me see once more this beautiful greenery,
> Said he; never has such a beautiful day shone on me;
> I see God; I hear him; this God calls me to him."
> He expires; and for three days, on these extinguished ashes,
> Shone the imprint of the glory of the just man.]

These lines reproduce several commonplaces of Rousseau's mythical death: his equanimity in the face of death, his love of nature, and his serene belief in a providential God. Much of Roucher's imagery was inspired by the influential account of Rousseau's final moments penned by his host at Ermenonville, the Marquis de Girardin, who would go on to profit substantially from Rousseau's death when his property became a popular site of pilgrimage.[75] Girardin did not witness Rousseau's final moments, and in fact he borrowed liberally from the unpublished manuscript of the *Rêveries* in composing his account.[76] As Leigh observes, this account, like so many others, must be read as a fiction, since the only person who actually witnessed Rousseau's final moments was his wife, Thérèse Le Vasseur.[77] In her down-to-earth account, published two decades after the fact in the *Journal de Paris,* she recounted that Rousseau offered no dramatic final speech, but simply asked her to close the door and open the window:

> Upon my return, it wasn't yet ten o'clock, I heard, in mounting the staircase, the plaintive cries of my husband. I entered precipitously, & saw him lying on the tiles, I called for help, he told me to contain myself, that he didn't need anyone, because I had come back; he also told me to close the door & open the windows, which I did; then, I used all my strength to help my husband get up onto his bed; I made him take drops of Carmelite water; he poured out the drops himself; I offered him an enema, he refused it; I insisted; he consented to take it; I gave it to him the best I could; but to bring it up he got down himself from the bed without my help, & went to place himself on the toilet. I went to him, holding his hands; he brought up the remedy, & at

the very moment I thought he was greatly relieved, he fell with his face to the ground with such force that he knocked me over; I got up; I let out piercing cries; the door was closed. Monsieur de Girardin, who had a copy of the key to our quarters entered, & not Madame de Girardin; I was covered in the blood that flowed from my husband's brow. He died holding my hands gripped in his without uttering a single word.[78]

However prosaic this account is (with Rousseau releasing an enema just before his death), it does share one motif with the popular iconography of Rousseau's death. An engraving of Rousseau's final moments, based on a drawing by Jean-Michel Moreau, shows him sitting in front of an open window to view nature for the last time. This image, like the poetic renderings indirectly inspired by the *Rêveries,* is an artistic invention. Nonetheless, it is tempting to take the open window mentioned by Rousseau's widow and depicted by Moreau as a metaphor for Rousseau's silence at the end of the tenth promenade: nature, or a final reverie inspired by it, has taken the place of language, and Rousseau looks out onto a vast spectacle of which he knows his existence, and his philosophical writing, can only be fragments.[79]

Thérèse Le Vasseur's letter to the *Journal de Paris* also details her trying financial circumstances at the end of her life: "The only thing remaining to the widow of your friend, the widow of Jean-Jacques Rousseau, nearly in her eighties, to live off is a modest life annuity from private individuals from Geneva; paid with difficulty, & a pension of 1,500 that the nation accorded her from the rent and pensions of the great book. Thus she lives in a humble cottage, where she is lacking in almost everything."[80] Before his death, Rousseau himself had been

Les dernières paroles de J. J. Rousseau. After Jean-Michel Moreau le
Jeune, print by Heinrich Guttenberg, late eighteenth century.
(Courtesy of the Bibliothèque nationale de France)

deeply preoccupied with providing for his wife. He had exposed
the couple's dire financial straits, and his wife's declining health,
in a document circulated to various acquaintances in 1777.[81]
And in his final will and testament, written in his own hand in
1763, he had left everything he owned, including his writings
and any proceeds from them, to the woman who had been his
companion and caretaker since 1745:

> This is the Testament of myself, Jean Jacques Rous-
> seau, citizen of Geneva, written in my hand.
>   I hope to die as poor as I have lived. A few
> rags and a little money will most likely make up my

entire bequest, and it is hardly worth making a Testament for so little. But the little there is does not belong to me. I must dispose of it according to my engagements and the laws of gratitude. I hope that such a just motive will overcome in the mind of the judges a few flaws in the formalities into which I may fall due to ignorance in making the declaration of my last wishes. I institute and name as my sole Heiress and universal legatee Thérese le Vasseur my Governess: wanting that everything that belongs to me and can be transmitted of whatever nature and in whatever place it may be, even my Books and Papers and the proceeds of my works, belong to her as to myself, most sorry not to be able to pay better for twenty years of services, care, and attachment that she devoted to me and during which she never even received from me any wages.[82]

Just as he had pledged to pay his debts to Madame de Warens in his earlier testament, Rousseau devotes this testament to the decades of assistance he received from Thérèse Le Vasseur and to his final wish that she be compensated for her services to him. His bequest of his writings is especially striking when one considers his obsessive preoccupation with preserving them for posterity as documented in *Rousseau juge de Jean-Jacques*. Thérèse Le Vasseur was only passably literate and could hardly be seen as the ideal reader or literary executor of Rousseau's oeuvre. But she was nonetheless the person to whom Rousseau left his writings, a bequest that would lead to bitter struggles and quarrels among the various men in possession of Rousseau's papers and manuscripts at the time of his death. Just as Rousseau could only pay his debts to Madame de Warens by evoking their fragile years of happiness together, he could not ensure that Thérèse would be provided for after his death. Nonetheless, his last will and testament mirrors and illuminates his writing in the *Rêveries,* where we see him concluding his entire corpus on the question of how his talents could allow him to provide for his loved ones. This is not the received image of the solitary walker, but it is nonetheless Rousseau's final ending.

On October 11, 1794, after several years of delays and controversy, Rousseau's mortal remains were transferred from Ermenonville to the Panthéon in Paris. The tomb erected there, which can still be visited today, is a curious one. It consists of a house-like structure in wood, rather than the expected stone. One side bears the inscription "Here lies the man of nature and truth," along with a bas-relief sculpture of four figures, from the youngest to the oldest, placing various offerings from nature (flowers, fruit, birds) onto the grave. It is the front of the crypt, however, that is the most dramatic. Framed by two vine-encrusted columns and topped with Rousseau's name are two doors. One of them is slightly ajar and emerging from it is a large, muscular, yet aging hand, somehow recognizably Rousseau's. The hand is holding an object so large it takes up more than half the adjoining door. This strange object appears to be a torch. As one tourist-oriented website dramatically proclaims, "Even death apparently can't stop the torch of Enlightenment!"[83] In keeping with the image of the philosopher in the *Encyclopédie,* Rousseau illuminates the path ahead of him with the torch of truth, even from beyond the grave. This image reflects the common perception that the Enlightenment philosophers paved the way for our modern world. But what if we imagined that the object in Rousseau's hand were not a torch, but a flower? What if he left us not with an enlightened path toward the future, but simply with the fragile remains of the last flower he held in his dying hands?

Tomb of Jean-Jacques Rousseau in the Panthéon, Paris, late eighteenth century. (Courtesy of Hemis/Alamy Stock Photo)

4

Voltaire's Butterflies

After spending much of his adult life in exile, Voltaire returned to Paris in February 1778 at the age of eighty-three. The occasion for his visit was the production of his tragedy *Irène* at the Comédie-Française. Shortly after his arrival, his long-time correspondent Marie de Vichy-Chamrond, marquise du Deffand, sent her secretary to pay her respects. Jean-François Wiart found Voltaire already attended by some three hundred visitors. In letters to Walpole, Deffand predicted that the crowds would kill Voltaire before she got a chance to visit him, or that anything less than the brilliant success of his tragedy would hasten his demise.[1] In the event, whether due to an excess of visitors, fatigue from his journey, or overwork in preparing for the production of his play, Voltaire fell sick in March and was unable to attend the premiere. Only at the sixth performance was he well enough to go to the theater, where he found himself crowned with laurels by an adoring public. A possibly apocryphal anecdote quotes him thanking the audience "for the glory under which I will expire."[2] When he died just a few months later, Deffand quipped to

Horace Walpole, "He died of an excess of opium, which he took to calm the pains of his strangury, and, I would add, of an excess of glory, which unduly shook his frail machine."[3] Irony aside, Deffand's witticism reflects the received idea that Voltaire's eternal glory was all but guaranteed from the moment of his death. This idea was confirmed during the French Revolution, when his remains were transferred to the Panthéon to consecrate his status as a *grand homme*.[4] The occasion was celebrated by some million followers, even though Voltaire's ignominious burial as a nonbeliever made the material reality of the transfer doubtful.[5]

The image of Voltaire's posthumous glory was also perpetuated by apocryphal testaments that preceded and accompanied his demise. A *Dernier testament de M. de Voltaire, contenant ses sentimens à la fin de sa vie, & ses volontés après sa mort* (*Last Testament of M. de Voltaire, Containing His Sentiments at the End of His Life & His Wishes for after His Death*), published in Geneva in 1778, included Voltaire's alleged signature from his residence in Ferney on March 18. In fact, Voltaire had already been in Paris for over a month by that date and would be crowned at the Comédie-Française soon after. Despite this factual inconsistency, the *Dernier testament* contributed to a broader mythology, in part self-perpetuated, surrounding Voltaire's death.[6] The apocryphal Voltaire, who speaks in the first-person in the *Dernier testament,* has no doubt, despite the attacks of his enemies, that his glory will only continue to grow after his death: "I will not descend into the grave without deserving and enjoying some consideration. My reputation, attacked in the first moments, will be like a young wine, which improves with age. After lying dormant for a little while, it will live again, never to die. I will pass for an enlightened genius and a good citizen."[7] This Voltaire also dictates a seemingly endless series of monuments to his own glory, including a copper plaque

marked "HERE LIES V . . . . . .," topped with literary trophies
and a crown of laurels; a medallion that is said to avoid the
imperfections and bad taste of earlier ones stamped in his
honor; an oil portrait to be hung in the halls of the Académie
française; an engraving to be made by the monarchs of Europe
depicting Voltaire surrounded by Homer, Virgil, Tasso, and
Milton at a Banquet of Epics; a marble statue representing
Voltaire larger than life and "jesting with one hand with a young
Genius who will caress [him]"; a stipend for a deserving actor
to train his younger colleagues in the performance of Voltaire's
plays; and several named chairs in philosophy at the Collège
Mazarin.[8] Yet even as these monuments appear to celebrate
Voltaire's glory, their excessive accumulation carries an ironic
edge, in keeping with Deffand's quip. Was Voltaire's posthumous
glory truly secure, or would the satirists who mocked him
throughout his life have the last word? As Rameau's Nephew
uttered in his own famous last words, *"Rira bien qui rira le
dernier"* (Laughs best who laughs last).[9]

Despite their lifelong friendship and correspondence, Deffand was pitiless in her assessment of Voltaire's legacy. On June
28, 1778, less than a month after his death, she wrote to Walpole that he had already been forgotten: "Voltaire is forgotten as
if he had never appeared; the encyclopedists would have wanted
him to live at least a few more months; he had plans that would
have made the Académie more useful; he was a leader for all the
supposed beaux esprits, whose objective is to become a corps
like the nobility, the clergy, the robe, etc."[10] Voltaire appears in
this account not as the great poet and philosopher Deffand believed him to be, but as an ephemeral bit player in the cultural
and political power struggles of his day. Although this judgment
may seem flippant, or even heartless, it is in fact entirely consistent with the singularly bleak philosophy of human existence
Deffand laid out in her correspondence with Voltaire. Moreover,

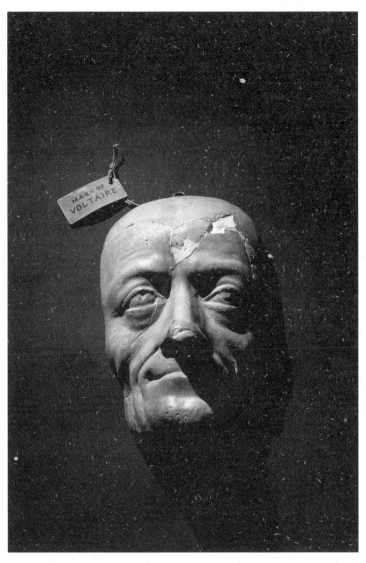

Death mask of Voltaire, 1778. (© The Hunterian, University of Glasgow)

as I will show in what follows, Voltaire came, by the end of his life, to share Deffand's philosophy. In two late poems, he echoed her view of death as an embrace of nothingness, devoid of any compensatory faith in the rewards of posterity.

Voltaire and Deffand were born two years apart, in 1694 and 1696, respectively. They also died two years apart, both at the age of eighty-three, in 1778 and 1780. They first met in their thirties at the Sceaux court, as members of the Duchesse du Maine's inner circle. But given Voltaire's prolonged exiles, and Deffand's sedentary lifestyle, especially after she went blind at mid-century, their friendship was largely confined to the letters they exchanged regularly until the last years of Voltaire's life. Their correspondence is marked by a singular brilliance, both literary and philosophical, and has been unjustly neglected, despite a number of modern editions.[11] It touches on a wide range of topics, from the weather, to gossip, to their bodily ailments, to literature and politics. But central to the correspondence is a problem that obsessed Deffand throughout her life: how could she, as a nonbeliever, bear the prospect of death? Although she paid homage to Voltaire as a great philosopher in turning to him for answers, it was Deffand who ended up serving as his teacher on the topic of death. His last poems show how deeply he was influenced by her thinking about death, and all the more so when he was facing his own.

Throughout the three decades of their correspondence, Voltaire expressed the greatest admiration for Deffand, above and beyond the formulas typical of eighteenth-century gallantry. In November 1775, three years before his death, he pledged to remain attached to her for as long as his corporeal envelope would permit: "Rest assured that even if I have lost everything that makes one live, passions, amusements, imagination, and all the trifles of this world, I remain seriously attached to you, and I will be so as long as my little apoplexies will allow. I will regard you as the person of my century who is the most suited to my heart and my taste, supposing I still have taste and heart. I will ask for your kindness as the first of my consolations, and I will say: it is by her side that I would have liked to spend my life."[12] Deffand was equally effusive, especially when one considers the harshness with which she typically judged her contemporaries. At the beginning of their correspondence, in October 1759, she sang Voltaire's praises as a writer and philosopher: "Your last letter, monsieur, is divine; if you often wrote me similar ones, I would be the happiest woman in the world and I would not complain about lacking reading material. Do you know the desire it gave me, along with your *Parable of the Brahmin*? It is to throw into the fire all those immense volumes of philosophy, except Montaigne who is the father of them all; but in my opinion, he produced stupid and boring children."[13] This early letter showcases Deffand's contempt for the philosophers of her day. Like Rousseau (for whom she also had little patience), she found them dogmatic. Nor did she appreciate their literary style, as someone who cared deeply about style and was herself a brilliant stylist. It is perhaps in part because of this antipathy for the *philosophes* that Deffand does not figure in Dena Goodman's groundbreaking study of the *salonnières*, *The Republic of Letters*. Yet this omission is unfortunate, because Deffand's letters to Voltaire reveal an incisive thinker who was deeply engaged with philosophical questions, despite her desire to throw most books of philosophy into the fire.

As Isabelle and Jean-Louis Vissière observe in their precious stand-alone edition of the Deffand-Voltaire correspondence, "The year 1764 marks a turning point in [this] correspondence. In March, Voltaire solicits a true philosophical dialogue."[14] This exchange arrived at a painful moment in

Deffand's life: barely two months after Voltaire's invitation, she definitively broke ties with Julie de Lespinasse, the younger companion and relative who for the past decade had assisted her in hosting her salon at the Saint-Joseph convent. Deffand had brought Lespinasse to Paris in 1754, when she found herself losing her eyesight. But the decade-long collaboration came to an abrupt end when Deffand discovered that some of the most eminent members of her salon had been covertly visiting with Lespinasse in the hours preceding their visits to her. The break with Lespinasse was consequential, not only because Deffand no longer had someone to assist her in her hosting duties, but also because a good number of her regulars chose to leave her salon to follow Lespinasse. The defection of the encyclopedist Jean le Rond d'Alembert was especially painful, and undoubtedly exacerbated Deffand's scorn for the *philosophes*. It was in this context of isolation and bitterness that her philosophical dialogue with Voltaire took root.

It was Voltaire who initiated the exchange, by volunteering his own philosophical conception of human existence:

> I have always noticed that we are masters of nothing. No one ever gave themself a taste for anything; that doesn't depend on us any more than our size or our face. Haven't you ever reflected that we are pure machines? I have sensed this truth through a continual experience. Sentiments, passions, tastes, talents, manners of thinking, of talking, of walking, all this comes to us in a manner I do not understand; everything is like the ideas we have in a dream, they come to us without our getting involved. Meditate on that, for we who have poor eyesight are better suited for meditation than other men who are distracted by objects.[15]

The philosophy of human existence sketched out here is one we might tend to associate with radical materialists like Diderot and d'Holbach, rather than a moderate deist like Voltaire. Yet it was one he reiterated regularly in his correspondence with Deffand, and one she shared, despite her traditional convent education and her hostility to the *philosophes*. At the same time, as Voltaire clearly recognized, Deffand had her own distinctive philosophy, which she developed over the course of their exchanges. Convinced that this philosophy would be superior to that of her male counterparts, Voltaire urged her to dictate her reflections, while also promising his discretion:

> You should dictate what you think when you are alone and send it to me. I am convinced I would find in it more true philosophy than in all the systems by which we are lulled to sleep. It would be the philosophy of nature. You wouldn't take your ideas from anywhere but yourself. Anyone who has, like you, imagination and accuracy of mind can find in himself [*dans lui seul*], without any other help, knowledge of human nature, for all men [*tous les hommes*] resemble each other deep down, and differences of nuance don't change anything of the original color. I assure you, Madame, that I would very much like to see a sketch of humankind in your manner. Dictate something, I beg of you, when you have nothing else to do; what more beautiful use of your time than to think? You cannot play, nor run around, nor receive company all day long. It would not be a trivial satisfaction for me to observe the superiority of a naive and true soul over so many arrogant and obscure philosophers. What is more, I promise you secrecy.[16]

It is worth noting that Voltaire invites Deffand to dictate what she thinks when she is alone, not when she is engaged in conversation with her salon guests. He makes his esteem for her intellect abundantly clear, placing her above the (primarily male) philosophers of their day. At the same time, he remains attached to a universalist view of human nature—"all men resemble each other deep down"—which elides any form of difference. This view may well have prevented him from realizing the extent to which Deffand felt confined in her social role as a woman and salon hostess. Voltaire also reproduces a number of received ideas about women in praising Deffand: her philosophy would be that of nature; she has a naive and true soul; she spends her days playing, rushing about, and receiving callers. Yet, as her more intimate correspondence with Walpole reveals, it was precisely the apparently frivolous existence of the salon hostess that plunged Deffand into the ennui she dreaded so intensely. Her disquiet only increased when she went blind in her fifties, a circumstance Voltaire refers to obliquely when he invites her to dictate (rather than write) her philosophy. As he well knew, Deffand was dependent on her secretary, Wiart, to read and write for her. Unfortunately, despite Wiart's devotion and their harmonious relations, it was an imperfect solution, above all because Deffand suffered from terrible bouts of insomnia and could not keep Wiart by her side during her long, sleepless nights. Occasionally, when the desire to write was too strong, she scribbled letters to Walpole during the night, only to discover the next morning with dismay that what she had written was largely illegible. These experiences may well have contributed to the depth of Deffand's philosophical reflections on nothingness, a topic to which I will return in my next chapter. She described the ennui she dreaded almost more than death itself as "a foretaste of nothingness [*un avant-goût du néant*]."[17] It was perhaps also her blindness and the loss of everything she had written during the night that gave her an acute sense of what Rousseau called "the nothingness of human things [*le néant des choses humaines*]."[18]

Deffand responded to Voltaire's invitation to a philosophical dialogue over a month later, at the very moment of her break with Lespinasse:

> Your last letter (which you surely don't remember) is charming. You tell me that you would like me to share my reflections with you. Oh, Monsieur, what are you asking of me? They are limited to a single one, it is quite sad, it is that there is, when considering it, only one misfortune in life, which is to be born. There is no state whatsoever that seems to me to be preferable to nothingness [*le néant*]; and you yourself who are M. de Voltaire, a name that comprises all kinds of happiness: reputation, respect, celebrity, preservation from boredom, finding in yourself all sorts of resources, a well-thought-out philosophy, which allowed you to predict that riches would be necessary in old age; well, Monsieur, despite all these advantages, it would have been better not to have been born, for the simple reason that one must die, that one is certain of it, and that nature finds death so repugnant that all men are like the woodcutter.[19]

If one wanted to capture Deffand's philosophy, with its nihilistic overtones, in a single phrase, one could not do better than this: "There is no state whatsoever that seems to me to be preferable to nothingness." Deffand takes Voltaire's existence as a test case for this radical principle, considering it rich in the many forms of happiness her own is lacking. No matter how many advantages Voltaire possesses, even his life is no more worth

living than Deffand's, because they both know they must die.
To illustrate this idea, Deffand evokes a fable by Jean de La
Fontaine, an author from the French neoclassical period she
especially admired. In "La Mort et le Bûcheron" ("Death and
the Woodcutter"), adapted from Aesop, an old woodcutter calls
upon Death to free him from the burden of his labors. But when
Death arrives to grant his wish, he suddenly changes his mind
and asks for help in putting his woodpile back up on his shoul-
ders. The fable concludes with the moral "Rather suffer than
die, / that is man's motto."[20] Deffand saw truth, but also paradox,
in this motto: if no human existence could be preferable to
nothingness, why would men (and women) invariably make
the woodcutter's choice? Deffand was evidently aware of the
singular power of her letter on the woodcutter: it is one of only
two letters to Voltaire that she kept among the personal papers
she bequeathed to Walpole.[21]

Voltaire's response to this bleak disquisition is characteristically both witty and full of pathos. Barely a week later, he
replies with an anecdote about one of his relatives, who had
been paralyzed after falling from a horse, but who "got accus-
tomed to his state and . . . loves life like a madman." He then
responds directly on the topic of nothingness, with one of the
finest examples I have seen of his bittersweet irony:

> It is not that nothingness has no good in it, but I
> think it is impossible to truly love nothingness, for
> all its good qualities.
>   When it comes to death, let us reason a bit,
> I beg of you: it is very certain that one doesn't feel it
> at all, it is not at all a painful moment, it resembles
> sleep like two peas in a pod, it is only the idea that
> one will never wake up again that is painful, it is the
> funereal pomp surrounding death that is horrible,

it is the barbarity of the extreme unction, it is the
cruelty of people warning us that everything is finished for us. What good is there in coming to us to
pronounce our death sentence? It will be accom-
plished whether or not the notary and the priests
get involved. One should make one's arrangements
early on, and from then on think no more about it.
People sometimes say of a man, he died like a dog,
but in fact a dog is very lucky to die without all the
abominable accoutrements with which we are per-
secuted at the last moment of our lives. If people
had a bit of charity for us they would let us die
without saying anything to us about it.[22]

Voltaire's ironic tone at the beginning of this passage belies the
seriousness with which he seeks to allay Deffand's concerns. He
relies on several commonplaces purveyed by the *philosophes* in
seeking to reassure her: death is not painful, it is just like sleep,
and it is above all the trappings of religion that make it so fear-
some for us. At the same time, he opens a window onto his own
fears when he evokes the horror, barbarity, abomination, and
persecution of a person's final moments. His evocation of a dog's
death may have held special resonance for Deffand, whose
attachment to her own dog, Tonton, was so great that she bequeathed him, along with a snuffbox adorned with his wax
portrait, to her beloved Walpole.

Voltaire again broached philosophical topics in February
1766, when he described his inquiries into metaphysics. He
admitted his ignorance in such matters, setting himself apart
from his fellow philosophers, those "fabricators of systems" who
posture self-importantly and deny their own ignorance.[23] Writing from his wintry retreat in Ferney, and suffering from declining eyesight, he beseeches Deffand to tell him whether she too

engages in such metaphysical meditations: "So, amidst mountains of snow eighty leagues around, besieged by the harshest of winters, and with my eyes refusing to serve me, I have spent all my time meditating. Don't you also meditate? Madame, don't there sometimes come to you hundreds of ideas about the eternity of the world, matter, thought, space, infinity?"[24] Voltaire does not explicitly link the metaphysical questions he raises here to his earlier exchanges with Deffand on the topic of death. But it is clear from Deffand's response that this topic remains foremost in her mind. Seemingly perplexed by Voltaire's interest in metaphysics, she asks if he really finds these studies necessary to him. She then rejects metaphysical speculation by insisting on her own adherence to empiricism, questioning whether we can ever hope to attain truths that lie beyond the teaching of our senses. In conclusion, she returns to her basic philosophical principle that nothing in human life can ever be preferable to nothingness:

> As for me, Monsieur, I'll admit it, I have only one fixed thought, one sentiment, one sorrow, one misfortune: it is the pain of having been born; there is no role one could play on the world's stage to which I would not prefer nothingness; and what will seem quite illogical to you is that even when I have definitive proof that I must enter into it, I will have no less of a horror of death; explain me to myself, enlighten me, share the truths you discover with me, teach me how to bear life, or how to view its end without repugnance; you have always had clear and accurate ideas, you are the only person I want to reason with, but, despite the high opinion I have of your brilliance [*vos lumières*], I would be quite mistaken if you were able to satisfy what I am asking of you.[25]

Within this remarkable single sentence, Deffand encloses a lifetime of metaphysical anguish. She revisits the paradox of La Fontaine's fable, but this time expresses it in unsettlingly personal terms. She goes so far as to evoke the very moment of her death, the moment when she will become aware that she is "entering" nothingness. Even as she adopts the position of supplicant to the great Voltaire, she emerges as a philosopher in her own right, as someone who has meditated so deeply on death and nothingness that she already knows the limits of Voltaire's reply. Just as she would turn later in life to religion, briefly and fruitlessly, here she turns to Voltaire and philosophy to assuage her fears of death, even as she knows full well he will be incapable of satisfying her.

It is clear that both Voltaire and Deffand were deeply engaged in their philosophical dialogue. But in order to grasp the extent of Deffand's influence, hitherto neglected in Voltaire scholarship, we must consider the place of death and nothingness in his corpus more broadly. A good place to start is Voltaire's abridged version of the bible of radical thought in eighteenth-century France, the *Testament de Jean Meslier*. The original dense, three-volume work was purportedly written by an obscure parish priest on his deathbed. The *Testament* promoted atheism and denounced all forms of religion. It began circulating in clandestine manuscript form shortly after Meslier's death in 1729, but did not gain prominence until Voltaire anonymously published a heavily abridged and modified version in 1761. Deffand had a manuscript copy of a different abridgment of the work in her personal papers, dated to 1755.[26] Voltaire saw the *Testament* as an ideal vehicle for converting readers to radical philosophy, his own moderate deism notwithstanding. As he wrote to d'Alembert in July 1762, this was because it was

written at death's door: "It seems to me that the testament of
Jean Meslier is having the greatest effect. Everyone who reads
it is convinced. This man discusses and proves his points. He
speaks at the moment of death, when even liars tell the truth.
Therein lies the strongest of arguments. Jean Meslier will convert
the entire earth."[27] Thanks in no small part to Voltaire's abridgment, Meslier's testament became a potent symbol of the
philosophical movement we know as the Enlightenment. More
specifically, the original work is notable for its stark depiction
of a nonbeliever facing death. Like Deffand, who did not shy
away from evoking the very moment she would enter into
nothingness, the first-person narrator of the *Testament* conjures
nothingness in his dying words by repeating the word *nothing*
(*rien*): "The dead, with whom I am on the point of going, burden themselves with *nothing* and worry about *nothing*. I will
thus finish this with *nothing*, also I am barely more than *nothing*, and soon I will be *nothing* etc."[28] This enigmatic conclusion
combines an insistent drumbeat of *nothings*, italicized and
placed at the end of each clause, with an unsettling final "etc."
The effect is to make the word *nothing* echo into perpetuity,
even as Meslier consigns himself to oblivion. This radical conclusion seems to have troubled more than one reader, in Voltaire's time and our own. The historian of death Michel Vovelle
drops the final "etc." when he quotes the passage.[29] Voltaire cut
the entire final chapter and concluded his abridged version with
a prayer. Instead of insisting on nothingness, the priest beseeches God to bring him and his readers back into the fold of
a natural religion. His very last words are: "God gave us this
religion in giving us reason. May fanaticism no longer pervert
it! I will die more filled with these desires than with hopes."[30]
After the priest falls silent, an unidentified third party concludes
the *Testament* by claiming that Meslier asked for forgiveness
from God in his final moments: "Here is the exact summary of

the folio Testament of Jean Meslier. Let us judge how weighty is the testimony of a dying priest who asks to be pardoned by God. *This 15th of March 1742.*"[31] This coda undercuts the radical nothingness of Meslier's original ending, and reflects what Jonathan Israel has characterized as Voltaire's rejection of radical Enlightenment in favor of a more moderate position.[32] It also lays the groundwork for the reception of Voltaire's own death, which was attended by speculation about whether he would renounce his philosophical beliefs and ask to be pardoned in his final moments.

Two years before he died, Voltaire wrote a short philosophical dialogue on the topic of death, *Sophronime et Adélos.* He presented it in the guise of a translation by the fourth-century North African teacher of Saint Augustine, Maxime of Madaure, a staunch pagan who raised objections to Christianity in letters to his former pupil. In the dialogue, Adélos (the Uncertain One) is wracked with anxiety about death at the age of seventy-five. He seeks out the counsel of the older Sophronime (the Wise One), who at eighty-six has attained an equanimity that eludes Adélos. As he puts it to Sophronime, "I admit to you that I have not been able to force myself to see death with the indifferent eyes with which so many sages contemplate it."[33] The situation of Adélos is in fact not unlike that of Deffand, who turned to the (slightly) older Voltaire to help her assuage her fears of death. The dialogue as a whole is suffused with a deep sense of Adélos's unrelenting anguish. In Stéphane Pujol's words, "The figure of Adélos, an old man wasted by metaphysical anxiety, is one of sincere and touching humanity."[34] But Voltaire concludes the work on a note of serenity. Just as he had sought to allay Deffand's fears of death, Sophronime urges Adélos to join him in embracing death with equanimity. Although he recognizes the impending nothingness death entails, he takes solace in the alleged last words of the Greek Stoic Epictetus:

I thus love truth when God makes it known to me;
I love him who is the source of it; I annihilate myself [*je m'anéantis*] before him who made me so
akin to nothingness [*si voisin du néant*]. Let us re-
sign ourselves together, my dear friend, to his universal and irrevocable laws, and let us say in dying,
like Epictetus:

"O God! I have never accused your providence. I was sick because you wanted it so, and I
wanted it in the same way. I was poor because you
wanted it so, and I was content with my poverty; I
was laid low, because you wanted it so, and I never
desired to elevate myself.

"You want me to leave this magnificent spectacle, I leave it, and I render unto you a thousand
very humble favors for deigning to admit me into
it and show me all your works, for spreading before
my eyes the order with which you govern this
universe."[35]

The last words Sophronime attributes to Epictetus are adapted
from the latter's *Discourses* and reflect the pervasive influence
of Stoicism on late Enlightenment thought.[36] But the language
of nothingness the sage adopts in accepting his death as God's
will ("I annihilate myself before him who made me so akin to
nothingness") has a more ambiguous filiation. It resembles the
bleak view of death put forth by Meslier and Deffand. But just
as he had rewritten the end of Meslier's *Testament,* Voltaire
tempers the stark view expressed at the end of *Sophronime et
Adélos* by introducing the figure of a munificent God, who
imbues the universe with order and bestows the gifts of nature
on man. His formulation echoes the spiritual language of a
Quietist like Jeanne Guyon or a Jansenist like Blaise Pascal, for

whom the nothingness of the human creature can only be understood in relation to the infinity of God.[37] This is a far cry from the atheist Meslier's radical drumbeat of nothings, or Deffand's near-nihilist philosophy of human existence.

One might thus take away from *Sophronime et Adélos* the idea that even as late as 1776, Voltaire remained largely unaffected by Deffand's stark view of death. That he, in other words, was the Sophronime to her Adélos. But this was not his last word on death. Two late poems, the second probably written during his last stay in Paris in 1778 just before he died, show how deeply Deffand influenced his final thinking on death and perhaps even the way he faced his own death. The first of these poems is "Le songe creux" ("The Hollow Dream"), most likely composed in 1776 or later, and which René Pomeau has described as "a fantasy on nothingness."[38] For Ralph A. Nablow, "Le songe creux" is "one of Voltaire's most searching poems," representing "by far his most significant statement on the concept of nothingness [and] revealing an aspect of his state of mind in the closing years of his life."[39] In the first two parts of the poem, the poet dreams he has died and sets out to explore the pagan underworld. Relying on classical imagery and influenced by Virgil and Ovid, among others, he traverses three rivers, meets the three Fates, and finds himself disappointed by both Tartarus and the Elysian Fields. It is not until the poem's dramatic conclusion that the allegorical figure of nothingness (*le néant*) emerges:

que me veux tu di-je a ce personage.
rien me dit il. car je suis le neant.
tout ce pays est de mon apannage.
de ce discours je fus un peu troublé
toy le neant! jamais il na parlé.
Si fait je parle, on m'invoque et j'inspire

tous les savants qui sur mon vaste empire
ont publié tant d'enormes fatras.
eh bien mon roi je me jette en tes bras [je ne t'invoque pas]
puisqu'en ton sein tout l'univers se plonge
tien prend mes vers ma personne et mon songe.
je porte envie au mortel fortuné
qui t'apartient au moment qu'il est né[40]

[what do you want from me I said to this personage.
nothing, he said to me. for I am nothingness.
this whole country is mine by right.
by these words I was a bit troubled
you nothingness! never has he spoken.
but of course I speak, I am invoked and I inspire
all the savants who on my vast empire
have published such an enormous jumble.
well then my ruler I throw myself into your arms [I do
not invoke you]
since into your breast the whole universe plunges itself
here take my lines my person and my dream.
I envy the fortunate mortal
who belongs to you the moment he is born]

It is striking that the poem lacks a final punctuation mark, leaving the poet's bleak final statement hanging in suspension. Nablow sees in Voltaire's evocation of *le néant* a reference to Seneca's *Trojan Women,* in keeping with the classical imagery of the first two parts of the poem. Nonetheless, he is at pains to explain the "cynical note" with which the poem ends.[41] And it is precisely this aspect of the poem that he and other critics find sublime. As he observes, "It was not easy for Voltaire to have to admit that life leads to nothingness. *Le Songe-creux* is indeed a poem of courage, not devoid of the sublime."[42] In support of this view, Nablow quotes Sylvain Menant, for whom "there is something sublime in the refusal of illusions and in the lyrical appeal to annihilation [*anéantissement*]."[43] Critics have been especially struck by the severity of the poem's ending, with Charles Vahlkamp characterizing it as "perhaps Voltaire's most pessimistic comment on the human condition."[44] They have also noted its novelty in Voltaire's corpus; for Nablow, "Le songe creux" is "unique among the [verse tales]" and "strikingly novel" in its embrace of nothingness.[45]

And yet these critics have failed to recognize Deffand's influence, even as Nablow quotes from Voltaire's side of the correspondence on the topic of nothingness.[46] We find in the opening lines quoted above the same delicious irony on the topic of nothingness found in Voltaire's correspondence with Deffand ("what do you want from me I said to this personage. / nothing, he said to me. for I am nothingness"). We also find an echo of Voltaire's conviction that any philosophy authored by Deffand would inevitably be superior to that of her male counterparts, in *le néant*'s scornful dismissal of the heap of rubbish published about his reign. Above all, we find in the last two lines a poetic distillation of Deffand's guiding philosophical principle: that we would be better off not to have been born. It is striking that the conclusion to "Le songe creux" offers none of the redemptive prayers of *Sophronime et Adélos* or Voltaire's revised version of Meslier's testament. Nor does it hold out any promise of posthumous poetic glory. On the contrary, the poet consigns his verses and his dream to oblivion, giving them up to *le néant*. In doing so, he in effect destroys his poetic legacy and effaces the poem we have just read. This interpretation is confirmed by a variant in the sole autograph manuscript in the Morgan Library. This manuscript reveals that Voltaire left open two possible versions of the line in which he consigns himself to *le néant*. Neither is crossed out, and there is no indication in the manuscript as to which version Voltaire favored. The line reads either: "well then my ruler I throw my-self into your arms" (the version preferred by Voltaire's editors), or alternatively, "well then my ruler I do not invoke you." The latter version is especially significant in that it erases the figure of *le néant,* in effect reducing him to nothingness. In its conclusion, "Le songe creux" is thus indeed a hollow dream, holding nothing, not even the figure of nothingness itself.

The last poem Voltaire wrote before he died is "Adieux à la vie" ("Farewell to Life"). Or at least that is the title the editors of the posthumous Kehl edition seem to have given it, for no title appears on either of the two autograph manuscripts. It should be noted that the word *adieu,* which opens the poem and is then repeated in the third line, never appears in the plural. So a more fitting title might simply be *adieu,* in keeping with the humble and intimate opening lines and Voltaire's use of a lowercase *a:*

> adieu je vais dans ce pays
> dont ne revint point feu mon pere.
> pour jamais adieu mes amis
> qui ne me regretterez guere.[47]

> [farewell I go into this land
> from which never returned my late father.
> forever farewell my friends
> who will miss me hardly at all.]

Nothing definitive is known about the date or circumstances of the poem's composition, but the critical consensus is that Voltaire wrote it during his last stay in Paris just before he died.[48] It was not published during his lifetime, and exists in only two, slightly different autograph manuscripts. The more complete of these, held in the Morgan Library, gives precious indications as to the meaning and import of the poem and its state of completion. As I will show in what follows, "Adieux à la vie" is the fullest expression of Deffand's influence over Voltaire's final thinking on death. It annuls the consoling words he offered her in an effort to assuage her own existential anguish. Astonishingly, it also presages her unsparing assessment of Voltaire's legacy, as the poet predicts he will be forgotten as soon as the derisive laughter of his enemies falls silent. His works will be consigned to oblivion and his existence will be reduced to the momentary fluttering of a butterfly's wings. No lasting glory will temper the nothingness that engulfs him.

The poem lends itself to being divided into four parts, the first two relatively straightforward, in both poetic form and presentation on the manuscript page, and the last two presenting more complex problems of interpretation. In the first part, consisting of ten octosyllabic lines, the poet bids farewell to his readers and friends, as we have seen. He then shifts his attention to his enemies, whose derisive laughter he calls the "ordinary requiem" of the dying man. He concludes this section by predicting that their laughter will be turned back on them, when they discover in dying that their own life's works have been consigned to the murky underworld they now inhabit:

> vous en rirés mes ennemis
> c'est le requiem ordinaire.
> vous en taterez quelque jour,
> et lors qu'aux tenebreux rivages
> vous irez trouver vos ouvrages,
> vous ferez rire à votre tour.

> [you will laugh at it my enemies
> it is the ordinary requiem.
> you will taste of it someday,
> and when at the murky shores
> you go and find your works,
> you will be laughed at in turn.]

These lines mirror the negation of poetic immortality expressed in the closing lines of "Le songe creux." It is not only the bodies (and possibly the souls) of the poet's enemies that are relegated to the darkness of the underworld, but also their works. In this sense, the first part of the poem bears all the marks of Deffand's influence. At the same time, her stark view of nothingness is tempered by the familiar classical imagery of the underworld. It is not until the second and especially final parts of the poem that the term *le néant* appears, this time presented not as an allegorical figure as in "Le songe creux," but simply in the abstract, as the expression of man's ultimate fate.

The second part of the poem, set apart from the first by an indent and a rare use of a capital letter, consists of twenty octosyllabic lines. It draws on the familiar "All the world's a stage" metaphor and zeroes in on man's final role as he lies dying.[49] Here, Voltaire echoes his lament to Deffand about the dreadful trappings of religion that surround a man on his deathbed. The *abominable attirail* (abominable paraphernalia) in the correspondence becomes the *attirail de la sacristie* (paraphernalia of the sacristy) in the poem:

> Dans leur derniere maladie
> j'ay vu des gens de tous etats
> vieux eveques vieux magistrats
> vieux courtisans a l'agonie.
> vainement en cerémonie
> avec sa clochette arrivait
> l'attirail de la sacristie;
> le curé vainement oignait
> notre vieille ame a sa sortie.
> le public malin s'en moquait,
> la satire un moment parlait
> des ridicules de sa vie;

puis a jamais on l'oubliait.
ainsi la farce etait finie.
le purgatoire ou le neant
terminaient cette comedie?

[In their final sickness
I have seen men of all estates
old bishops old magistrates
old courtiers in death's throes.
vainly in ceremony
with its little bell came
the paraphernalia of the sacristy;
the priest vainly anointed
our old soul on its exit.
the malicious public mocked it,
satire for a moment spoke
of the foibles of his life:
then forever it was forgotten.
thus the farce was finished.
purgatory or nothingness
ended this comedy?]

In the opening lines of this passage, the poet places himself not in the position of the dying man, but in that of an eyewitness to innumerable deathbed scenes of others (*"j'ay vu"* [I have seen]). But with the ninth line comes a shift in perspective, when he includes himself in the plural first-person possessive (*"notre vieille ame a sa sortie"* [our old soul on its exit]). This is a significant choice, and all the more so that in the manuscript, Voltaire crossed out *"cette vieille ame"* (this old soul) and replaced it with *"notre vieille ame"* (our old soul). The death becomes a collective one, in which the poet participates. It is also a farce or a comedy that provokes momentary laughter, before ending in purgatory or nothingness. With the first appearance of the term *néant* (which is written in tiny letters above crossed-out lines in the manuscript and is practically illegible), Deffand's vision begins to emerge. This word stands out as the only one in this section of twenty lines, with its insistent use of words ending in "-ie" and "-ait," that lacks a rhyming partner. It should also be noted that this part of the poem ends with a question mark, which Voltaire's editors have chosen to suppress, but which paves the way for the ambiguous and questioning tone of the poem's conclusion and recalls the searching questions Deffand put to Voltaire.

It is in the last two parts of the poem that we see Voltaire's ultimate response to Deffand's philosophy of human existence. It is also here that the poem poses the most complex questions of formal and semantic interpretation. This is due in part to the arrangement of the words on the manuscript page, an aspect of the poem that is not reflected in printed editions. On the left-hand verso side of the folded manuscript page, following the section just discussed, there are four lines, set apart from the preceding section by an indent. Below these lines is a small, straight dash that seems to indicate the end of the poem, with the rest of the page left blank. On the right side of the page there are five additional lines, under which there is a decorative dash that again seems to indicate the end of the poem, with most of the page left blank. What meaning are we to attribute to this arrangement? Did Voltaire hesitate between two alternative endings to the poem? Although it cannot be discounted, this possibility is belied by the fact that the two endings work quite well together, and by the rhyme scheme that links the second part of the poem to the fourth through the rhyming repetition of the word *néant*. Nonetheless, the question of the two dashes and the unexplained blank spaces remains.

The lines on the left-hand side leave behind the collective death scene described in the preceding section and directly evoke the poet's death in the first person. They begin with a question, and end with an answer, although, as in "Le songe creux," there is no final punctuation mark:

> au terme ou je suis parvenu
> quel mortel est le moins a plaindre?
> c'est celui qui scait ne rien craindre
> qui vit et qui meurt inconnu
>
> [at the end I have reached
> which mortal is least to be pitied?
> it is he who knows to fear nothing
> who lives and dies unknown]

The first line brings us right up to the moment of the poet's death. It echoes the simplicity of his opening *adieu*, "farewell I go into this land / from which never returned my late father." But, significantly, it is in the past tense. In this it recalls Hume's curious formulation, "I am, or rather was (for that is the style I must now use in speaking of myself . . .)."[50] Rather than setting out for a distant land, the poet has already reached his end. This prompts him to ask which mortal is least to be pitied. The first answer to this question is classical, inherited from the Stoics and, as we have seen, recycled in several of Diderot's late works. It is he who does not fear death. It is Sophronime, or Voltaire as he depicted himself in his "Épître à Horace," impassive in the face of death even as his doctor, Tronchin, trembled on his behalf. The second answer is more unexpected. It is he who lives and dies in obscurity. In evoking this obscure life, Voltaire does not seem to be referring to himself. After all, he, like his nemesis, Rousseau, was one of the first and foremost celebrities in Europe.[51] But according to Deffand, for all his glory, even Voltaire was soon to be forgotten. A life of obscurity was also what she envisioned for herself, when she wrote to Walpole that she did not wish to be spoken of. Perhaps in the end the distance separating Voltaire from Deffand was not so great after all.

The last five lines of the poem are the most disorienting, both formally and in their juxtaposition of unexpected images. Unlike the first and second parts, with their easily recognizable classical underworld imagery and world's a stage metaphor, the closing lines seem to flit from image to image:

> petits papillons d'un moment
> invisibles marionetes
> qui volez si rapidement
> de Polichinele au neant
> dites moi donc ce que vous etes
>
> [little butterflies of a moment
> invisible marionettes
> who fly so rapidly
> from Polichinelle to nothingness
> tell me then what you are]

Here we move rapidly, from butterflies to marionettes to the anarchic Commedia dell'arte character Polichinelle into nothingness. While the image of the marionette is consistent with the world's a stage metaphor, the butterflies seem to emerge out of nowhere, and do not fit seamlessly within the poem as a whole.[52] One clue as to the personal meaning of this image can be found in Voltaire's notebooks, where he mused, "It may be that we become something after our death: does a caterpillar suspect it will become a butterfly?"[53] But the faint hope for an afterlife held out by this passing remark is belied by the conclusion to the poem, in which the butterflies flitter in an instant from Polichinelle into nothingness. The fleetingness of a mortal's life is expressed through the intricate rhyme scheme around the word *néant*, the only rhyming word to be repeated twice in the poem. After its first instance in line 29 ("*le purgatoire ou le neant*"), we must wait an unusually long six lines for the resolution of the rhyme in line 35 ("*petits papillons d'un moment*"), with the pairing of *néant* and *moment* reinforcing the sense of the brevity of human life. This protracted delay can also be linked to the purgatory evoked in the earlier line. In contrast, the second instance of *néant* in line 38 follows immediately after *rapidement* in line 37 to form a rhyming couplet: "*qui volez si rapidement / de Polichinele au neant.*" This couplet creates an effect of acceleration that mirrors the mortal's nearly instantaneous passage from butterfly to marionette to Polichinelle to nothingness. And the concept of passage was apparently on Voltaire's mind as he composed this part of the poem: on the manuscript he replaced "*passageres marionettes*" with "*invisibles marionnettes*" and "*qui passez si rapidement*" with "*qui volez si rapidement.*" The unusual rhyme scheme, along with the way the word *néant* bridges the blank space between the two sides of the folded manuscript page, draws attention to the place of nothingness in the poem and its capacity for poetic disruption. Both sides of the page are filled with emptiness, and each one contains the word *nothing.* The unsettling impression is exacerbated by the last line of the poem,

dites moi donc ce que vous etes

[tell me then what you are]

This line creates an effect of suspension, not only because this question, unlike the earlier one, remains unanswered, but above all because it has no final question mark. At the same time, the decorative dash below this line seems to suggest that the poem is complete. The last line is both ironic and angst-ridden, in keeping with Voltaire's responses to Deffand: this final question is posed just after the addressee has flown away into nothingness,

Adieu je vais dans ce pays, autograph manuscript. By Voltaire, [1778?]. (Courtesy of the Morgan Library and Museum, New York. MA 638.87. Purchased by Pierpoint Morgan, 1900.)

such that the only answer to it must be nothing. It is thus that the poem's suspended meaning takes on a heightened poetic significance: the poet's addressees cannot answer the question because they have already entered a state of nothingness. There is, in the end, no possible answer to the questions raised by Deffand. Or perhaps, the poet's only answer is to fall silent and fill the rest of his page with blank space.

Deffand undoubtedly never had the occasion to read Voltaire's final *adieu*. What would she have thought of a poem that so perfectly expressed the philosophical reflections she shared with Voltaire at his urging? This question too must remain unanswered. What we do know is that she staunchly defended Voltaire for receiving the visit of a priest during one of his final illnesses. This was in response to Walpole's charge of religious hypocrisy in March 1778: "I am not at all of your opinion on the visit he received from the priest, it seems to me he did the right thing; he called upon him in his affliction, he is supposed to have confessed; the priest asked him for a declaration conceived more or less in these terms: *I will die in the religion I was born in; I respect the Church; I disavow and I repent the scandal I may have caused.*"[54] In another letter, Deffand specified that Voltaire recanted "everything he did, said, and wrote that could have caused some scandal and been harmful to religion."[55] Unlike Walpole, she did not see this declaration as hypocritical, nor did she believe it signaled some actual change in Voltaire's beliefs. Rather, she insisted that he had met with the priest and recanted his writings out of respect for social decorum, and above all in order to be left in peace at his final hour: "You have a very great and good mind, but which nonetheless does not prevent you from making a few mistakes in your judgments; I know it from experience, and most recently on the topic of

Voltaire; you don't judge his motives correctly; he would be very sorry for anyone to believe he changed his way of thinking, and everything he did was for the sake of decorum, and so that he would be left in peace."[56] This defense of Voltaire's final comportment may well have reflected Deffand's own intention to die in a manner that respected social decorum while also limiting the abominable paraphernalia with which dying men and women were surrounded on their deathbeds.[57] At the end of her life, Deffand conducted herself in a similar manner to Voltaire. She showed outward respect for religious conventions, accepting the visit of a parish priest and asking for God's forgiveness in her testament. At the same time, she dictated in her testament an unusually modest ceremony to follow her death and she gave no indication of any change in her religious beliefs in her correspondence with Walpole.[58] As her secretary, Wiart, wrote to Walpole after her death, "Far from desiring honors after her death, Monsieur, she ordered in her testament the simplest of funerals."[59] Perhaps, like Voltaire, she would have preferred to die a dog's death, something she hinted at by bequeathing her dog, Tonton, to Walpole along with her writings. It is to her correspondence with Walpole, and to the meaning of that final bequest, that I now turn.

5
Deffand's Nothingness

It may seem strange to include Marie de Vichy-Chamrond, marquise du Deffand, in this book. She did not think of herself as a philosopher, and she did not make any obvious contribution to the Enlightenment. Although she was one of the most well-known salon hostesses of her day, she does not figure in Dena Goodman's feminist account of the ways the *salonnières* governed philosophical discourse in the Enlightenment Republic of Letters.[1] While she maintained an active correspondence with Voltaire throughout much of their lives and was close to Jean le Rond d'Alembert in the early years of the *Encyclopédie,* her break with her younger companion, Julie de Lespinasse, in 1764 distanced her from the encyclopedists and, according to the standard account, accentuated the conservative and aristocratic leanings of her salon.[2] As Lytton Strachey put it in a 1913 essay on Deffand, "The truth is that d'Alembert and his friends were moving, and Madame du Deffand was standing still."[3] In recent years, the view of Deffand as a conservative, worldly hostess who was hostile to Enlightenment ideas has found support in the work of Antoine Lilti, who in his critical riposte to Goodman questions the intellectual seriousness of the *salonnières* and their contribution to the Enlightenment.[4] Deffand appears in Lilti's book as the epitome of the worldly sociability that is central to his account of the salons: in his rendering, beginning in the late 1740s, when she set up her quarters at the convent of Saint-Joseph on the rue Saint-Dominique, she gave her distinguished guests the occasion to share gossip and news and engage in the worldly diversions of *mots d'esprit*, gambling, theatricals, and literary readings, all the while eschewing serious intellectual discussion and the fomenting of radical ideas.

Yet the received view of Deffand is an impoverished one, failing to account both for the intellectual richness of her correspondence and her distinctive take on Enlightenment philosophy. Deffand has pride of place in this book because, more than any of her male counterparts, she grappled with the quintessentially Enlightenment question of how to die as a nonbeliever. Her obsession with ennui—a mind-body condition she suffered from daily but also reflected on in the starkest metaphysical terms—gave her a unique perspective on the obliteration of the human soul that was the logical consequence of materialist thought.[5] At the same time, her position as a woman and salon hostess, whose life was devoted to ephemeral social exchange rather than the production of a lasting oeuvre, denied her the traditional compensations for death enjoyed by famous male philosophers such as Hume and Voltaire.[6] Although she produced a voluminous correspondence and had full confidence in her exacting literary judgments, Deffand did not think of herself as a writer and had no wish to be remembered by posterity. Her expectation that she would not be remembered—along with her conviction that her social existence as a salon hostess was essentially meaningless—gave her an unflinching view of Enlightenment philosophy, in its materialism and its cult of sociability.

That Deffand's writings have been preserved at all is thanks to the efforts of her cherished correspondent, the English man of letters Horace Walpole, and his literary executrix, Mary Berry. Deffand's encounter with Walpole in 1765, when she was sixty-nine years old, was in many ways the determining event of her life.[7] In Walpole, who was twenty years her junior, Deffand found both the object of her most ardent affections and an outlet for the existential ennui that increasingly plagued her in her later years. She also found in Walpole an intellectual and aesthetic equal, someone with whom she could share her ideas and literary judgments. The friendship was a stormy one, with Walpole fearing the ridicule his attachment to an older woman might bring and frequently scolding his friend for her effusive expressions of tenderness. But the two maintained an assiduous correspondence for fourteen years, until Deffand's death in 1780, and Walpole traveled to Paris several times for the express purpose of visiting her. During her last illness he broke his habitual reticence to express the depth of his affection for her, writing to his nephew Thomas Walpole, who was in Paris at the time of her death, "Should she be capable of hearing it, when you receive this, I entreat you to tell her—but I do not know how to express, how much I love her and how much I feel."[8] He also recognized her literary achievement, making every effort to obtain the personal manuscripts she had bequeathed to him and ensuring the publication of her letters after both of their deaths, despite his insistence that his own side of the correspondence be destroyed. For Walpole, Deffand's letters rivaled those of the most esteemed epistolary writer in all of French letters, Madame de Sévigné, a writer they both adored. And he found in her literary portraits the quintessence of the elegant classical style of the French seventeenth century: "They are written with all the graces, ease, and elegance of the best period of Louis XIV, accompanied by a profound penetration into character, and she accounts with unequalled solidity for the assertions she makes."[9] This appraisal was echoed in the mid-nineteenth century by the Romantic critic Charles-Augustin Sainte-Beuve, who lauded Deffand as "one of our classics by the language and by the thinking, and one of the most excellent."[10] Such judgments of Deffand's literary genius have ensured the preservation of her letters, contrary to her expectations. But, to the extent that she is remembered at all, they have also contributed to the distorted impression of her as a conservative throwback to an earlier era. In this way, her unique perspective on the philosophical questions of her day has long been obscured.

In an effort to uncover that perspective, this chapter focuses on Deffand's correspondence with Walpole, some 840 letters composed between 1766 and her death in 1780, and on a brief, impersonal journal she kept in the last year of her life. My purpose is to evaluate Deffand's contribution to the Enlightenment, from the perspective of her late reflections on ennui, aging, and the diminution of the senses, the ultimate destruction of the soul, the ephemeral nature of social relations, and the craft of letter writing.[11] The chapter concludes with a discussion of Deffand's moving last letter to Walpole, read in conjunction with the journal of daily events she kept during the last year of her life. Although these are not last works in the traditional sense, they were written with death in view and offer a window onto the distinctive ways Deffand chose to craft the end of her life in writing, even as she believed she would soon be forgotten.

The most widely reproduced portrait of Deffand depicts her holding out her empty hands with her eyes closed. In fact, this portrait was based on an earlier watercolor by Louis Carrogis

Portrait of Madame du Deffand. Print by Samuel Freeman, after
Louis Carrogis Carmontelle, July 1810. (Courtesy of the Lewis
Walpole Library, Yale University)

Carmontelle, in which she is holding out her hands to receive a doll from her closest female friend, the Duchesse de Choiseul. But in the amended portrait, by the printmaker Samuel Freeman, both the doll and Choiseul have been removed. The result is an enigmatic image in which Deffand appears to be contemplating nothingness, not with her eyes, due to her blindness, but by holding it in her hands. Whether by accident or design, the portrait captures something essential about its subject. Throughout her long life as a salon hostess, Deffand was haunted by the specter of nothingness. In the last years of her life, the diminution of her social circle, combined with her blindness and encroaching deafness, made this specter loom ever larger. As she wrote to Walpole in May 1780, less than four months before her death, "I myself have not been feeling too bad, especially for the past two days, but I have nothing to do, nothing to read, and nothing to think about. Of all these nothings the sum total is ennui."[12] Deffand had long feared ennui. The scandals of her early years, when she was allegedly mistress to the Regent Philippe d'Orléans, have been seen as dizzying attempts to head off boredom on the part of a young noblewoman whose limited convent education and worldly occupations were no match for her corrosive intelligence. But in her last years, in her soul-baring correspondence with Walpole, her reflections on the emptiness of her existence took on a new poignancy, as she came to see the ennui she had long fled as prefiguring the nothingness she would soon enter. In response to Walpole's somewhat perverse claim that happiness is the source of ennui, she wrote in October 1779 that on the contrary, "It is ennui that destroys all happiness, it is idleness that is the true source of it. ... Ennui is a foretaste of nothingness [*un avant goût du néant*], but nothingness is preferable to it."[13]

For Lilti, Deffand's expressions of ennui are symptomatic of the worldly sociability of eighteenth-century French high society, in which a "frenzy of sociability" fills the void of empty, aristocratic lives.[14] But this interpretation fails to account for the philosophical and aesthetic understanding of ennui that underpinned Deffand's reflections on the topic. The article "Ennui" in the *Encyclopédie,* classified under the rubric of philosophical morals, borrowed heavily from Jean-Baptiste Du Bos's aesthetic treatise, *Réflexions critiques sur la poésie et sur la peinture (Critical Reflections on Poetry and Painting),* which Deffand had in her library.[15] Du Bos devoted his opening chapter to ennui as a prime motive in people's natural inclination to pursue the stimulation of their passions, through art among other means. For Du Bos, ennui resulted from failing to satisfy the intrinsic human need to occupy one's mind, either through the sensory impressions created by objects outside the mind, or through internal reflection and meditation. The latter posed a special challenge, which Du Bos described in terms borrowed from Lockean epistemology and psychology: "The soul finds it difficult, and even impracticable at times, this second way of occupying itself, principally when it is not a current or recent sentiment that is the subject of its reflections. The soul must in this case make continual efforts to follow the object of its attention, and its efforts, often rendered fruitless by the disposition of the organs of the brain, results only in a vain and sterile strain."[16] To avoid this natural physiological resistance to reflection and meditation required both a particular temperament and a program of meditative study beginning in one's youth. For those not lucky enough to possess such a temperament or education, the only means of avoiding ennui was to pursue the stimulation of the senses and the excitement of the passions. The desire to avoid ennui, while also avoiding the deleterious effects of the passions, explained the human attraction to the arts of poetry and painting.

Du Bos was thus interested in ennui only insofar as it explained the human need for painting and poetry; the main focus of his treatise was the arts that could serve as a means of avoiding it. In the *Encyclopédie,* Louis de Jaucourt built on Du Bos's account, but prescribed hard work, rather than the pursuit of pleasures, as the best remedy for ennui: "But he who has made for himself the kind of life of which work is both the nourishment and the support, is dependent only on himself, and doesn't need the pleasures I've been speaking about to chase away ennui, because he doesn't know it at all. Thus, every kind of work is the true remedy for this ill."[17] Jaucourt outlined a program designed to exercise the body and mind for those suffering from ennui. Although like Du Bos he presented his physiological theory of ennui as universal, he did acknowledge in passing that this program might need to be tailored to suit the needs of various individuals, notably depending on their age and sex:

> Since it is rare and near impossible always to be able to fill the soul with meditation alone, and since the manner of occupying it, which is to feel, in giving oneself over to the passions that affect us, is a dangerous and fatal option, let us seek a practicable remedy against ennui, within reach of everyone, and that brings no disadvantages with it; this will be that of work for the body combined with cultivation of the mind, through the execution of a well-thought-out plan that each person can form and fulfill early on, according to his rank, position, age, sex, character, and talents.[18]

By acknowledging that his plan for combatting ennui must take individual traits into account, Jaucourt undercut the universalism of Du Bos's prescriptions against ennui. Deffand would develop this insight in her own discussions of ennui, emphasizing the way her social position, age, sex, and especially her blindness contributed to her difficulties in overcoming ennui.[19] Even more than Du Bos and Jaucourt, Deffand saw ennui as the primary motive of human behavior: "It is ennui that rules the world, because everything we do is only to avoid it; we lose ourselves, we are almost always mistaken in the means we have recourse to."[20] Echoing Jaucourt's characterization of ennui as "the most dangerous enemy of our being," she observed that it leads to self-destructive behavior: "It is quite miserable to be by one's character subject to ennui; it is a state that cannot be borne, and that causes us to fall into every pitfall imaginable in order to relieve ourselves of it."[21] She also concurred with Jaucourt and Du Bos that the only cure for ennui was to occupy the body, mind, or heart. Yet she was much less sanguine than her male counterparts about the possibility of overcoming ennui: "If I have given in to the folly of searching for the philosopher's stone, I will not blush, and I will perhaps not repent. If in being unable to find out how to make gold, one managed to discover other secrets, one has not wasted one's time; there is no other remedy for ennui than exercising the body, applying the mind, or occupying the heart; to forgo all three is to be an automaton; but one becomes one, or at least one should become one, when one pushes one's career further than one should."[22] Although unable to vanquish ennui, Deffand suggests here that she may have made other discoveries along the way. Principal among these was her insight that old age—when one can or should no longer avoid being reduced to an automaton—poses a special challenge to the traditional prescriptions for ennui.

In addition to old age, Deffand's blindness also shaped her understanding of ennui. For Du Bos, engaging the senses with external objects—notably by looking at paintings—was one of the easiest ways to occupy the mind. But Deffand had lost her eyesight at the age of fifty-seven, a loss that became especially bitter to her in her old age. In June 1776, she explained to Walpole that she considered deafness preferable to blindness in old age, because it allowed one to engage in activities apart from the social exchanges she considered ill-suited to old age: "It would be better, in old age, to be deaf rather than blind; deafness is contrary to society, but when one is no longer suited to it, it would be only a slight disadvantage to be forced to do without hearing, and to have instead eyes to be able to keep oneself occupied in retirement."[23] Deffand's concern with keeping herself occupied was a constant throughout the years of her blindness. Reading and writing were among her most regular activities, but her blindness made her dependent on her secretary and valet, Jean-François Wiart, a man about whom little is known, but who served her loyally for nearly thirty years and was with her on her deathbed. Although she could write using a device to guide her hand, and in this manner occasionally wrote a letter in her own hand, Wiart had to be called in to decipher and recopy any writing she did on her own.[24] This limitation was all the more painful to her that as a perpetual insomniac, she sometimes spent up to fourteen hours in bed with nothing to do but mull over the meaning of her existence. And yet as she saw it, she was by character and education fundamentally ill-suited to the kind of sustained internal reflection and meditation Du Bos prescribed as the best antidote to ennui.

Deffand thus found herself obliged to confront ennui not as a temporary, remediable condition, but as a permanent state of being. As a blind woman and salon hostess, she constantly lamented her inability to *do* just about anything. Her existence, as she described it to Walpole in April 1777, was limited to the apparently empty social exchanges of eighteenth-century salon culture: "Anyway, don't worry, I'm not claiming to be a philosopher. I only know two afflictions in this world, pain for the body, and ennui for the soul. I have no passions of any kind;

almost no taste for anything, no talents, no curiosity, almost no reading pleases me or interests me. I cannot play or work; what then should I do? Try to distract myself, listen to small nothings, say them and tell myself that all this won't last much longer."[25] Deprived of the resources that would have allowed her to combat ennui, Deffand defined her existence in terms of everything it lacked. Despite her belief that old age was antithetical to sociability, she clung to the social exchanges that shaped her life as a salon hostess, even as she defined them as small nothings that served merely to fill the emptiness of her remaining years.

As we have seen, Deffand's view of ennui was informed by the physiological perspective of Du Bos and Jaucourt, which was itself grounded in Lockean epistemology and psychology. But she added a distinctly metaphysical dimension to this Enlightenment perspective. She defined ennui not simply as a condition caused by the deprivations of the body or mind, but as an active, destructive force whose physical presence in the body she compared to a tapeworm (significantly called *ver solitaire,* or solitary worm, in French): "What gets in the way of my happiness is an ennui that resembles the tapeworm and that consumes everything that could bring me happiness. This comparison would require an explanation, but I cannot unravel this thought."[26] Although Deffand failed to develop her idea further, the image of ennui as a parasite that consumed its victim from within implicitly linked this malady to the eventual destruction of the body and soul that was the logical consequence of materialist thought. In marked contrast to so many Enlightenment accounts, from Locke's blank slate to Condillac's statue, of sensorial impressions and ideas entering and taking shape within the human mind, Deffand defined ennui as a sort of material nothingness in the mind: "Taking myself as an example, when my soul is without sentiment, I am without ideas, without taste, without thoughts, I fall into the nothingness I call ennui."[27] Deffand's depiction of the mind suffering from ennui also stands in stark contrast to recent scholarship on the rich metaphors and overstuffed material collections that shaped eighteenth-century conceptions of mind. If we borrow Sean Silver's metaphor of the mind as a collection, Deffand's mind during a bout of ennui would amount to an empty collection, defined by what it lacks rather than by what it encloses within its case.[28] What is most intriguing about her account of ennui is the way it borrows tropes of Enlightenment empiricism, while subtly reconfiguring them to take on elusive metaphysical questions. In defining ennui as "a foretaste of nothingness," Deffand takes the sensorial impression of taste as a conduit for a metaphysical awareness of the ultimate nothingness of death that lies beyond all human experience. Ennui is thus in a certain sense a logical contradiction: it is a foretaste of death, an experience that can never truly be tasted until all sensorial impressions have ceased. If Deffand finds death preferable to ennui, it is because the saving grace of death is that it cannot be experienced at all.

Deffand's reflections on ennui were thus integral to her broader engagement with the Enlightenment problem of how to die as a nonbeliever. In this respect, she deserves to be recognized as a philosopher, in the tradition of the Stoics and Montaigne, who took the Ciceronian precept "*Que philosopher c'est apprendre à mourir*" as the title of one of his essays. Although she derided the encyclopedists and considered Rousseau a charlatan whose eloquence hid the speciousness of his thought, the extent to which she rejected the radical philosophical thinking of her time has been greatly exaggerated.[29] In her own day she was known as a skeptic and nonbeliever. Her close friend the

Comte de Forcalquier wrote in his portrait of her that "she took to reason as women ordinarily take to devotion."[30] And in one of the rare anecdotes from her early years in a convent, she is said to have "preached irreligion to her small companions."[31] She would remain a nonbeliever throughout her life, often referring to her lack of faith in her correspondence with Walpole. Although she never professed anything resembling the radical materialism of Diderot or d'Holbach, she defined the soul in purely material terms, as the union of the five senses. Writing to Walpole of her blindness and encroaching deafness in 1778, she implied that her soul would eventually die along with her senses: "All my senses will die before me; we shall see what will become of my soul, which according to me must be the perfect accord of our five senses."[32] She even described her life aspirations in terms that resemble the cynicism of Rameau's Nephew: "My wishes are limited to digesting well, sleeping well, and not finding myself bored."[33] And although she found Buffon's innumerable descriptions of quadrupeds tiresome, she echoed his subversive erasure of the religious distinction between man and beast, comparing herself to her dog, Tonton: "I am sometimes astonished at the uselessness of my life, and at the small difference there is between me and Tonton."[34] This comparison makes all the more poignant Deffand's decision to bequeath Tonton, along with a snuffbox adorned with the dog's portrait, to Walpole at her death. It is as if she were sending him a living substitute for her own body, in the spirit of Montaigne's *Essais*.

These various remarks in Deffand's letters to Walpole do not amount to a coherent philosophical position and do not make of her a materialist in the traditional sense. Nonetheless, they are not simply superficial witticisms scattered across her correspondence. They are symptomatic of a profound and restless questioning that was rooted in Enlightenment philosophy and in Deffand's preoccupation with learning how to die. In

May 1767, in the early years of her friendship with Walpole, Deffand reflected on her fear of death and the challenges it posed to enlightened reason:

> You want me to have hopes of living ninety years? Oh good God, what cursed hopes! Are you unaware that I hate life, that I regret having lived so long and that I cannot console myself for having been born? . . . Despite all that, one fears death, and why does one fear it? It is not only the uncertainty of the future, it is the strong aversion one has for one's destruction [*destruction*], which reason cannot destroy [*détruire*]. Oh! reason, reason! What is reason? What power does it have? When does it speak? When can we listen to it? What good does it bring? Does it triumph over passions? That is not true; and if it stopped the movements of our soul, it would be a hundred times more contrary to our happiness than our passions can ever be; to live that way would be to feel only nothingness, and nothingness (which I hold in high esteem) is only good because we do not feel it. Here is a threepenny metaphysics, I humbly beg your pardon for it; you are entitled to tell me: "Content yourself with being bored, refrain from boring others."[35]

Passages like this one undercut Strachey's assertion that Deffand belonged more to the first half of her century than the second.[36] Her fear of death, and her experience of ennui, had taught her that the Lucretian injunction not to fear death—which had become one of the watchwords of the Enlightenment—could not erase our natural aversion for death. Deffand chose her words carefully to convey an ironic edge: nature brings about the *destruction* of our bodies and souls far more effectively than reason can *destroy* our fear of death. This insight led her to a broader reflection about the tension between the Enlightenment ideals of reason and happiness: what is the purpose of reason if all it manages to do is destroy our passions and, along with them, any hope for happiness? Once again, Deffand reconfigures empiricist tropes: to live without passions would be to *feel* nothingness, whereas the only good in nothingness is that we cannot feel it. Despite the gravity of the topic, she concludes by displaying her ironic wit, alluding to her esteem for nothingness and apologizing to Walpole for provoking in him the very ennui she sought so desperately to avoid.

A few years later, Deffand revisited these questions in a letter Sainte-Beuve admiringly dubbed "her Hamlet monologue":

Farewell. I have a headache, pains in my gut, I feel very hot; this is nothing to me; it seems to me that I am all ready to pack my bags and go. This frame of mind may come from my still being far from that; it is as one wishes.

Tell me why, hating life, I dread death? Nothing indicates to me that all will not end with me; on the contrary I notice the impairment of my mind, as well as that of my body. Everything said for or against makes no impression on me. I listen only to myself, and I find only doubt and obscurity. *Believe*, people say, *it's the safest bet*; but how does one believe what one doesn't understand? What one doesn't understand can undoubtedly exist; so I don't deny it; I am like a person born deaf and blind; there are sounds and colors, he acknowledges; but does he know what he is acknowledging? If it were enough not to deny, that's all well and good,

but it is not enough. How can one decide between
a beginning and an eternity, between the plenum
and the vacuum? None of my senses can teach me
this; what can one learn without them? At the same
time, if I do not believe what must be believed, I am
in danger of being a thousand times more unhappy
after my death than I am during my life. What is to
be chosen, and is it possible to choose? I ask you,
you who have such a true character that you must,
out of sympathy, find the truth, if it can be found. It
is news of the other world that you must teach me
and tell me if we are destined to play a role there.[37]

Here, the full extent of Deffand's engagement with the philosophical questions of her day becomes apparent. She takes the
decline of her mind and body as evidence against the immortality of the soul. Foreshadowing Kant's answer to the question
"What Is Enlightenment?" she claims to rely on her own understanding rather than outside authorities. In keeping with
the intellectual modesty characteristic of Enlightenment empiricism, she insists that human knowledge is limited to what
can be known through the senses. Alluding to contemporary
debates around the Molyneux problem, she imagines herself as
a person born deaf and blind and asks how knowledge of the
other world can possibly be gained without sensory input.[38]
And she concludes by inviting Walpole into dialogue with her,
in keeping with the Enlightenment practice of philosophy as a
dialogic, collective enterprise. The letter is not devoid of irony,
as Deffand alludes to her actual blindness in imaging herself as
someone born blind and requests news of the afterlife from a
man twenty years her junior. But it is also filled with pathos—
in the words of Sainte-Beuve, "she has her view of the depths
like Shakespeare."[39] To the quintessentially Enlightenment

question—how can I believe what lies beyond my experience?—
she adds an existential one: what is the meaning of such an
unhappy life if I cannot believe?

Walpole's response to this letter is one of the rare fragments
from his side of the correspondence that was preserved by the
sparing choices of his literary executrix, Mary Berry. It high-
lights the gulf separating Deffand's restless questioning from
Walpole's less critical acceptance of received religious beliefs:

> And it is to me that you turn to resolve your doubts!
> Not being a priest, nor a philosopher, I won't tell
> you anything positive, nor anything negative. I be-
> lieve firmly in an all-powerful God, who is just and
> full of mercy and kindness. I am convinced that the
> spirit of benevolence and charity is the least un-
> worthy offering one can bestow upon him. As for
> the rest, that is to say, everything that is a matter of
> conjecture, I await his will with submission, and
> I have no intention of guessing for others what I
> am uncertain of myself. The vacuum, the plenum,
> eternity—oh! when it comes to all those questions,
> I will get mixed up in them when I prefer the
> ineptitudes of Messieurs of the Encyclopedia to the
> tales of Mother Goose.[40]

Although Walpole did leave some room for doubt in his response, on the question of religious faith he simply asserted his
belief in a benevolent God, without addressing Deffand's fun-
damental Enlightenment question: how can I believe what I
can neither understand nor observe with my senses? He also
failed to respond to the painful evocation of an unhappy life
on the part of a seventy-two-year-old woman who clearly had
death in view. Instead of engaging with Deffand's metaphysical

questions, he sought to steer her away from philosophy altogether. Knowing that she was hostile to the encyclopedists
following her break with Lespinasse, he mocked them as mere
purveyors of nursery rhymes.

But Deffand's metaphysical questions only grew more
urgent as she advanced in age. In May 1779, she wrote to Walpole that the despondency of old age, blindness, and deafness
had led her to seek out religious faith, or at least the illusion of
it. In describing her state of mind, she referred to one of the
most famous scenes from Jean Racine's *Athalie*, in her eyes the
most perfect work of literature:

> Remember Athalie's dream, reread it if you have
> forgotten it, you will find this:
>
> Dans le temple des Juifs un instinct m'a poussée,
> Et d'apaiser leur Dieu j'ai conçu la pensée.
> [An Instinct drove me to the *Hebrews* Temple;
> I cherish'd Hopes to pacify their God;][41]
>   I thus sought to satisfy this inspiration or this
> whim, I wanted to see, and I saw an ex-Jesuit, a
> good preacher; I found he had a lot of intelligence,
> reason, and kindness, he didn't tell me anything
> new, but his conversation pleased me; I think he is
> in good faith, I plan to see him from time to time.
> Who knows what will come of it? If indeed there is
> grace, I will perhaps obtain it; failing that, if I can
> have the illusion of it, that will already be some-
> thing.[42]

Even in describing this rare (and ultimately fleeting) religious
impulse, Deffand retains her usual skepticism and irony, hesitat-
ing between inspiration and whim, grace or the mere illusion

of it. Her reference to Athalie casts further doubt on her spiritual quest, as she quotes from a scene in which the heretical queen's visit to the temple is prompted less by religious repentance than by her fear of death. In her dream, she has seen a wretched vision of dogs disputing Queen Jezebel's corpse:

> . . . je lui tendais les mains pour l'embrasser.
> Mais je n'ai plus trouvé qu'un horrible mélange
> D'os et de chair meurtris, et traînés dans la fange,
> Des lambeaux pleins de sang, et des membres affreux,
> Que des chiens dévorants se disputaient entre eux.[43]

> [. . . I stretch'd my Arms to meet her;
> But Nothing caught besides a horrid Heap
> Of Bones, and mangled Flesh bedawb'd with Mire,
> Garments all-dy'd with Blood, and shatter'd Limbs,
> Which greedy Dogs seem'd eagerly to fight for.][44]

When read in light of this gory passage, Deffand's allusion to Athalie's dream appears as an implicit acknowledgment that her turn to religion was prompted above all by her aversion to the physical realities of death. As she wrote to her most intimate female correspondent, the Duchesse de Choiseul, "I do not like life any more than the next person, I am sorry to have been granted it, but I do not for that have any less aversion to death. If we could go up in smoke, that kind of destruction would not displease me, but I do not like burial. Ah! fie, fie, let us talk about something else!"[45]

In September 1779, a year before her death, Deffand revealed to Walpole that she had made little progress in her attempts to believe: "I am making attempts [essais] to manage to believe what cannot be understood; I am not, I admit, making any great progress; in any case, I am doing my best to be the least unhappy I can be. I know well what would be most

necessary to me, and the only thing I desire, it would be to see
you again; however I often tell myself I am wrong to desire it."[46]
Deffand's unusual choice of the word *essais* to convey her attempts to believe can be read as an implicit homage to Montaigne, who composed his essays in part as a means of preparing for death. Montaigne's influence can also be seen in the shift
from religion to friendship. Her evocation of her sole desire to
see Walpole before her death is all the more poignant that in
1779, in the context of the Anglo-French War, Deffand knew
that a final visit from Walpole was almost as unlikely as a visit
from God himself.

In the last years of her life, Deffand also sought out a model for
how to *write* in the face of death. For this she turned to the late
writings of David Hume. She was acquainted with the Scottish
philosopher and had exchanged a few letters with him, one of
which took his side in his famous quarrel with Rousseau.[47] But
she had never shown much interest in his writings and found
his *History of England,* which she owned in French translation,
boring.[48] In this context, the keen interest she took in two
pieces Hume wrote shortly before his death is all the more
notable. The first was a brief letter he wrote to Deffand's friend,
the Comtesse de Boufflers (nicknamed the Idol by Deffand), to
express his condolences for the death of her lover, the Prince
de Conti, and to inform her of his own impending death. In
September 1776, just a few weeks after Hume's death, Deffand
wrote to Walpole of her great admiration for this letter and her
desire to obtain a copy of it: "The day before yesterday the Idol
gave me to read a letter from M. Hume, on the occasion of the
Prince's death; he bid her farewell, as if he had only a few more
days to live. This letter seemed to me of the greatest beauty; I
asked her for a copy, and I will get it."[49] Deffand did indeed

obtain a copy of the letter, and later included a translation of it in a manuscript compendium of letters in Wiart's hand, bearing the title *Recueil de lettres choisies de différentes personnes* (*Collection of Chosen Letters by Different People*). This volume was among the personal papers she bequeathed to Walpole at her death. In it, Hume's letter was explicitly framed as a last letter, written in the face of death, under the heading "From David Hume written a few days before his death, to Madame la Comtesse de Boufflers."[50] Deffand's admiration for Hume's letter is all the more striking when one reads the letter itself, as it is marked not by the *mots d'esprit* so prized in salon society, but by its simplicity and directness. The conclusion to the brief letter reads as follows: "My distemper is a diarrhoea, or disorder in my bowels, which has been gradually undermining me these two years; but, within these six months, has been visibly hastening me to my end. I see death approach gradually, without any anxiety or regret. I salute you, with great affection and regard, for the last time."[51] A concise description of physical symptoms, an expression of equanimity in the face of death, and a final, understated expression of social affections: Hume's letter incarnates the enlightened philosopher's response to death in which neither fear nor religious feelings have any place. Deffand would have this model foremost in her mind when she composed her own last letter to Walpole.

The second piece of writing Deffand took a special interest in was Hume's last work, *My Own Life*. Of course, she was not alone in paying close attention to the final moments of a religious skeptic who had claimed he would face death with equanimity. But her interest in Hume's death is notable given that she barely mentioned the deaths of other famous contemporaries such as Rousseau and the *salonnière* Marie Thérèse Geoffrin.[52] As we have seen, Hume conceived of *My Own Life* in part as an answer to the question of how he would comport himself on his deathbed. He addresses this question toward the end of the work in the same sober, direct style Deffand admired in his letter to Boufflers:

> In spring 1775, I was struck with a disorder in my bowels, which at first gave me no alarm, but has since, as I apprehend it, become mortal and incurable. I now reckon upon a speedy dissolution. I have suffered very little pain from my disorder; and what is more strange, have, notwithstanding the great decline of my person, never suffered a moment's abatement of my spirits; insomuch, that were I to name the period of my life, which I should most choose to pass over again, I might be tempted to point to this later period. I possess the same ardour as ever in study, and the same gaiety in company. I consider, besides, that a man of sixty five, by dying, cuts off only a few years of infirmities; and though I see many symptoms of my literary reputation's breaking out at last with additional lustre, I know that I had but few years to enjoy it. It is difficult to be more detached from life than I am at present.[53]

These words were first published in March 1777, in a work originally titled *The Life of David Hume, Esq. Written by Himself.* But Deffand had already heard of the work as early as December 1776, when she asked Walpole to request a copy of it from their mutual friend Henry Seymour Conway: "Couldn't I acquire, through him, the Memoirs of M. Hume? I have a very good translator all ready. I know that these Memoirs are not much of anything; but those of madame de Staal are not very important, and never cease to bring the greatest pleasure: in any case I want them, and if M. Conway wants to get them for me, he will do me the greatest pleasure."[54] Deffand's interest in Hume's last work reflects her long-standing preference for memoirs over works of history and philosophy. By drawing a parallel between Hume's memoirs and those of her close friend, Madame de Staal-Delaunay, she inscribes Hume's work into a tradition of women's writing, while also asserting that works deemed "not much of anything" are worthy of our attention. This begs the question of whether she may also have been interested in *My Own Life* as a self-portrait, given her own widely praised practice of literary portraiture and self-portraiture.

A letter written in March 1777 confirms that she received a copy of the work in English and sent it to Boufflers to have it translated.[55] And her bequest to Walpole included a manuscript French translation of the work, entitled *La vie de David Hume écrite par lui-même traduite de l'anglais* (The Life of David Hume Written by Himself and Translated from English).[56] It also included Adam Smith's letter to Hume's publisher, William Strahan, about Hume's death, but in a different translation from the one published with *My Own Life* in 1777.[57] All of this confirms the intense interest she took in Hume's last work and his death. But, curiously, she made no further mention of the work in her correspondence with Walpole, contrary to her habit of sharing her impressions as a reader with him. This silence leaves us with something of an enigma, especially when one considers that she did share her reaction with her closest female correspondent. In April 1777, she wrote to the Duchesse de Choiseul: "Have you been sent the Life of Mr. Hume? Aren't you pleased with his simplicity? With his courage in facing his death, with his gentleness, with his gaiety? I would have accorded him much more esteem if I had known how well he would know how to die."[58] It is impossible to know why Deffand did not share this reaction with Walpole: was she generally more forthcoming on the topic of death with her closest female correspondent? In any case, the letter to the Duchesse de Choiseul confirms the significance of *My Own Life* in her eyes and suggests that she may have looked to Hume's death as a model for her own.

At the same time, it is worth asking to what extent acclaimed male authors like Hume or Voltaire could in fact serve as a model for Deffand as she approached her own death. Hume ended his life with an optimistic assessment in *My Own Life*, describing his existence as one fruitfully devoted to the pursuit of learning and letters. Although he cast his posthumous glory into doubt, he nonetheless held out the possibility of his works surviving him as a form of progeny. In contrast, Deffand had no expectation, nor even desire, of being remembered after her death. As she wrote to Voltaire in May 1775, "I am very little affected by the memory one leaves of oneself. The late madame de Staal said she would be very pleased to be able to invest her reputation, her consideration with no hope of a return; that is more philosophical than heroic."[59] Once again, it is significant that Deffand allied herself with a close friend and minor woman writer she greatly admired in professing her indifference to being remembered. In this way, she points to the gulf separating her and Staal-Delaunay from authors like Hume and Voltaire and suggests that not all writing is made to be remembered.

Six months after Deffand received a copy of *My Own Life* and sent it out for translation, she wrote to Walpole on the occasion of her eighty-first birthday. In her letter she offered a bitterly negative appraisal of her own life that stood in stark contrast to Hume's optimistic self-portrait:

> Today is the day of my birth; I never would have believed I would see the year 1777: I have reached it. What use have I made of so many years? It is pitiful. What have I acquired? What have I preserved? I had an old friend to whom I was neces-

sary, it is the only connection one can count on; I lost him, without any hope of replacing him, and never did anyone have such a need for support and counsel. I spend my bouts of insomnia thinking, searching for what I should do; I am, by character, indecisive, anxious; but what does this matter to you?[60]

Unlike Hume, Deffand depicts her life not as a productive accumulation of literary works, but as a succession of wasted years devoid of anything acquired or preserved. Even her friendship with Walpole is erased from this bleak picture, as she suggests that her late friend, the Comte de Pont-de-Veyle, was her only true social tie and that she is lost without him. Hers is a life marked by emptiness and loss. She spends her sleepless nights ruminating anxiously over what she should do with the rest of a life whose meaning continues to elude her.

One possibility Deffand envisaged during these years was to abandon her position as an eminent Parisian salon hostess and retreat from society. It was the solution advocated by Voltaire, who in March 1775 expressed his firm intention to die in his retreat at Ferney: "You will do with me anything you want, except to make me come to Paris. My imagination takes me on a stroll there from time to time, because you are there; but reason tells me I must end my life at Ferney. One must hide oneself from the world, when one has lost half one's body and soul, and make room for the young."[61] Although Deffand dreaded loneliness and inactivity, the prospect of retirement was not without appeal for her. As she wrote to Walpole in June 1776, "The idea of retirement comes to me often; I would like a fixed state, that this day, the day before, and the day after be the same."[62] Unlike Madame de Lafayette, a writer she greatly admired and felt a certain affinity for due to their shared experience of vapors—another word for *ennui* in Deffand's idiom—Deffand did not hold a religious conception of the retreat from worldly affairs.[63] Her idea of retirement was more terrestrial, closer in kind to the solitary botanical reveries of Rousseau at the end of his life. As she approached death, and as she retreated within herself, she aspired simply to vegetate: "All the events of my life happen in my head: it alone produces my joy or my sadness; everything external to me I forget almost as soon as it has happened. . . . I hate high society, and I observe with pleasure the truth of the proverb *God tempers the wind to the shorn lamb*. Solitude doesn't frighten me as much, and I will manage, I hope, to vegetate."[64] Although Deffand cited a religious proverb in describing her newfound hatred for high society, her aspiration to vegetate marks the materialist underpinnings of her conception of retreat. To vegetate was not to prepare for a spiritual communion with God, in the manner of the Princesse de Clèves, but, in the spirit of the Enlightenment, to lose one's human capacity for reason and sentiment and descend into the lesser sensations of plant life.[65] Instead of the dog's death advocated by Voltaire, Deffand aspired simply to die in the manner of a plant.

Like her religious aspirations, however, Deffand's project of vegetative retreat was short-lived. In April 1777, less than six months after forming her project, she declared to Walpole that despite her growing distaste and inaptitude for high society, she was too dependent on it to consider any form of retreat: "I don't flaunt retirement; I hate high society because I am out of place in it, but I fear solitude even more. I like society, it is necessary to me, and I always think I'm on the point of missing it."[66] In a subsequent letter she elaborated on the reasons she now considered retirement impossible for her:

I don't have any plans for retirement. The other day
I found a line in a comedy that pleased me. A man,
tired of the world, sad, discontent, says he wants to
retire to the countryside to find tranquility and
peace. *You must bring it there,* someone answered
him, *if you want to find it there.* Nothing is more
painful to bear than the emptiness of the soul; thus,
I conclude that retirement (which can only increase
it) is of all the states the one that would suit me
least; I don't plan to make any change in the life I
lead; there is none more idle, more devoid of every
kind of occupation and interest.[67]

Once again, Deffand draws on a literary example to explain why
she has come to believe she will never find inner peace in retirement. The comedy in question, *L'amant anonyme* (*The Anonymous Lover*), was written by one of her acquaintances, Stéphanie
Félicité, comtesse de Genlis.[68] Deffand finds confirmation in
this play that to move to the countryside would only further
oblige her to confront the unbearable emptiness of her soul.
She thus finds herself caught between two different forms of
emptiness: the emptiness of her soul, and the emptiness of her
life as a salon hostess, which is far too idle to keep ennui at bay.

How then was Deffand to fill her remaining years? Although she often claimed that her blindness prevented her from
doing just about anything, she frequently occupied herself with
the quintessentially feminine handicrafts popular in the salons.
The first of these was *faire des noeuds,* knot-making or tatting,
a craft in which a woman used a small shuttle to make a tight
row of knots along a cotton or silk thread, which could then be
used to trim a garment. Although it is surprisingly difficult to
find precise descriptions or diagrams of this craft (notably, there
is no reference to it in Diderot and d'Alembert's *Encyclopédie*),

a number of eighteenth-century portraits and novels depict society women engaging in it. Deffand referred to her own practice of knot-making both in her correspondence and in the journal of daily events she kept in the last year of her life. She also recounted an amusing anecdote about knot-making to several of her correspondents. The occasion was her first acquaintance with Joseph II, the Holy Roman Emperor and brother to the French queen, Marie Antoinette, during his trip to Paris in May 1777: "When I entered the room, he came before me and said to M. Necker: Introduce me. I made a deep curtsey; I was conducted to my seat: the Emperor, wanting to talk to me and not knowing what to say, and seeing me with a bag of knots, said to me: 'You are making knots?'—'I cannot do anything else.'—'That doesn't prevent one from thinking.'—'No, and above all today when you give so much to think about.'"[69] The humor of this anecdote stems in part from the way it revisits a scene from a popular novel Deffand despised, *Les égarements du coeur et de l'esprit* (*The Wanderings of the Heart and Mind*) by Claude-Prosper Jolyot de Crébillon. In the novel, the older Madame de Lursay casually displays her body in the act of knot-making in an effort to seduce the naive protagonist, Meilcour. In asking the very same question as the emperor, Meilcour reveals his ignorance of the ways of women and the world: "So you are making knots, Madame? I asked her with a trembling voice. To this interesting and spiritual question, Madame de Lursay looked at me with astonishment. Whatever notion she had formed of my timidity and lack of knowledge of the ways of the world, it seemed to her inconceivable that this was all I could find to say to her."[70] In Deffand's case, in contrast, she seems to have been especially struck by the emperor's witty and knowing reply—"That doesn't prevent one from thinking"— given her own perpetual frustration with the gap between the relentless activity of her mind and the lack of any serious occupation for it. As she wrote to Walpole in April 1776, "Unfortunately my soul doesn't at all grow old like my body; it would require an occupation, and today nothing occupies me nor interests me."[71] In realizing that knot-making might not prevent a woman from having her own thoughts, the emperor was more perceptive than both Meilcour and Voltaire. The latter explicitly set knot-making in opposition to philosophical thinking when he invited Deffand to share her reflections with him: "Don't blush to join the graces of your person to the force of your mind. Make knots with the other women but speak reason to me."[72]

Deffand's anecdote is all the more telling in that knot-making was conceived in her time as tantamount to doing nothing at all. As Rousseau wrote in his *Confessions,* "To make knots is to do nothing, and it takes as much care to amuse a woman who is making knots as one who has her arms crossed."[73] In their nostalgic view of eighteenth-century salon culture, Edmond and Jules de Goncourt observed that knot-making was a charming craft precisely because it allowed a woman of leisure to display her body to advantage in the *semblance* of activity: "It allows her to give herself in coquettishly to the graces of a lively nonchalance, of a laziness that appears to be doing something."[74] Viewed in this light, knot-making seems emblematic of the triviality and emptiness that Deffand lamented in her existence as a salon hostess. Another craft that was all the rage in the late eighteenth century, *effilage,* gave even more eloquent expression to Deffand's bleak view of her existence. *Effilage,* as the Goncourt brothers later described it, consisted simply in unweaving the threads of a cloth, especially one with valuable gilt thread, to be set aside for future use. In the last year of her life, Deffand referred on a number of occasions to this craft in lamenting the triviality of her existence: "*Effilage* and the lottery, those are my occupations and my distractions, is there anything more puerile?"[75] For a woman obsessed with nothingness, *effilage* was an especially poignant metaphor for her existence: instead of making something, the woman who engaged in *effilage,* as Deffand so often did in her last years, was unmaking something, or crafting nothing.

Viewed in this light, the feminine handicrafts practiced by Deffand beg the question of how she understood her own practice as a writer. As Elena Russo has observed, one of the challenges of engaging in a historical reconstruction of the salons is that this institution was by its nature an ephemeral phenomenon that "left scant written evidence of its oral practices."[76] Deffand was acutely aware that the *petits riens* of her life as a salon hostess—from the *mots d'esprit* to the social bonds—would not survive the destruction of her body and soul. For her, the feminine crafts of knot-making and *effilage* came to symbolize an existence that lacked both meaning and permanence. At the same time, someone as widely read as Deffand could not fail to recognize that these crafts also resonated with some of the earliest depictions of female authorship and self-determination in Western literature, from Helen's woven tapestry of the Trojan War to Penelope's weaving and unweaving of Laertes's funeral shroud to keep her suitors at bay. In Deffand's day, the association between weaving (or knotting) and female authorship was given new life in a popular philosophical novel, Françoise de Graffigny's *Lettres d'une péruvienne* (*Letters of a Peruvian Woman*). The heroine, Zilia, uses *quipos,* or knots, to write to her fiancé after her kidnapping by Spanish conquerors. As a metaphor for women's writing, the Peruvian *quipos* resemble both knot-making and *effilage* in the sense that they are marked by impermanence: the knots formed to write a letter must be undone by the addressee to write a response.

How, in this context, did Deffand view her own immense epistolary production? As we have seen, she declined to contribute her letters from Voltaire to a posthumous edition of his correspondence, writing to Walpole in April 1779, "I don't want to give those I have from him, I don't want to give any occasion for myself to be spoken of."[77] And she showed no interest in publishing her own letters during her lifetime or after her death. Does this mean that she saw her letters simply as an ephemeral feature of the social exchanges she engaged in throughout her life as a salon hostess, analogous to the craft of *effilage* and soon to be unraveled at her death? Or did she develop over the course of her correspondence with Walpole an awareness of herself as a writer whose letters had enduring literary value? When Walpole compared her letters to those of Madame de Sévigné, she scoffed at the comparison, claiming to have neither the taste nor the talent of her epistolary predecessor: "If I were more in the swing of writing, I could tell you a thousand little nothings; but I have neither the taste nor the talent of Mme de Sévigné: she would find today material for eight pages. Everything interested her, and me, nothing interests me."[78] Yet despite her claim to be lacking in taste, Deffand was supremely confident in her literary judgments, which in her eyes were not, as her modern critics have asserted, formed in accordance with a classical, rule-based canon. On the contrary, they were dictated solely by her personal impressions: "Every day I become more certain in not relying on anyone else's judgment; not that I believe I have more taste, but at least I only judge according to myself, by my own impressions, and never by rules that I don't even know."[79] This claim is borne out by her eclectic literary preferences, which were by no means strictly classical: in addition to Montaigne and Racine, she admired writers as diverse as Shakespeare, Lafayette, Sévigné, the English novelists of her day, including Samuel Richardson, and her contemporaries in France Staal-Delaunay and Marie-Jeanne Riccoboni.[80] The number of women on this list begs the question of whether

Deffand had a special affinity for women writers. She clearly shared Walpole's veneration of Sévigné, writing of her style, "As far as that of madame de Sévigné, it is unique and has a charm that resembles nothing else."[81] And although she did not see herself in Sévigné, she did acknowledge a certain affinity between herself and Lafayette. This was in part because both women suffered from vapors: "Mme de la Fayette suffered from vapors; I find myself to correspond closely with her."[82] But it was also because she saw a certain resemblance between their literary styles, to the extent that she admitted to having a style at all: "I have no style; but if one absolutely wanted to suppose I did, it would be closer to that of Mme de la Fayette than Mme de Sévigné."[83] Such remarks suggest she did have some conception of herself as a writer, and as one who belonged to a feminine tradition, despite the fact that she had no wish to be remembered.

The question of Deffand's self-conception as a writer is also raised by her decision to bequeath her personal manuscripts to Walpole, along with her dog, Tonton, and a snuffbox adorned with the dog's wax portrait. She made this decision carefully, knowing that Walpole's fear of ridicule might make him reluctant to accept a bequest that would publicly testify to the depth of their attachment. In June 1778, she wrote to ask him if he would be comfortable with such a bequest: "Tell me simply if you are concerned about the one I am intending for you, and if you feel any aversion to having your name written in a manuscript that cannot remain unknown; I expect from your candor that you will tell me in all simplicity how you feel about it."[84] It is tempting to read Deffand's bequest as a belated coming into authorship. Yet she left no indication as to what she wanted Walpole to do with her manuscripts. It is thus impossible to

Madame du Deffand's snuffbox with a portrait of Tonton. Louis Roucel (box) and Isaac Gosset (wax sculpture), late eighteenth century. (Courtesy of the Lewis Walpole Library, Yale University)

know whether she intended her bequest simply as a final expression of the ephemeral social bonds of friendship that connected them during their lives, like the living body of her dog, Tonton, or whether she finally came at the end of her life to recognize that she had produced a corpus of writings worthy of being preserved.

The meaning of Deffand's bequest is all the more enigmatic that she left to Walpole not only her letters, literary portraits, and other occasional writings, but also a journal she began dictating in the last year of her life. To the modern eye, this journal does not appear as a work of literature, nor even as an especially revealing autobiographical document. In stark contrast to Deffand's letters, in which she claimed to lay bare for Walpole "everything I think," the journal is almost entirely devoid of any trace of Deffand's inner life.[85] At the same time, it does convey something essential about the way she perceived her life, to the extent that it consists almost entirely of the *petits riens* that made up her day-to-day existence as a salon hostess: visits, guests, letters sent and received, gambling gains and losses, new dresses, and news items from her social circle such as pregnancies, illness, deaths, and political events. Why, in the last year of her life, did Deffand decide for the first time to start keeping such a record? As she suggests in a letter to Walpole, it may have been simply as an antidote to her failing memory.[86] But this would not explain why she chose to include the journal in her bequest, along with the rest of her personal manuscripts. This choice seems to indicate a desire on her part to preserve something of the ephemera of her quotidian existence as a salon hostess.

The journal provides an especially intriguing point of contrast to Deffand's letters when read alongside the last letter she wrote to Walpole before her death. This letter was written on August 22, 1780, a month before Deffand's death on September 23. In the interim, her secretary, Wiart, sent regular bulletins to Walpole detailing the progress of the illness that would take her to her grave. According to his account, she retained her full mental faculties until September 20, when he reported that her "head [was] totally lost, the ideas entirely eclipsed."[87] Yet during that month-long period, as her condition waxed and waned and she continued to receive numerous visitors, she never dictated another word to Walpole. While this may have been due to her medical condition (she was suffering from a persistent fever and kept largely to her bed, despite her many visitors), it is notable that she continued to dictate her journal on a daily basis until September 10. When placed alongside Deffand's correspondence, the journal reveals more by what it omits than by what it contains. Notably, there is not a single reference to the illness that would take Deffand to her grave, even as a minor migraine suffered by one of her guests is duly recorded. On the day Deffand composed her final farewell to Walpole, her journal entry reads simply: "*Tuesday 22.* Supped at home. Alone. Visit from M. de Toulouse, from Bouvart. Took cassia. Received a letter from M. Walpole from the 14th."[88] It is only by reading between the lines that we can find any signs of Deffand's condition on that fateful day: this is the only entry where the word *alone* appears, even though she supped alone with increasing regularity in the last month of her life; it refers to a visit from her doctor, Bouvart, and to the laxative, cassia, he prescribed; and it omits any mention of the letter she wrote to Walpole on that day.

It is difficult, and perhaps fruitless, to speculate about the significance of an absence. Deffand often recorded the letters she wrote in her journal, but she did not always do so. Nonetheless, the lack of any reference in the journal to Deffand's last letter to Walpole is striking, insofar as she clearly conceived of it as a final farewell. Wiart also understood it as such. In a letter to Walpole written a month after Deffand's death, he described the touching scene this last letter occasioned between him and the woman he had served for nearly three decades: "I cannot tell you the pain I felt in writing this letter under her dictation; I could never finish rereading it to her after having written it, my words were broken with sobs. She said to me: *You love me then?* This scene was more sad for me than a real tragedy, because in the latter one knows it is a fiction; and in the former I saw only too well that she told the truth, and this truth pierced my soul."[89]

Earlier that week, on August 17, Deffand had written to Walpole of having felt unwell for several weeks, but concluded that her condition was no cause for alarm: "That is my state, which is not alarming except to the extent it matches my age, for which there is no remedy."[90] Just five days later, however, she interpreted the very same symptoms as presaging her death:

> I have received your letter of the 13th and 14th. I sent word to you, in my last letter, that I was unwell, it is even worse today. I don't have a fever, at least one judges it so, but I am of an excessive weakness and despondency; my voice is extinguished, I cannot support myself on my legs, I cannot make any movement, my heart is constricted; I have a hard time believing that this state does not inform me of an impending end. I don't have the strength to be afraid of it, and, being unable to see you again for the rest of my life, I have nothing to regret [*Je n'ai pas la force d'en être effrayée, et ne vous devant revoir de ma vie, je n'ai rien à regretter*].[91]

In tone and content, this letter resembles Hume's last letter to the Comtesse de Boufflers, which Deffand had so admired and included in her compendium of chosen letters. Like him, she offers a precise description of her physical symptoms and calmly predicts her coming death. Like him, she notes her lack of fear and regret in the face of death. And like him, she expresses her parting affection for Walpole in a sober, straightforward manner. Deffand departs from Hume's model, however, in envisaging the future after her death and in prescribing how Walpole should behave and feel after she is gone: "Amuse yourself, my friend, as much as you can; don't be at all distressed by my condition; we were nearly lost to each other; we were never to see each other again; you will miss me, because one is very pleased to know oneself loved [*nous ne nous devions jamais revoir; vous me regretterez, parce qu'on est bien aise de se savoir aimé*]."[92] In projecting herself into Walpole's future, from which she knows she will be absent, Deffand repeats two verbs—*revoir* and *regretter*—she had used earlier in her letter to describe her own feelings in the face of death. This double parallelism, with an important difference, allows her to highlight the continuing connection between herself and Walpole at the moment of her writing, while also evoking the unbridgeable gap that will soon separate them. The parallel is clear: she has nothing to regret because she was never to see him again ("*ne vous devant revoir de ma vie, je n'ai rien à regretter*"), and he must not be afflicted because they were never to see each other again ("*nous ne nous devions jamais revoir*"). But the gap is equally clear: he will regret her because, and this is the significant part, "one is delighted to know one is loved [*vous me regretterez, parce qu'on est bien aise de se savoir aimé*]"). By repeating the same verb, *regretter*, in the future tense, to designate a time when she will no longer exist, Deffand subtly calls attention to the fact that, unlike Walpole, she will die with no certain knowledge of his love for her.

Deffand closed her letter by passing the baton to Wiart: "Perhaps later Wiart will send you word of my news; it is tiring for me to dictate."[93] But the letter does not end there. It includes a postscriptum, evidently composed by Wiart but consisting in a sort of dialogue—curiously in the third person—between him and Deffand about whether such a sad letter should even be sent at all:

> *P.S.*—Wiart didn't at all want such a sad letter to be sent; but he couldn't gain the point; he admits, undoubtedly, that Madame is very weak, but not as sick as she thinks; there's a lot of vapors in it, and she sees everything darkly. M. Bouvart just prescribed her two ounces of cassia, she took half this evening, and she will take the other half tomorrow morning; she has just eaten a good plate of soup and a small biscuit, she is stronger than earlier; she was in a bad disposition when she wrote.
>
> Wiart will take care to send a bulletin every day by post, until her health has been restored to its ordinary state.[94]

Wiart's use of the third person in this postscriptum is unsettling, as it is initially unclear whose perspective is being represented. The ambiguity is all the more jarring that the postscriptum clearly seeks to undo the moving farewell Deffand has just dictated. From Wiart's perspective, there is no reason to believe Deffand will die, all this is just a terrible bout of vapors; as soon as she is feeling better she will undoubtedly resume her correspondence with Walpole. Just as in *effilage* a woman unweaves the threads of a cloth, Wiart's postscriptum pulls apart the carefully woven threads of a letter Deffand crafted as her final farewell.

Walpole, however, was not reassured by Wiart's postscriptum and immediately read the letter as Deffand's taking leave of him. Although his response was destroyed along with most of his side of the correspondence, we can gauge his reaction from a contemporaneous letter he wrote to his nephew, Thomas Walpole, who was visiting Paris at the time:

> I cannot but be infinitely obliged to you, my dear Sir, for the very friendly trouble you have given yourself, though the subject is so exceedingly afflicting to me. My dear old friend's last letter shocked me as much as possible: it was a kind of taking leave of me, when I had no notion of her being ill; for though the preceding letter had talked of her being out of order, she has so often written in the same manner after a restless night, that it had given me no sort of apprehension. . . . My only satisfactions are that she does not suffer, and that she is so tranquil—should she be capable of hearing it, when you receive this, I entreat you to tell her—but I do not know how to express, how much I love her and how much I feel.[95]

Although not a direct response to Deffand's letter, Walpole's letter to his nephew implicitly responds to her plea that he not be afflicted by her death by using the very same word, *afflicting*, to describe his pain. The letter makes it clear that Walpole never doubted that Deffand's last letter to him was conceived as a final farewell, not unlike the one Hume had written to the Comtesse de Boufflers and that Deffand had taken as her model.

In the weeks that followed, Walpole wrote frequently to both Deffand and Wiart, with increasingly urgent pleas that Deffand try the English remedy of James's powder that he hoped might cure her. Wiart's replies allow us to follow the progress of Deffand's illness and to get some sense of how she might have reacted to Walpole's letters. On September 10, Wiart wrote to assure Walpole that he had communicated his latest letter to Deffand and that she had been deeply moved by it: "I read to her the day before yesterday, Monsieur, your letter [of August 17] where you express to her the greatest interest and the most tender friendship. I can assure you that she was quite affected by it. As soon as she is able to dictate a few words to me, she will certainly do it, but she is currently in the midst of taking her medicine."[96] There is something very moving about reading this part of the correspondence, as Deffand's voice falls silent, and we are only able to gauge her reaction to Walpole's letter via Wiart's third-person account of it. The idea that Walpole might have expressed the depth of his affection in his last letters is all the more poignant in that Deffand had revealed to him, two years before her death, her secret need to love and be loved: "You are right to be astonished that at my age my soul hasn't aged at all; it has the same needs it had at age fifty, and even at forty: it was from that point freed from those kinds of impressions of the senses, of which M. de Crébillon was such a vile painter. I had then, and I will have until the last moment of my life a need to love and a desire to be loved; but that is a secret reserved for you, and which I don't have the slightest desire to tell anyone."[97] For Sainte-Beuve, the beauty and pathos of Deffand's letters to Walpole stem from the combination of her corrosive incredulity about the possibility of love and her secret need for love. He found evidence for this in the anecdote Wiart recounted to Walpole about the dictation of Deffand's final letter: "I only want to recall one thing more, it is that last letter, so restrained and so touching, that she dictated for Walpole. The loyal secretary Viart [sic], who had just written it out, could not reread it aloud to his mistress without breaking down in tears; she then said to him those words that are so profoundly sad in their naïve astonishment: 'So you love me?' The wound of her entire life is there: incredulity and desire."[98] The scene Sainte-

Beuve describes allows us to see Deffand witnessing her secretary's tears as the physical evidence of his affection for her, just
after she had dictated a letter to Walpole highlighting her lack
of certain knowledge of his love. As readers of the correspondence, we are deprived of a similar scene between Deffand and
Walpole and must content ourselves with Wiart's claim that she
was deeply moved by Walpole's final expressions of friendship.

Even more cruelly, we learn from Wiart that he opted to
withhold Walpole's last letter from Deffand, fearing that it would
pose too great of a risk to her health by revealing how close she
was to death: "Monsieur,—How terribly sorry I am not to have
been able to read the letter you addressed to me to your friend.
It would have caused her too great a turmoil, because it would
have informed her of her state. She is not suffering, she even
says that she is much better. Only true friendship can express
pain so strongly. Your letter made me cry and I would not have
had the strength to read it to her. The slightest emotion could
cause her a great deal of harm."[99] In a curious substitution, it is
Wiart who becomes the recipient of Walpole's final expression
of friendship and who sheds tears in response to his pain at
losing his friend. This is strangely fitting given Wiart's constant
presence as a third party throughout their intimate correspondence; as Deffand had once written to Walpole, "Keep in mind
that I am speaking right into your ear, and that with the exception of Wiart, who is a sort of wall, no one else hears me."[100]
That threesome has now been reduced to two, and Deffand dies
without any knowledge of Walpole's last letter to her. According
to Wiart, she also dies without any awareness of her coming
death: "What is fortunate is that she does not suffer at all, and
she doesn't know her state; she didn't notice at all (even in her
right mind) that she was in grave danger. She is passing away
without realizing it."[101] It is of course impossible to know
whether Deffand indeed slipped out of life in the vegetative

state she aspired to, entering nothingness without the terrible
foretaste she so dreaded during her life. But Wiart's claim notwithstanding, the testimony of her final letter to Walpole must
not be forgotten, as it was evidently written with a full knowledge of her coming death and with the clear intention of crafting a final farewell. This letter, when read alongside her silence
toward Walpole in the last month of her life, suggests that
whatever others may have said on her behalf, Deffand died as
she had lived, facing nothingness head-on. The nothingness she
held in her empty hands in Carmontelle's portrait is mirrored
by a poignant material trace of her silence: the last 206 pages
of her journal, bound in beautiful green vellum, have been left
blank.

Of *King Lear*, Deffand wrote, "It darkens my soul to a degree I
cannot express."[102] In the tragedy, Lear responds to his Fool's
query—"Can you make no use of nothing, nuncle?"—with
"Why, no, boy, nothing can be made out of nothing." Yet Shakespeare built an entire tragedy out of Cordelia's initial response—
"Nothing, my lord"—to her father's demand that she speak more
eloquently of her love for him than her sisters had done.[103]
Deffand would undoubtedly have scoffed at any comparison
between her letters and the work of Shakespeare, just as she
rejected Walpole's comparison between herself and Madame
de Sévigné. But for a critic as astute as Sainte-Beuve, Deffand
"has her view of the depths like Shakespeare."[104] What Sainte-
Beuve, along with so many of Deffand's commentators, failed
to perceive, however, was the extent to which Deffand's version
of Shakespearean nothingness was conceived in dialogue with
the modern philosophy she claimed to despise. In writing of
her experience of ennui, Deffand laid bare the hidden underside
of optimistic Enlightenment accounts of the workings of the
mind. What happened when the mind was not an overstuffed

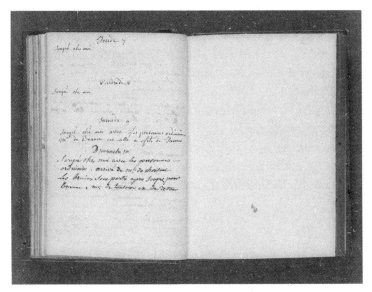

Madame du Deffand's journal, 1779–80. (Courtesy of the Lewis
Walpole Library, Yale University)

collection, but emptied of any sensations or ideas? When instead
of receiving sensations from the outside world and recombin-
ing them in multiple forms, it was overtaken by a tapeworm
that seemed intent on destroying everything in its midst?
In describing ennui as a foretaste of nothingness, Deffand did
not abandon the empirical, sensationist framework of her
century. Instead, she subtly reconfigured it, asking how the mind
could ever gain experience of the ultimate nothingness that
was the endpoint of human life in the materialist worldview. At
the same time, Deffand's social existence as a salon hostess
gave her a disenchanted view of the Enlightenment ideal of
sociability. Just as the mind suffering from ennui was emptied
of sensations and ideas, Deffand saw her life as a salon hostess
as one of irredeemable loss, as the social exchanges and bonds

she cultivated were gradually destroyed with the decline of her senses and the death of her friends. In this context, her letters to Walpole appear not as an effort to be remembered by posterity, but as a quotidian craft analogous to the feminine handicrafts of knot-making and *effilage* that she practiced to bide her time until her death. Nonetheless, for all her belief that nothing would survive of her after her death, Deffand realized the Fool's prophecy by making something out of nothing, in the form of a corpus of letters that remains as a testimony to one woman's devastatingly lucid foretaste of nothingness.

EPILOGUE

Roland's Death

Speak; it is something to know one's fate, and with
a soul like mine, one is capable of envisaging it.

—MADAME ROLAND'S *last, unsent letter to*
Maximilien Robespierre, from the infirmary
at the Sainte-Pélagie prison, October 14, 1793

Marie-Jeanne Phlipon, the future Madame Roland, was born in 1754, nearly half a century after the writers discussed in this book. But she died just five short years after Buffon, in 1793. Unlike them all, she did not die of natural causes, and did not reach the age of forty. Instead, she died under the guillotine, where she uttered her famous last words: "Oh Liberty, what crimes have been committed in your name!"[1] Roland's lifespan could not have been predicted by Buffon's mortality tables, and her cause of death lay beyond the scope of his physiological theory of death as the gradual hardening of the bones and flesh. It was brought about, quite abruptly, by historical and political

forces and events that the major figures of the Enlightenment
did not live to witness. Their generation, and their self-conception
as philosophical subjects, had drawn to a close. She died as a
modern political subject, facing execution by the state and
knowing that her fate was tied to that of her country. In almost
every way, then, Roland's death does not belong in this book.
But I end with her because the way she came into her identity
as a writer in the face of death, and her efforts to shape her
posthumous political legacy in her prison writings, throw into
sharper relief, by contrast, the radical embrace of nothingness
and silence on the part of Enlightenment philosophers. Unlike
them, she wrote her last pages with the express intention of
ensuring that her name would be remembered, and vindicated,
by posterity. Unlike them, she did not choose silence: on the
contrary, she wrote more and more frenetically as she approached
death, multiplying the texts that could be considered her last
words. And unlike them, she renounced her philosophical incredulity in the face of death, expressing full confidence in the
afterlife in her last writings. She came into authorship at a time
when the incipient cult of revolutionary martyrs was emerging,
and she used her last words to cement her status as a sacrificial
figure in the image of Socrates. For her, at her particular historical and political moment, death was not so much an ending
as a sacrifice that, she believed, would eventually allow for a new
beginning.

Roland is instructive, as a counterexample, in part because, as a
brilliant autodidact, her mind was formed by reading the Enlightenment philosophers. Although she aspired as a girl to a
life behind convent walls, in part due to an early experience
of sexual molestation, her readings of the materialists, notably
Diderot, but also d'Alembert, d'Holbach, and Claude Adrien
Helvétius, converted her to incredulity in her late adolescence.

From the age of nine, she shared Rousseau's love of the Greek Platonist Plutarch, and after the death of her beloved mother she became an ardent reader of Rousseau himself. Writing during the Terror, imprisoned for her part as a behind-the-scenes leader and strategist of the Gironde, she modeled her memoirs of childhood on his *Confessions*, while also highlighting how her experiences as a girl and young woman set her apart from him. Like the Enlightenment philosophers, Roland cultivated Stoicism, a philosophy that served her well during her imprisonment and in her final hours. Yet the circumstances under which she put the lessons of the *philosophes* to the test could not have been more different from those they faced at the end of their lives.

The structure of what we call the *Mémoires* of Madame Roland was dictated by a combination of her personal choices as a writer and the extreme circumstances under which they were written. Roland was arrested in the night of May 31, 1793, at the start of the insurrections that brought about the fall of the Girondin party in favor of the Montagnards. She made no attempt to escape from her captors, later explaining that she sought in this way to facilitate the flight of her husband and assuage the anger of his political enemies. Exhibiting the fortitude that characterized her behavior throughout her imprisonment, Roland began documenting the circumstances of her arrest from her very first hours in the Abbaye prison (she would later be briefly released, only to be re-arrested and imprisoned in the Sainte-Pélagie, and then transferred to the Conciergerie shortly before her execution). Her initial project, however, was not to write her personal memoirs. She titled her work *Notices historiques* (*Historical Notes*), and described it as follows:

> I used the first period of my captivity to write; I did it with such speed and in such a happy disposition that within barely a month's time, I had enough

manuscripts to make up a duodecimo volume. It was, under the title *Notices historiques,* the details of all the facts and all the people connected to public life that my position put me in a situation to know; I shared them with the freedom, the energy of my character, with the abandon of frankness, the ease of a spirit above all particular concerns, with the pleasure of depicting what I had sensed or what I felt; lastly with the confidence that, in any event, this collection would be my moral and political testament.[2]

In designating her prison writings as a moral and political testament, Roland inscribed her work into an illustrious tradition exemplified by the Cardinal Richelieu and picked up by her contemporary Olympe de Gouges. Yet her use of the conditional ("*would be* my moral and political testament") points to the extraordinary contingency surrounding the survival of her manuscripts. After making valiant efforts to have the *Notices historiques* smuggled out of her prisons little by little, she learned in August that the friend charged with copying and safeguarding the work had thrown it into the fire amid the panic surrounding his own arrest:

I had just completed the whole thing, bringing matters right up to these last moments, and I had entrusted it to a friend who valued it highly; the storm came down on him suddenly; in the moment he saw himself being arrested, he thought only of the dangers; he felt only the need to ward them off and, without thinking of expedients, he threw my manuscripts into the fire. I admit that I would have preferred he throw me into it instead.

> This loss agitated me more than the harshest or-
> deals I am still enduring; this is understandable if
> one conceives that the crisis is approaching, that
> I can be massacred on the first day, or dragged
> somehow to the tribunal the dominators use to rid
> themselves of those they find troublesome; that
> these writings were a pillow on which I rested the
> justification of my memory and that of many inter-
> esting personages.[3]

Roland's dismay at the burning of her manuscripts recalls Deffand's distress when she discovered her nighttime scribblings
to Walpole were illegible. Yet Roland's claim that she would
rather have been burned alive than lose her manuscripts sets
her apart from Deffand, who never sought to publish her work,
and the late Rousseau, who claimed to care little for the fate of
his *Rêveries*. As a martyr to the revolutionary cause, Roland was
prepared to die to ensure the survival of her writings. Looking
into the future, she believed these writings would support her
vindication in the eyes of posterity, along with her fellow
Girondins.

Roland reacted to the catastrophic burning of her manuscripts with a determination to rewrite her work in a new form.
And it is here that we find one of the most subtly moving passages in her memoirs: "Certainly! The death of Lauzun's spider
in the Bastille was no more cruel, and that was a loss for him
alone. However, since one must succumb to nothing, I am going to use my leisure to jot down carelessly, here and there,
whatever comes into my mind. This cannot replace what I have
lost but will be the tatters that will serve to remind me of it, and
one day help me to make up for it, if I still have the ability to
do so."[4] The underlying meaning of this passage will remain
obscure for most readers today. But eighteenth-century readers

versed in philosophy would have known the anecdote of Lauzun's spider from Adam Smith's *Theory of Moral Sentiments* or
Claude Adrien Helvétius's *De l'esprit* (*On Mind*), the explosive
work that led to the suppression of the *Encyclopédie* in 1759.[5]
In Helvétius's telling, Lauzun sought to assuage "the boredom
and horror of prison" by taming a spider, only to see his inhu-
mane warden sadistically squashing it. But rather than expressing sympathy for the prisoner, Helvétius uses the anecdote to
illustrate his claim that we are often mistaken about the motives
determining our actions. He compares Lauzon crying over his
spider to a bereaved mother crying over the child she has lost:
"The prisoner feels a bitter sorrow at this; there is no mother
who would be affected by a more violent pain at the death of
her son. Now where does this conformity of feelings for such
different objects come from? It is that, in the loss of a child, as
in the loss of a spider, one often cries only over the boredom
and idleness one falls into."[6] When one reads this passage in
light of Roland's own dire circumstances—torn apart from her
eleven-year-old daughter and mourning the loss of a work that
was to restore her reputation in the eyes of posterity—her reference to Lauzon's spider takes on an added pathos. However
much she admired Helvétius as a philosopher, she can hardly
have been impervious to the lack of feeling he displayed for an
imprisoned man and a bereaved mother.

A few days later, Roland learned that some pages of the
Notices historiques had been rescued from the fire. But by that
time, she had already reconceived her project along new lines.
She now set out to write two different works: one entitled *Portraits et anecdotes* that sought to restore the lost work in a different form, and another entitled *Mémoires particuliers* that
marked a new direction entirely. Although the *Portraits et anecdotes* was intended as a reprise of the lost work, its new title
inscribed it into a predominantly feminine tradition of literary

portraiture. The *Mémoires particuliers* was a memoir of Roland's childhood and young adulthood, explicitly modeled on Rousseau's *Confessions*. The completed portion of the work took the reader up through Roland's engagement to be married in 1779. But the rest could only be sketched out, under the heading "Outline of what remains for me to cover, to serve as a final supplement to the Memoirs."[7] In a footnote appended to the sketch, she explained why she had recourse to this expedient: "To follow things step by step in this way, I would have a long job to do, for which I no longer have enough time in my life; I content myself with an outline."[8] This outline (or *aperçu*—literally a glimpse) briefly fills in the years of the Rolands' marriage up to 1789, but only mentions the Revolution once, in a passing reference to the enthusiasm with which the couple greeted it.

The "Aperçu" concludes with a paragraph that appears to constitute Roland's parting words. It marks a rare moment when she renounces her project of completing the memoirs: "Thirteen years spent in various places, working continuously, with very varied relations, and of which the latest ones are connected to the history of the day, would supply the fourth and most interesting part of my Memoirs. The disparate parts that can be found in my *Portraits et anecdotes* will have to stand in for it: I no longer know how to advance my pen amidst the horrors that tear my country apart, I cannot live on its ruins, I prefer to bury myself in them. Nature, open your breast! . . . Just God, receive me! At age thirty-nine."[9] Like the Enlightenment philosophers she emulated, Roland knew that she would not be able to bring her last work to completion. Unlike them, however, she bid her final farewell with an acute sense that the fate of her country was hanging in the balance. Her sense of an ending was inextricable from her awareness of her position as a modern political subject. As such, it was entirely oriented toward the future. The image of her burying herself in the ruins of her country paved the way for her status as a martyr to the revolutionary cause. At the same time, Roland's distinctly modern political consciousness was offset by her traditional evocation of death as a return to God. In this, she was closer to the *Confessions* of Saint Augustine than to those of her avowed model, Rousseau.

Paradoxically, it was at the very moment that Roland renounced writing and accepted her coming death that she embraced for the first time her identity as a writer. Certainly, Roland had had ample occasion to write and prove her skills as a writer before being imprisoned. She describes with pride in the "Aperçu" how she responded incognito to the Académie de Besançon's question of "how the education of women could contribute to making men better." This was a contest to which Rousseau's disciple Bernardin de Saint-Pierre also applied; surprisingly, despite these two talented contestants, no prize was awarded that year. From the very beginning of the Revolution, when the Rolands were still in Lyon, excerpts of her letters were published as articles in the revolutionary press, again anonymously or signed simply "a woman from the south." When her husband served as minister of the interior, she likely wrote most of his letters and memoranda, including the famous letter of protest to Louis XVI in 1792 that brought his ministry to an end. But until her imprisonment, Roland never wrote in her own name, and despite her influential role within the Gironde, she ostensibly maintained the attitude of a conventional, supportive wife, whose involvement in politics should only be in the service of her husband's glory. Once in prison, however, she signed her writings and explicitly evoked her aspirations as a writer. In this too, she offers a striking point of contrast to the Enlightenment philosophers, who became less concerned with preserving their writings and their names for posterity in the face of death.

Roland's self-conception as a writer found its most dramatic expression in a note appended to the "Aperçu." This note makes clear that just before her death, when she no longer had the time nor the heart to write, she finally formed ambitions that were on par with her prodigious talents:

> If it had been granted to me to live, I would have had, I believe, only one temptation: it would have been to write the *Annals* of the century, and to be the Macaulay of my country; I was going to say the Tacitus of France, but that would not be at all *modest*, and the rogues who don't consider themselves as such, would say, proving the contrary, that in order to do that I am missing *a certain something*. I developed in prison a veritable passion for Tacitus: I cannot sleep without reading a few passages from him; it seems to me that we see things in the same way, and that with time, on an equally rich subject, it would not have been impossible for me to express myself in imitation of him.[10]

This ironic and even playful evocation of Roland's literary models—the Roman historian Tacitus and the English historian Catharine Macaulay—points to her emerging self-awareness as a writer, and as a woman writer. Her sense that Tacitus was the historian to emulate in documenting the dramatic events of the Revolution was shared by her contemporaries. Her fellow Girondin, Louis Sébastien Mercier, wrote in the preface to his *Nouveau Paris* (*New Paris*): "There's no doubt that to paint so many contrasts would require a historian like Tacitus or a poet like Shakespeare. If he appeared in my lifetime, this Tacitus, this Shakespeare, I would say to him: forget your own idiom, for you must paint what has never been seen before, man touching at the same moment the two extremes of ferocity and human greatness."[11] Yet Roland took her emulation of Tacitus as an occasion to mock her contemporaries for believing women were incapable of writing as well as men. She underscored her point by evoking an alternative female model, Macaulay, the first published woman historian in England. At the same time, Roland chose to omit Macaulay's first name, thereby subtly signaling the historian's fame and declining to designate her as a woman. However tragic Roland's untimely death, this passage suggests that we have her imprisonment and the looming threat of her execution to thank for her coming to conceive of herself as a writer who could sign in her own name, and who, had circumstances been different, could have attained Macaulay's status. As Goethe wrote in 1820, at the height of the Romantic fervor for Roland, "The works of Madame Roland inflamed my admiration. The appearance of such talents and such characters will perhaps be the principal advantage that such unhappy times will have procured for posterity."[12]

Yet even the "Aperçu" was not to be Roland's final word. In lieu of the partially destroyed *Notices historiques*, which she intended as her moral and political testament, she wrote an additional testament entitled "Dernières pensées" ("Last Thoughts"). Roland wrote this brief text the day she decided to let herself die of starvation, on October 8, 1793, following the Convention's eradication of the Girondins.[13] On that same day, she also composed brief letters of farewell to her daughter, Eudora, and her maid, Fleury. As Jules Michelet observed, drawing a rapprochement between Roland and the man who brought down the Girondins, Maximilien Robespierre, Roland wrote constantly, and all the more so when she was under the immediate threat of death: "Both of them were always writing, *they were born scribes.* Concerned, as we shall see, with style as much as with political affairs, they wrote night and day, living and dying, amidst the most terrible crises and almost under the knife; the plume and style were for them an obstinate thought."[14] With his play on the double meaning of *style* in French—both style and stylus—Michelet implies that Roland used writing as a weapon to combat the threat of the guillotine. Unlike the Enlightenment philosophers, whose last words could not reverse the inevitable process of aging and decline, Roland had some hope of changing her fate through the exercise of her stylus. It is significant, in this context, that a week after writing her "Dernières pensées," Roland composed a final letter to Robespierre. Ultimately, however, she decided not to have it delivered, concluding that to do so would "compromise me fruitlessly with a tyrant who can sacrifice me, but cannot debase me."[15]

The "Dernières pensées" is a moving and politically fraught text. It offers Roland's last thoughts on her country's political turmoil and reflects her steadfast resistance to tyranny in her final hour. It also contains Roland's parting words for her husband—an apology for "taking into [her] own hands a life [she] had devoted to him"—and for her lover, the younger Girondin François Buzot. It includes pathetic details such as her wish that the rented harp Eudora played be purchased for her with the thousand paper *écus* Roland had set aside. And it contains a poignant farewell to her maid, Fleury, the person whose care she wishes she could repay in kind before she dies. Yet it cannot be denied that read alongside the last works discussed in this book, the "Dernières pensées" is much more conventional in its manner of confronting death. Renouncing her unbelief, Roland declares her expectation that she will be reunited with some form of divinity after her death: "Divinity, Supreme Being, soul of the world, principle of what I feel is great, good, and happy, you whose existence I believe in because it must be true that I emanate from something better than what I see around me, I

am going to be reunited with your essence!"[16] She concludes
her "Dernières pensées" with a moving passage in which she
evokes everything in this world she regrets leaving behind, but
then closes with the redemptive thought that she and Buzot will
transcend death to be reunited in the world beyond:

> Farewell, my child, my husband, my friends; fare-
> well, sun whose brilliant rays brought serenity into
> my soul as they called it back into the sky; farewell,
> solitary countryside of which the spectacle so often
> moved me; and you, rustic inhabitants of Thézée,
> who bless my presence, whose sweat I wiped away,
> whose misery I softened and whose illnesses I tend-
> ed to; farewell, peaceful rooms where I nourished
> my mind with truth, captivated my imagination
> with study, and learned in the silence of meditation
> to take command of my senses and despise vanity.
>
> Farewell . . . No, it is from you alone that I will
> not be separated; to leave this earth is to bring us
> closer to each other.[17]

In this last of her many last texts (and there would be still
others—notably a letter to the woman charged with caring
for Eudora, written the day before she died), Roland leaves no
gaps and no unanswered silences. She interrupts the ellipsis
of her final farewell to negate the solitude of her coming
death. She renounces her adherence to the most radical
strains of Enlightenment philosophy, consoling herself with
the prospect of a shared afterlife. There is something para-
doxical about the fact that the very political circumstances
that led Roland to assert for the first time her identity as a
woman author—as the Macaulay of her country—also led her
to adopt such conventional language at the moment of her

death. I emphasize her reliance on a shared language of convention not to deny her extraordinary courage in the face of death. Her death remains a formidable example of the human spirit. But it does not confront the urgent questions Deffand wrestled with and put to Voltaire. And there is little doubt in my mind that while Deffand might well have admired Roland's last words, she would not have been satisfied with them.

The image that has come down to us of the Enlightenment philosophers is a confident, forward-looking one. They, like the philosopher depicted in the *Encyclopédie,* bear a torch that illuminates the path ahead of them. For many interpreters of the Enlightenment, that path is our modern world. Yet the twilight moment of Enlightenment philosophy has been largely ignored. At the end of their lives, and as their generation came to a close, the philosophers discussed in this book cast a backward glance over their lives and their historical moment. Whereas many of them, like Diderot, had been deeply preoccupied with their image in the eyes of posterity at earlier points in their lives, in this twilight moment they seemed to relinquish their ties to the future. What did it matter whose statue was erected or whose name was inscribed on its pedestal? As Étienne Maurice Falconet observed, many women, and even men, died completely, leaving nothing to posterity.[18] Even Suzanne Curchod Necker, who believed in the afterlife, saw in the death of her famous friend "the spectacle of the nothingness of M. de Buffon," irrespective of the statues raised in his honor.[19] One might, in the face of death, make desperate efforts to control one's legacy, as Rousseau did in *Rousseau juge de Jean-Jacques,* and as Diderot accused him of doing in the *Confessions.* Yet the Rousseau of the *Rêveries* was an entirely different writer. Cut off from all human ties, writing for himself alone, he conceived of a text that was just as fragile as his aging body, or as the pressed flowers in his herbarium. This fragility was embodied in the last promenade, a fragment that expressed the ephemeral moments of Rousseau's happiness with Madame de Warens but broke off with the evocation of his unpaid debt to her. No words could fill that silence.

To fall silent in advance of death is to embrace the nothingness these writers believed was their ultimate fate. After long seeking to temper that nothingness with ironic quips and reassuring platitudes, Voltaire finally confronted *le néant* head-on in two of his last poems. Paradoxically, these poems paid homage to Deffand at the very moment he came to accept that she, and even he, would ultimately be forgotten. As Voltaire himself recognized, Deffand was unparalleled among the Enlightenment philosophers in grappling with what it meant to die as a nonbeliever. She lived her day-to-day life with an acute, even visceral sense of the nothingness that awaited her. Her experience of ennui was a sort of nothingness in the mind, a material emptiness she experienced in bodily terms. This gave her a highly original take on materialism, even though she did not embrace the materialists themselves. Her philosophy of nothingness was further informed by her identity as a woman and salon hostess, whose existence was filled with those tiny nothings of social exchange. Although she was plagued by the fear of death to an almost unbearable degree, she never turned her blind eyes away from it, belying François de La Rochefoucauld's maxim that "Neither the sun nor death can be looked at fixedly."[20] It is in this sense that I have characterized her as the most radical of Enlightenment philosophers.

And so it is that at the end of their lives, the writers in this book leave us with questions not usually associated with the Enlightenment. What are their lives, what are their words, after they have fallen silent? What are these butterflies that flitter from Polichinelle to nothingness in the space of eight syllables? I cannot say that writing this book has given me any answers to these questions. But it has renewed the intensity with which I have attended to the last words these writers left us with, and to the emptiness that follows. The rest, their rest, is silence.

Acknowledgments and Credits

Rousseau ends his last promenade with an evocation of debts that cannot be repaid. My circumstances over the last several years have made me indebted to all those who have supported me in the writing of this book to an exceptionally high degree. For a time, I placed myself quite literally in the hands of others. How much would I like to offer the people named here a collage, or a quilt, or some other material form of thanks where language seems inadequate. In lieu of that, please accept these heartfelt words of gratitude.

To my surgeons, Dr. Brett Youngerman and Dr. Matei Banu, for giving me back to myself; to my nurses, Mira and Nico, for getting me through that long night, which stretched from 3023 to 1923 to—finally—2023; and to Dr. Maria Diaz Ordoñez for accompanying me into the future.

To the members of the eighteenth-century reading group headed by Jeffrey Freedman—Basile Baudez, David Bell, Flora Champy, Andrew Clark, Charly Coleman, Madeleine Dobie, Thomas Dodman, Julia Doe, Lynn Festa, Jeff Horn, Laurence Marie, Thierry Rigogne, David Troyansky—for insightful, generous feedback, and to Jeff in particular, for starting and shepherding the group into its current form.

To the New York Eighteenth-Century Seminar at Fordham, and especially to Andrew Clark, for providing an unusually stimulating and convivial forum for the exchange of ideas.

To Jackats for offering a space of retreat, friendship, and intellectual companionship unlike any I have known.

To Dena Goodman, Thomas Laqueur, Deidre Lynch, and Helen Vendler for inspiring me with their scholarship.

To Katie Graves at the Morgan Library and Museum, for the opportunity to touch Voltaire's last manuscript page, bringing me closer to the topic of my book than I had ever been before, and to the unparalleled staff at the Lewis Walpole Library at Yale—Nicole Bouché, Colleen Collins, Kristen McDonald, Scott Poglitsch, Cynthia Roman, and Susan Walker—for allowing me to hold Deffand's snuff box in my hands and for insightful questions that changed the way I saw it.

To David Bates, Andrew Clark, Dan Edelstein, Marcie Frank, Victoria Höög, Alison James, Laurence Mall, Heather Meek, Pierre Saint-Amand, Sandrine Roux, Martin Rueff, Jimmy Swenson, and Caroline Warman for invitations to speak about my work and learn from the best of audiences.

To Lauren Kopajtik for her insights on Hume and Adam Smith and for craft-making inspiration.

To Fayçal Falaky and Glenn Roe for generous help with permissions and images.

To Gillian Pink and Brian Johnson for helping me to track down elusive references, from Voltaire to Epictetus.

To Jonathan Kramnick and Pierre Force for helping me to imagine this book in a new form when I had nearly lost hope, and to Adina Popescu for not giving up on me.

To Laura Hensley for making the copy editing process more seamless, stress-free, and even pleasurable than I could have imagined.

To Alison MacKeen for getting me an advance contract way back when, for helping me to envision a future for my writing, and for being the best of company.

To Dan Edelstein and Thomas Kavanagh for supporting this book at its earliest stages.

To the anonymous readers of the press for insightful reports that truly moved me and made me feel understood.

To Madeleine Dobie for serving as an exceptionally benevolent Chair at my worst moments and for insightful and generous feedback on my work.

To Nicholas Cronk, Lynn Festa, Bob Hymes, Roosevelt Montás, Sophie Queuniet, Philippe Roger, Emmanuelle Saada, and Caroline Warman for so many things: friendship, good conversation, precious feedback, and model scholarship.

To Richard Wolin for listening, making me laugh and think, and believing in my work.

To David Bates for transcendent meals and conversation over many years.

To Andy Curran for tai chi and laser-beam help with Diderot references, and for being my twin brother.

To Andrew Clark for exceptionally generous and transformative feedback, advice on life and death, and true friendship.

To Elisabeth Ladenson for being better than Percocet and for making me laugh at the absurdity of it all, even in times of irreparable loss.

To Kate Tunstall for telling me I had spinach in my teeth.

To Nan and Bob Stalnaker for philosophy, Manet, good cooking, a loving family, and the model of a meaningful life.

To Tom and Aimee Stalnaker for all their love and support over the years and for the many holidays we have spent together.

To the Leveau, Watrigant, and Clees families for welcoming me with love and acceptance.

To Donna Younger for gracing me with boundless empathy, intelligence, and love at age ninety-six.

To Léon Leveau for asking the best questions at the right time ("So, who is this Madame du Deffand?") and for having a creative spirit and a heart of gold.

To Felicity Leveau for saying, "This too shall pass" and for having a vibrant, colorful mind peopled with stories, costumes, and characters.

To Eric Leveau for this life, together.

Saskia Hamilton excerpt from "All Souls" from *All Souls: Poems.* Copyright © 2023 by Saskia Hamilton. Reprinted with the permission of The Permissions Company, LLC on behalf of Graywolf Press, Minneapolis, Minnesota, graywolfpress.org, and Little Brown Book Group Limited through PLSclear.

I am grateful to the publishers for permission to republish, in revised form, material from the following of my articles:

"Un avant-goût du néant: Madame du Deffand et Voltaire, deux philosophes face à la mort," ed. Marcie Frank, Heather Meek, and Sandrine Roux, *Lumen: Selected Proceedings from the Canadian Society for Eighteenth-Century Studies* 43 (2024).

"Emotions, Mortality, and Vitality: Two *Salonnières-Philosophes* Facing Death," in *A Cultural History of Death: In the Age of Enlightenment,* ed. Jeffrey Freedman (London: Bloomsbury Academic, an imprint of Bloomsbury Publishing PLC, 2024), 67–88.

"Diderot's Brain," in *Mind, Body, Motion, Matter: Eighteenth-Century British and French Literary Perspectives,* ed. Mary Helen McMurran and Alison Conway (Toronto: University of Toronto Press, 2016), 230–53.

"Buffon on Death and Fossils," *Representations* 115 (Summer 2011): 20–41.

"Diderot's Literary Testament," *Diderot Studies* 31 (2009): 45–56.

Notes

Abbreviations

Shortened titles are used in most of the Notes, with complete publication details in the Bibliography. Frequently cited works are referred to using the following abbreviations:

CCR   *La correspondance complète de Jean-Jacques Rousseau,* Leigh edition

CEM   *The Complete Essays of Montaigne,* Donald M. Frame translation

CV   *Cher Voltaire,* Voltaire-Deffand correspondence, Vissière and Vissière edition

EP   *Éléments de physiologie* by Diderot, Hermann edition

HNM   *Histoire naturelle des minéraux* by Buffon, Imprimerie royale edition

HNS   *Histoire naturelle, Supplément* by Buffon, Imprimerie royale edition

LWL   W. S. Lewis Collection of Marie du Deffand, The Lewis Walpole Library, Yale University

MOL   *My Own Life* by David Hume, in *Dialogues Concerning Natural Religion,* Macmillan edition

OCR   *Œuvres complètes* by Rousseau, Pléiade edition

OCV   *Œuvres complètes de Voltaire,* Voltaire Foundation edition

VC   *Voltaire's Correspondence,* Besterman edition

WDC   *Horace Walpole's Correspondence with Madame du Deffand,* Yale edition

Preface

Epigraph: My epigraph revises Montaigne's famous quotation about his friendship with Étienne de la Boétie—"Parce que c'était lui, parce que c'était moi" ("Because it was he, because it was I")—to make it about a friendship with a woman. Montaigne, *CEM,* 139; *Essais,* 195.

1. Deffand to Walpole, Paris, April 12, 1779, in *WDC,* 5:130.

2. Deffand to Walpole, Paris, October 8, 1779, in *WDC,* 5:180.

3. Diderot to Sophie Volland, Grandval, October 15, 1759, in Diderot, *Lettres à Sophie Volland,* 78–79. I am grateful to Kate E. Tunstall for pointing me to this beautiful letter.

4. Falconet to Diderot, December 1765, in Diderot, *Pour et contre,* 6.

5. Google search result for "Madame du Deffand," https://www.google .com/search?client=firefox-b-1-d&q=madame+du+deffand, accessed on April 23, 2023. This page has since been updated to identify Deffand simply as a "French presenter": https://g.co/kgs/mXE1kHk, accessed on October 1, 2024.

6. Woolf, *Mrs. Dalloway,* 248.

7. Deffand to Walpole, July 15, 1780, in *WDC,* 5:238.

Introduction

1. Kant, "What Is Enlightenment?," 54.

2. Foucault, "Qu'est-ce que les Lumières?," 4:568, 575.

3. See in particular, for the period under study, Israel, *Democratic Enlightenment.*

4. Edelstein, *Enlightenment: A Genealogy,* 2.

5. Diderot to Falconet, February 1766, in Diderot, *Pour et contre,* 33. See also Becker, *Heavenly City,* 119, 150. Becker takes this sentence as his epigraph and then quotes it in the body of his essay.

6. Diderot, *Essai,* 121.

7. Diderot, *Rêve de d'Alembert,* 139.

8. Deffand to Voltaire, May 2, 1764, in *CV,* 138.

9. Voltaire to Deffand, aux Délices, May 9, 1764, in *CV,* 140. Letter 11028 in *VC,* 55:22.

10. Voltaire, "Songe creux: autograph manuscript." I have reproduced the text as it appears in the manuscript, restoring only missing apostrophes and spaces to ensure readability. For the critical edition of the poem, see "Songe creux," in *OCV* 77B, 307–10.

11. Rousseau, *Rêveries,* 999–1001, 1073.

12. The literature on this topic, much of it from the 1970s and 1980s, is vast. See, most notably, Vovelle, *Mourir autrefois;* Ariès, *Homme devant la mort;* Chaunu, *Mort à Paris;* Favre, *Mort dans la littérature;* McManners, *Death and Enlightenment;* and Vovelle, *Mort et Occident.* Wilson reviews this literature in "Death and Social Historians." Wilson credits Emmanuel Le Roy Ladurie with coining the phrase "the new history of death" in the latter's "Nouvelle histoire de la mort." Laqueur responds to this earlier literature and traces a new path forward in *Work of the Dead.*

13. Voltaire to Deffand, aux Délices, May 9, 1764, in *CV,* 140. Letter 11028 in *VC,* 55:22.

14. On Lucretius and Locke on the problem of consciousness and its cessation in death, see Kramnick, "Living with Lucretius."

15. D'Holbach explicitly identifies the fear of death as a prejudice in his "Réflexions," 129. Favre notes that d'Holbach "is perhaps the only one to have drawn up a systematic plan to wrest the thought and sentiment of death from their exploitation by the church" in *Mort dans la littérature*, 162. See also Buffon, *Œuvres*, 279.

16. See d'Holbach, *Lettres à Eugénie*. For a discussion of the way d'Holbach's grief over his first wife's death may have influenced his philosophical preoccupation with death, see Favre, *Mort dans la littérature*, 162.

17. See my "Emotions, Mortality."

18. De Staël, *Mémoires*, 97.

19. See Freedman, "Limits of Tolerance."

20. Laqueur, *Work of the Dead*, 13.

21. Laqueur, *Work of the Dead*, 14.

22. Laqueur, *Work of the Dead*, xiii.

23. Quoted from Rousseau's correspondence in Fellows, "Buffon and Rousseau," 188.

24. Goodman, *Becoming a Woman*, 1.

25. Kramnick, *Criticism and Truth*.

26. Kermode, *Sense of an Ending*.

27. Outram, "Enlightenment Our Contemporary," 32.

28. I have discussed Israel's difficulty in placing Rousseau within his taxonomy of radical, moderate, and Counter-Enlightenment figures in "Jonathan Israel in Dialogue." In *Enlightenment Contested*, Israel claims that in the 1760s, Rousseau became "the moral 'prophet' as it were of one form of Counter-Enlightenment" (11). See also Garrard, *Rousseau's Counter-Enlightenment*; and, for what is in my eyes the most convincing view, Hulliung, *Autocritique of Enlightenment*.

29. Diderot, "Avertissement," vol. 8 in Diderot and d'Alembert, *Encyclopédie*.

30. Israel, *Enlightenment Contested*, 11. On Israel's neglect of the dialogic aspect of Enlightenment in his *Democratic Enlightenment*, and his unwillingness to enter into genuine dialogue with his critics, see my "Jonathan Israel in Dialogue." His reply to my and Helena Rosenblatt's critiques of his work in "Rousseau, Diderot, and 'Radical Enlightenment'" is a case in point. In the same volume, see Rosenblatt, "Rousseau the 'Traditionalist,'" and Wolin, "Introduction."

31. Laqueur, *Work of the Dead*, 182–210. See also Miller, *Three Deaths*.

32. Voltaire, "Épître à Horace," in *OCV*, 74B, 288.

33. Said, *On Late Style*.

34. Montaigne, *CEM*, 139; *Essais*, 195.

35. Montaigne, *CEM*, 268; *Essais*, 389.
36. Montaigne, *CEM*, 837; *Essais*, 1140.
37. Deffand to Voltaire, Paris, October 28, 1759, in *CV*, 56. Deffand had a manuscript copy of the "Histoire d'un bon Bramin" among the personal papers she bequeathed to Walpole. *LWL*, MSS 11, Series 3, Box 10, Folder 19.
38. See González Fernández, "Voltaire y Montaigne."
39. Walpole to Deffand, October 10, 1766, in *WDC*, 1:151.
40. Deffand to Walpole, Paris, October 27, 1766, in *WDC*, 1:164.
41. Beaujour, *Miroirs d'encre*.
42. Rousseau, *Rêveries*, 1000–1001.
43. Montaigne, *CEM*, 61; *Essais*, 845.
44. Rousseau, *Rêveries*, 1012.
45. Montaigne, *CEM*, 267–68; *Essais*, 388–89.
46. Rousseau, *Rêveries*, 1005.
47. Manent, "Montaigne and Rousseau," 315.
48. Montaigne, *CEM*, 219; *Essais*, 321.
49. This comparison is implicit and is developed over the course of the work. See Rousseau, *Rêveries*, 999–1001, 1073. My thinking about the materiality of the *Rêveries* has been influenced by the work of my former advisee, Célia Abele. See, notably, her "Rousseau's Herbaria."
50. Schwartz, "Diderot and Montaigne," 72. For nuanced treatments of Montaigne's presence in Diderot, see Tunstall, "Paradoxe"; and Knee, "Diderot et Montaigne" and *Parole incertaine*.
51. Diderot, *Essai*, 268.
52. Schwartz, "Diderot and Montaigne," 75.
53. Montaigne, *CEM*, 2; *Essais*, 27.
54. Montaigne, *CEM*, 62; *Essais*, 91.
55. Montaigne, *CEM*, 804; *Essais*, 1098.
56. Montaigne, *CEM*, 805; *Essais*, 1098.
57. Montaigne, *CEM*, 809; *Essais*, 1104.

Prologue. Hume's Life

1. Hume, *MOL*, 239. This edition also includes the preface by Strahan and the letter by Adam Smith.
2. Hume, *MOL*, 240.
3. Hume expressed his desire that *My Own Life* be "prefixed" to future editions of his works in letters to both Adam Smith and William Strahan. On the significance of this term, in the sense of "adding to the meaning of a text which follows," see Stanley, "Writing," 6.
4. These attempts are part of what Stephen Miller calls Hume's "deathbed project" in *Three Deaths*, 44–85. Miller devotes surprisingly little attention

to *My Own Life*, however. See also Mankin, "Maladie comme triomphe." Mankin died following a brief, brutal illness just two years after this article was published. He is missed.

5. Baier, *Death and Character*, 275.

6. Hume, *MOL*, 239.

7. In an article written in French, Mankin notes that Hume's use of the possessive is unnecessary in English and serves to emphasize his attempt to take ownership of his deathbed scene. See his "Maladie comme triomphe," 212.

8. Hume, *MOL*, 233.

9. Stanley, "Writing."

10. Hume, *Treatise*, 300. Baier has made the intriguing argument that the problems of personal identity Hume grappled with in the appendix to his *Treatise* were bound up with that work's "inadequate version of death." See her *Death and Character*, vii, 147–81.

11. On a particular conception of "prose immortality" that emerged in the eighteenth century, see Sider Jost, *Prose Immortality*. Sider Jost's argument offers an important counterpoint to my own.

12. Baier, *Death and Character*, 109.

13. Quoted in Rasmussen, *Adam Smith*, 5.

14. Hume, *MOL*, 234.

15. Hume, *MOL*, 236.

16. Hume, *MOL*, 236.

17. Hume, *MOL*, 237.

18. Hume, *Dialogues*, 173.

19. Hume, *MOL*, 237.

20. Hume, *MOL*, 239.

21. Hume, *MOL*, 239.

22. Hume, *MOL*, 239.

23. Stanley has emphasized the artfulness of Hume's writing in *My Own Life* in "Writing," 4.

24. See Lynch, *Economy of Character*.

25. Stanley, "Writing," 15.

26. Laqueur, *Work of the Dead*, 203–10; and Miller, *Three Deaths*, 86–89.

27. See Rasmussen, introduction to *Adam Smith*, 7.

28. Adam Smith, "Letter from Adam Smith, LL.D. to William Strahan, Esq.," Kirkaldy, Fifeshire, November 9, 1776, in Hume, *Dialogues*, 245.

29. Baier, *Death and Character*, 108. Baier convincingly demonstrates that Hume seems to have based his anecdote not on the *Dialogues of the Dead*, which depict long-dead figures who are worthy of emulation, but on another Lucian dialogue, "Kataplous" or "The Downward Journey," a work of a more satirical genre in which risible figures who are more recently deceased attempt to delay their departure across the River Styx.

30. Smith, "Letter," in Hume, *Dialogues,* 248.

31. Hume, *MOL,* 240.

32. Miller, "Two Philosophical Deaths."

1

Buffon's Stone

1. Necker, *Mélanges,* 3:287–88.

2. Haussonville, *Salon de Madame Necker,* 1:320–32.

3. An excerpt of this letter is included in Haussonville, *Salon de Madame Necker,* 1:327.

4. Necker, *Mélanges,* 3:375–76.

5. Buffon, *Œuvres,* 31. Although this edition offers a limited selection of Buffon's work, I refer to it when possible because of its accessibility.

6. Nadault de Buffon, *Correspondance inédite,* 2:614–15.

7. Necker, "Derniers moments," in Nadault de Buffon, *Correspondance inédite,* 2:613.

8. Quoted in de Baecque, *Gloire et effroi,* 245.

9. See Boon, "Last Rites" and "Performing the Woman"; and de Baecque, *Gloire et effroi,* 215–51. On Necker's role as a *salonnière* who shaped the Enlightenment, see Goodman, *Republic of Letters,* esp. 73–89.

10. Foucault, *Mots et choses.*

11. Schmitt, introduction to *Œuvres,* by Buffon, xl.

12. In his *Rhetoric and Natural History,* Loveland has convincingly demonstrated the ways that rhetorical and stylistic considerations shaped Buffon's presentation of his natural philosophy. In her *Language of Nature,* Roman has analyzed the literary and scientific implications of the motif of heat across Buffon's corpus.

13. Buffon, *Œuvres,* 263.

14. Grmek, "Idées de Descartes," 294–96; and "Ageing."

15. McManners, *Death and Enlightenment,* 114.

16. Buffon, *Œuvres,* 266–67.

17. Louis de Jaucourt, "Ossification, s.f. s'ossifier, v. neut. [Physiolog.]," in Diderot and d'Alembert, *Encyclopédie,* 11:687–89. Although Jaucourt did not acknowledge Buffon by name, he borrowed liberally from the chapter "De la vieillesse et de la mort."

18. Buffon, *Œuvres,* 1461n4.

19. Reill, *Vitalizing Nature,* 173; see also Porter, *Flesh,* 211–26. Although Buffon is sometimes characterized as a vitalist, Williams notes that "A detailed study of Buffon's relation to Montpellier vitalism is needed" in *Physical and Moral,* 53n133. Rey has linked Buffon's gradualist conception of death to that of the vitalist Xavier Bichat in "Buffon et le vitalisme," in *Buffon 88,* 407.

20. See Reill, *Vitalizing Nature*, 171–82; Ariès, *Homme devant la mort*, 389–99; and Boon, "Last Rites."

21. Buffon, *Œuvres*, 275.

22. Buffon, *Œuvres*, 279.

23. See Lucretius, *Nature of Things*, 91–121. For a discussion of Buffon's attempts to banish fear through rationalism and the control of nature, see Bremner, "Buffon and Fear."

24. Buffon, *Œuvres*, 276.

25. Buffon, *Œuvres*, 268.

26. Buffon, *Œuvres*, 262.

27. Hadot, *Philosophy*, 79–125.

28. McManners, *Death and Enlightenment*, 191; see also Porter, *Flesh*, 211–13.

29. See Condillac, *Traité des sensations*.

30. Buffon, *Œuvres*, 303.

31. Buffon, *Œuvres*, 305.

32. Buffon, *Œuvres*, 306.

33. Delon, preface to *Œuvres*, by Buffon, xi.

34. Ariès, *Homme devant la mort*, 317–46. For Ariès, the distancing of death initiated in the early modern period culminates in today's modern hospital death. There is a striking parallel between Buffon's (positive) account of the imperceptible nuances leading to death, and Ariès's (critical) account of the engineering of death in the modern hospital.

35. Buffon, *Œuvres*, 281.

36. Heller-Roazen, *Inner Touch*.

37. See McManners, *Death and Enlightenment*, 295–99. This conversation continues to this day in the anthropological literature. See, for example, Metcalf and Huntington, *Celebrations of Death*.

38. "Funérailles, [Hist. mod.]," in Diderot and d'Alembert, *Encyclopédie*, 7:371. Much of the material for the "Funérailles" articles was taken from Pierre Muret, *Cérémonies funèbres de toutes les nations* (Paris: Estienne Michallet, 1679).

39. See "Sépulture, [Droit naturel]," in Diderot and d'Alembert, *Encyclopédie*, 15:75.

40. Buffon, *Œuvres*, 366. With respect to the source of this information, Buffon remarks: "I took these facts from a relation communicated to me by M. de La Brosse who wrote the principal things he noticed during a trip he took to the coast of Angola in 1738" (366). The editors of the Pléiade edition note that they have been unable to identify this traveler. On Buffon's anthropological sources and reliance on travel literature, see Duchet, *Anthropologie et histoire*, 229–80.

41. Daston, *Classical Probability*; and Roger, introduction to *Un autre Buffon*, 93.

42. Daston, *Classical Probability*, xi.

43. Daston cites De Witt's *Waerdye van Lyf-Renten* (*Treatise on Life Annuities*) of 1671 as "one of the earliest attempts to extend the new mathematics of probability to other sorts of aleatory contracts besides games of chance," in *Classical Probability*, 27. Koselleck links the emergence of life insurance and studies of life expectancy to the conceptual relationship between present and future in the early modern period, with its characteristic focus on rational prognosis, in *Futures Past*, 18. See also McManners, *Death and Enlightenment*, 89–119.

44. The phrase "moral arithmetic" appears in Buffon's *Essai d'arithmétique morale* (*Essay in Moral Arithmetic*), published in the fourth volume of the Supplément to the *Histoire naturelle* in 1777. This work was symptomatic of the alignment of mathematical and moral expectation in classical probability theory. See Daston, *Classical Probability*, 90–95, and, on the application of classical probability theory to the moral sciences among later writers, 296–369.

45. Buffon, *HNS*, 4:149. Unfortunately, the Pléiade edition does not include this key supplement to the *Histoire naturelle de l'homme*.

46. Daston notes that d'Alembert criticized Buffon's method for failing "to coincide with psychological expectation, that is 'moral experience,'" in *Classical Probability*, 87. On d'Alembert's critique of probability theory more generally, see 76–90.

47. Buffon, *HNS*, 4:161.

48. McManners discusses the accuracy of these statistics in *Death and Enlightenment*, 10–11; see also 89–119. With respect to Buffon's surprising claim that those who die before age thirty-nine do not have a chance to propagate the species, McManners observes that the "postponement of marriage was the keystone of the old demographic structure, the essential contraceptive device keeping population and resources in equilibrium" (69).

49. In an editorial preface to the eighth volume published in 1766, Diderot writes: "May general instruction advance at such a rapid pace that twenty years from now there is hardly in a thousand of our pages a single line that is not popular!" Diderot and d'Alembert, *Encyclopédie*, 8:ii.

50. Buffon, *HNS*, 4:411.

51. Buffon, *HNS*, 4:411.

52. See the editor's "Notice" for the *HNM* in Buffon, *Œuvres*, 1645–46. Jacques Roger notes that Buffon neglected the *Histoire naturelle des oiseaux* (*Natural History of Birds*) in order to devote himself to what he called his "dear minerals" in *Buffon: Un philosophe*, 501.

53. Roger, *Buffon: A Life*, 399. For the original French, see *Buffon: Un philosophe*, 524.

54. "Notice," *HNM*, in Buffon, *Œuvres*, 1645–46.

55. See Roger, *Buffon: Un philosophe*, 469.

56. Gohau, *Sciences de la terre*, 212.

57. Rudwick, *Bursting the Limits*, 150.

58. The phrase is Rudwick's in *Bursting the Limits of Time*. De Baere addresses the epistemological paradoxes of Buffon's historicism in "Une histoire imaginée." Eddy contests Buffon's historicism entirely in "Buffon's *Histoire naturelle*." For the more traditional view that Buffon's late work is marked by an important shift toward a more historical understanding of nature, see Roger, *Buffon: Un philosophe*, 528–48.

59. Quoted in Rudwick, *Bursting the Limits*, 143.

60. Buffon, *Œuvres*, 1345.

61. Schmitt, introduction to *Œuvres*, by Buffon, xli. In *Buffon: A Life*, Roger gives a more pragmatic explanation for the publication of the supplementary volumes: "Certain volumes of the *Supplement* serve as a bit of a grab bag, and one cannot help thinking that Buffon made money for himself by reselling to Panckoucke old texts at the price of twelve thousand livres per volume" (384). Whether or not this was a factor, one might contest Roger's claim that "the old articles on the strength of wood, the eccentricities of ligneous layers, and the effect of frosts on plants . . . have nothing to do with what he was doing at the time," given the relevance of these texts to the imaginative association between death and fossils (384). For the original French, see *Buffon: Un philosophe*, 504.

62. On Buffon's motivations for cutting Daubenton's descriptive articles, see Laissus, "L'histoire naturelle," in *Buffon, 1788–1988*, 85; Fellows and Milliken, *Buffon*, 58; Roger, *Buffon: Un philosophe*, 298; and Mornet, *Sciences de la nature*, 128. Mornet is alone in suggesting that Buffon may have cut the descriptive articles for fear of being eclipsed by Daubenton's superior reputation in scientific circles.

63. Buffon, *Œuvres*, 427.

64. Buffon, *HNM*, 2:345. This tome is also labeled as volume 26 of the *Histoire naturelle*.

65. Buffon, *HNM*, 2:345.

66. See Sloan, "Buffon-Linnaeus Controversy"; Dawson, "Limits of Observation"; and Reill, *Vitalizing Nature*, 238–39. For Reill, Enlightenment vitalism is marked by a creative tension between broad views of nature and detailed empiricism.

67. On Buffon's attitude toward systematic approaches to natural history, see Hayes, *Reading French Enlightenment*, 30–39.

68. Even Buffon's highly speculative history of the earth in *Des époques de la nature* was based on a lengthy and apparently accurate investigation into the amount of time necessary for metal balls of various sizes and substances to cool. See Roger, *Buffon: Un philosophe*, 516–20.

69. Buffon, *Œuvres*, 1356.

70. De Baere, "Une histoire imaginée."

71. Eddy, "Buffon's *Histoire naturelle*," 657.

72. Buffon, *Œuvres*, 1364.

73. De Baere, "Philosophie," 203.

74. On Buffon's view of the rise and fall of human civilizations, see Eddy, "Buffon's *Histoire naturelle*," 658–61; and de Baere, "Philosophie."

75. Buffon, *Œuvres*, 1354.

76. Buffon, *Œuvres*, 1355.

77. Rudwick, *Meaning of Fossils*, 101.

78. This is Rudwick's subtitle for *Bursting the Limits of Time*.

79. See Spary, *Utopia's Garden*.

80. Rudwick, *Meaning of Fossils*, 25.

81. On Renaissance analogies, see Foucault, *Les mots et les choses*, 32–59. Rey notes that Buffon may have been influenced by Louis Bourguet's work on fossils in developing the concept of the *moule intérieur* within his theory of generation, in "Buffon et le vitalisme," 404.

82. Saban, "Testament," 98, 110.

83. Schmitt, introduction to *Œuvres*, by Buffon, xli.

2
Diderot's Brain

1. On the increasing radicalization of Diderot's political thought during this period and his contributions to the *Histoire des deux Indes*, see Strugnell, *Diderot's Politics;* Venturi, "Vieillesse de Diderot"; and Quintili, "Stoïcisme révolutionnaire." Recent scholarship has portrayed the *Histoire* as Diderot's crowning achievement, in a way that reflects a view of the Enlightenment as paving the way toward modern liberal political values. See, notably, Curran, *Diderot Thinking Freely*, 360–73, in which the *Histoire* is treated after the *Essai*, in a final chapter entitled "Last Words"; and Israel, *Democratic Enlightenment*, 413–42. Without discounting the importance of Diderot's political thought, I have emphasized a countervailing strain in his late writings that is much less confident in the legacy of Enlightenment.

2. See Vartanian, "Enigma," 300.

3. Ballstadt, *Diderot: Natural Philosopher*, 209.

4. Ballstadt, *Diderot: Natural Philosopher*, 209. Other important sources include the works of Paul-Joseph Barthez, Charles Bonnet, Antoine Le Camus, Robert Whytt, and Jean-Paul Marat. See Vartanian, "Enigma," 287.

5. Diderot, *Éléments*, ed. Quintili, 31.

6. Regarding the originality of the *Éléments*, Mayer writes: "The multiplicity of sources and their often textual use could make the *Éléments de physiologie* appear as a compilation completed with a very thin personal contribution. But the original proportion of the work is greater than it seems." See Diderot, *Éléments*, ed. Mayer, liii.

7. Fabre, "Deux frères ennemis."

8. Diderot, *EP,* 105.

9. For a detailed exposition of this view, see Vartanian, "Enigma," 288–95.

10. See Diderot, *Éléments,* ed. Quintili, 105n3.

11. Clark, *Diderot's Part,* 43. Another outstanding study in this and other respects is Warman, *Atheist's Bible.*

12. See Mayer, *Diderot homme de science,* 278; and Ballstadt, *Diderot: Natural Philosopher,* 180.

13. Mayer, *Diderot homme de science,* 279.

14. Ballstadt, *Diderot: Natural Philosopher,* 180. See also Diderot, *Éléments,* ed. Mayer, xxxi–xxxviii.

15. Clark, *Diderot's Part,* 41. Clark further argues that "Bordeu's and Haller's experiments helped Diderot to articulate scientifically a conception of the *part* as relatively autonomous with respect to the *whole*" (41).

16. On animal organization and self-organization, see Riskin, "Mr. Machine," 75–94; and Sheehan and Wahrman, *Invisible Hands.*

17. Diderot, *EP,* 310.

18. Diderot, *Rêve de d'Alembert,* 120–23.

19. Diderot, *EP,* 310.

20. Diderot, *EP,* 310–11.

21. Diderot, *EP,* 311.

22. Diderot, *EP,* 296.

23. Diderot, *Rêve de d'Alembert,* 139.

24. Diderot to Volland, Grandval, October 15, 1759, in *Lettres à Sophie Volland,* 78–79.

25. See Mayer, *Diderot homme de science,* 272, where he draws an opposition between the *Rêve de d'Alembert* as speculative philosophy and the *Éléments* as empirical science.

26. See Pangburn, "Bonnet's Theory of Palingenesis"; and Laplassotte, "Quelques étapes."

27. Diderot, *EP,* 311.

28. The collective project of the *Histoire des deux Indes* poses similar problems. Venturi has suggested that scholarly attempts to determine precisely which parts of the work were written by Diderot risk distorting the anonymous, collective nature of the enterprise as it was perceived by eighteenth-century readers. See his "Vieillesse de Diderot," 17–18.

29. Vartanian, "Enigma," 288.

30. Mayer, *Diderot homme de science,* 277.

31. Diderot, *EP,* 313.

32. Diderot to Volland, La Haye, September 3, 1774, in *Lettres à Sophie Volland,* 663.

33. Ballstadt, review of *Éléments,* 397.

34. Diderot, *EP,* 471.

35. Diderot, *EP,* 456.
36. Diderot, *EP,* 467.
37. Diderot, *EP,* 468–69.
38. See Shomrat and Levin, "Automated Training Paradigm." Regrettably, and ironically, I cannot remember which of my generous and brilliant colleagues sent me this reference many years ago.
39. Diderot to Volland, Grandval, October 15, 1759, in *Lettres à Sophie Volland,* 78.
40. Diderot, *EP,* 471.
41. Diderot, *EP,* 472.
42. Diderot, *EP,* 473.
43. Diderot, *EP,* 465.
44. Diderot, *EP,* 516.
45. Russo, "Slander and Glory," 1.
46. Diderot, *EP,* 516.
47. See Diderot, *Éléments,* ed. Quintili, 361–62n107.
48. Diderot, *EP,* 516.
49. Vandeul, *Mémoires,* 31.
50. Ehrard, "Pourquoi Sénèque?," 6. See also Chartier's introduction to a special issue devoted to the *Essai,* where he characterizes the *Essai* as an "unsettling personal testament" (5).
51. Wilson, *Diderot,* 692–93.
52. Russo, "Slander and Glory"; and Citton, "Retour sur la querelle."
53. Starobinski, "Diderot et la parole." Starobinski republished a modified version of this seminal piece in his *Diderot, un diable de ramage,* 58–82.
54. Diderot to Grimm, undated [end of August], Diderot, *Correspondance,* 218.
55. Diderot, *Essai,* 36. For a detailed analysis of this passage, see Chartier, "Je ne compose point."
56. Diderot, *Essai,* 204.
57. Diderot, *Essai,* 49.
58. Wilson, *Diderot,* 692.
59. In addition to Russo, "Slander and Glory," and Citton, "Retour sur la querelle," see Gatefin, *Diderot, Sénèque et Jean-Jacques;* and Mall, "Sénèque et Diderot." See also Said, *On Late Style.*
60. Diderot, *Essai,* 249.
61. D'Alembert, *Œuvres,* 260.
62. D'Épinay, *Contre-confessions.*
63. Fabre, "Frères ennemis," 203.
64. Russo, "Slander and Glory."
65. Citton, "Retour sur la querelle."
66. Diderot, *Essai,* 121.
67. Diderot, *Essai,* 176.

68. Diderot, *Essai,* 399.

69. Seneca, *Dialogues and Letters,* 3.

70. See Hadot, *Philosophy Way of Life;* and Foucault, *Herméneutique du sujet.*

71. Diderot, *Essai,* 369.

72. Diderot, *Essai,* 170.

73. Diderot, *Essai,* 229.

74. Diderot, *Essai,* 256–57.

75. Diderot, *Essai,* 35.

76. Diderot, *Essai,* 363.

77. Nouis, "Emploi du temps."

78. Diderot, *Essai,* 371.

79. Diderot, *Essai,* 270.

80. Diderot, *Essai,* 270.

81. Diderot, *Essai,* 429.

82. Starobinski, "Diderot et la parole."

83. Diderot, *Essai,* 363. As Starobinski has shown in "Diderot et la parole des autres," this is a general tendency in Diderot's work. But I am suggesting here that Diderot's use of others' words takes on a heightened resonance in his last work.

84. Diderot to Falconet, February 1766, in Diderot, *Pour et contre,* 37.

85. Diderot, *Essai,* 431. For a convincing but contrasting interpretation of this last sentence, and the tone of the *Essai* more generally, as manifestations of late style, see Hayes, "Aspects du style tardif."

86. Diderot, *Neveu de Rameau,* 109.

87. Diderot to Naigeon, July 28, 1780, Letter 913 in Diderot, *Correspondance,* 15:178. My thanks to Andrew S. Curran for helping me to track down this reference in a matter of minutes.

88. Seneca, *Dialogues and Letters,* 47.

89. Vandeul, *Mémoires,* 32.

90. Diderot, *EP,* 275.

91. Vandeul, *Mémoires,* 34–35.

92. Vandeul, *Mémoires,* 35.

3
Rousseau's Flower

1. On the significance of this reform for Rousseau's view of authorship, see Kelly, *Rousseau as Author.*

2. Rousseau, *Rousseau juge de Jean-Jaques* [sic], 933. The editors have respected the original spelling of "Jaques" from the manuscript. For the sake of brevity, subsequent notes refer to this work as the *Dialogues.*

3. Rousseau, *Dialogues*, 989.

4. Madeleine-Catherine Delessert, née Boy de la Tour, to Jean-André Deluc, March 14, 1777, Letter 7122 in Rousseau, *Correspondance complète*, 40:130.

5. Melzer, *Natural Goodness*, 4–9.

6. In addition to Melzer, see Goldschmidt, *Anthropologie et politique;* and Masters, *Political Philosophy*. For an overview of earlier work on the unity of Rousseau's thought (by Gustave Lanson, E. H. Wright, and Ernst Cassirer), see Gay's introduction to *The Question of Jean-Jacques Rousseau* by Cassirer.

7. Melzer, *Natural Goodness*, 7.

8. Rousseau, *Rêveries*, 1000.

9. On the *Rêveries* as one of Rousseau's "individualistic solutions" for recovering the sentiment of existence and the natural goodness of man, see Melzer, *Natural Goodness*, 91–94.

10. Rousseau, *Rêveries*, 1023.

11. Rousseau, *Rêveries*, 1012.

12. Rousseau, *Rêveries*, 1023.

13. The exact date of the composition of the "Profession de foi" remains uncertain, but Pierre-Maurice Masson dates the first draft to 1757. See Rousseau, *Œuvres*, 1:1781n2.

14. Rousseau, *Émile*, 569. See also Rousseau, *Rêveries*, 1018, where Rousseau offers a similar formulation of this method in the third promenade.

15. Rousseau, *Rêveries*, 1015.

16. Rousseau, *Rêveries*, 1015–16.

17. Similar claims are frequent in Counter-Enlightenment works of this period. See Israel, *Democratic Enlightenment*, 140–71.

18. See, for example, Rousseau, *Émile*, 576, where the vicar concludes the first stage of his profession of faith with "Here is my first dogma, or my first article of faith."

19. Rousseau, *Rêveries*, 1012–13.

20. Rousseau, *Rêveries*, 1018.

21. Rousseau, *Rêveries*, 1016.

22. Saint Augustine, *Confessions*, 145.

23. Rousseau, *Rêveries*, 1019.

24. On the reception of the *Dialogues*, see Masters and Kelly, introduction to *Rousseau Judge*, xiii; and Garréta, "Dialogues de Rousseau."

25. Horkheimer and Adorno, *Dialectic of Enlightenment*. Lilti remarks on this resemblance in his "Writing of Paranoia," 74. Recent work on *Rousseau juge de Jean-Jacques* has emphasized its contribution to our understanding of the public sphere, celebrity, and posterity in the Enlightenment. In addition to Russo, "Slander and Glory," and Citton, "Retour sur la querelle," see Perrin, *Politique du renonçant;* and Knee and Allard, *Rousseau juge de Jean-Jacques*.

26. Masters and Kelly, introduction to *Rousseau Judge of Jean-Jacques,* xxvi.

27. Edelstein, *Enlightenment: A Genealogy,* 2. For contrasting views on Rousseau's relationship to the Enlightenment, see Hulliung, *Autocritique;* Garrard, *Rousseau's Counter-Enlightenment;* and Israel, *Enlightenment Contested* and *Democratic Enlightenment.* Hulliung's account is in my view the most nuanced and convincing.

28. Rousseau, *Émile,* 578–81, 587–91.

29. Rousseau, *Dialogues,* 967.

30. Rousseau, *Dialogues,* 969.

31. Rousseau, *Dialogues,* 401.

32. Starobinski, *Transparence et obstacle,* 283–300.

33. Melzer, *Natural Goodness,* 43.

34. Rousseau, *Dialogues,* 936.

35. Rousseau, *Dialogues,* 974.

36. Rousseau, *Dialogues,* 976.

37. Rousseau, *Confessions,* 5.

38. Rousseau, *Rêveries,* 1001.

39. Starobinski, *Transparence et obstacle,* 270.

40. Rousseau, *Dialogues,* 987.

41. Rousseau, *Dialogues,* 987.

42. Rousseau, *Dialogues,* 985.

43. Rousseau, *Dialogues,* 989.

44. For Beaujour, the literary genre of the self-portrait, of which the *Rêveries* is one example, tends to resist the traditional rhetorical and poetic insistence that writing must be an efficacious mode of civic action. See his *Miroirs d'encre,* 14.

45. Kelly, *Rousseau as Author,* 8–28.

46. Rousseau, *Rêveries,* 1001.

47. For an interpretation of the *Rêveries* as belonging to the classical tradition of spiritual exercises in preparation for death, see Dornier, "Écriture de la citadelle."

48. Montaigne, *CEM,* 2; *Essais,* 27.

49. Clément asserts in his "Dixième promenade" that nothing allows us to conclude definitively that the tenth promenade is incomplete. I agree with him, not on the basis of manuscript research, but rather due to my reading of the meaningful design of the fragment.

50. See Eigeldinger, "Avatars du manuscrit." The Marquis de Girardin, who took possession of the notebook and other papers pertaining to the *Rêveries* after Rousseau's death, wrote that he was able to "add to the *Rêveries du promeneur solitaire* copied out by the author two promenades and the beginning of a third one" (150).

51. Rousseau, *Rêveries*, 1098.

52. Rousseau, *Rêveries*, 1060.

53. Rousseau, *Rêveries*, 1000. On the significance of the term *feuilles*, see Abele, "Rousseau's Herbaria."

54. Rousseau, *Rêveries*, 1000. See Beaujour, *Miroirs d'encre*, 7, where he observes that literary self-portraits such as the *Rêveries* are typically texts "that don't know how to designate themselves."

55. Rousseau, *Rêveries*, 1073.

56. Rousseau, *Rêveries*, 1001.

57. Rousseau, *Confessions*, 225.

58. Rousseau, *Confessions*, 226.

59. Rousseau, *Confessions*, 226.

60. Rousseau, *Rêveries*, 1003.

61. Rousseau, *Rêveries*, 1099.

62. Rousseau, *Rêveries*, 1099. See Clément, "Dixième promenade," 377–78, where he follows Robert Osmont in observing that the manuscript reveals that Rousseau removed a more explicit allusion to Madame de Warens's financial distress in revising this sentence.

63. Rousseau, *Confessions*, 277.

64. Rousseau, *Rêveries*, 1054.

65. Rousseau, *Rêveries*, 1059.

66. Kuhn, *Autobiography and Natural Science*, 43n1, 43. Kuhn himself departs from this interpretation, seeing the *Rêveries* "as part of a larger effort in Rousseau's final years not to escape history but to imagine and to communicate in a new language that combines the scientific and the poetic the possibility of a less alienating and fragmented future for the individual and for humankind" (45). I agree with this nuanced interpretation.

67. The document is included in Rousseau, *Œuvres*, 1:1209–12.

68. Rousseau, *Confessions*, 392.

69. Israel, *Democratic Enlightenment*, 21. See also Melzer, *Natural Goodness*, 4–9.

70. Rousseau, *Rêveries*, 1002.

71. Rousseau, *Rêveries*, 1003.

72. On Rousseau's request for an autopsy to uncover the source of the urinary disorder that plagued him throughout his adult life, see Starobinski, "Maladie de Rousseau," in *Transparence et obstacle*, 430–44.

73. Leigh, "Mort de Rousseau," 188. See also Trousson, "Rousseau, mort et œuvre."

74. Roucher, *Les mois*, 249. On another poem inspired by Rousseau's death, see Candaux, "Hommage."

75. See Ridehalgh, "Preromantic Attitudes"; and "Rousseau as God?"

76. See Eigeldinger, "Avatars du manuscrit," 146–47.

77. Leigh, "Mort de Rousseau," 196.

78. *CCR*, Letter 8344, 49:150. Part of this passage is quoted in Leigh, "La Mort de Rousseau," 197. This letter cannot have been penned as such by Le Vasseur alone, for she was nearly illiterate. The following quotation from a letter to Girardin gives a more accurate sense of her writing: "faitteu moi lamities deu meu randreu toules papier ela musique eles quon fesion ineu son pas a vous geu veu goiir deu mes droit ilialongtan que vous san gouisez et que vous faite quopier geu qite votteu mes son." Quoted in Eigeldinger, "Avatars du manuscrit," 153.

79. A version of this image in the Metropolitan Museum of Art's collection bears the following inscription (translated from the French): "THE LAST WORDS OF J.J. ROUSSEAU: My dear wife, do me the favor of opening the window so that I can have the pleasure of seeing the Greenery one more time. How beautiful it is! How pure and serene this day is! Oh, how great Nature is! Look at the Sun, of which the pleasant view calls to me: look yourself at this immense Light, there is God; yes God himself who opens his breast to me, and who invites me at last to go taste the eternal and inalterable peace that I had so desired . . ." See the Metropolitan Museum of Art, "*Les dernières paroles de J. J. Rousseau (The Last Words of J. J. Rousseau)* by Heinrich Guttenberg after Jean Michel Moreau le Jeune: Artwork Details," https://www.metmuseum.org/art/collection/search/425722, accessed October 1, 2024.

80. *CCR*, Letter 8344, 49:151.

81. This document can be found in *OCR*, 1:1187–89.

82. *OCR*, 1:1224.

83. Heymont, "Tomb of Rousseau."

4
Voltaire's Butterflies

1. Deffand to Walpole, February 12, 1778, in *WDC*, 5:18; and February 22, 1778, 5:21.

2. This anecdote is recounted in Standish, *Life of Voltaire*, 376. It is not found in two recent biographies of Voltaire, Pearson, *Voltaire Almighty*, 378–80; and Trousson, *Voltaire*, 698–99.

3. Deffand to Walpole, May 31, 1778, in *WDC*, 5:46.

4. See Bonnet, *Naissance du Panthéon*; and Flamein, *Voltaire à Ferney*. My argument in this chapter offers a counterpoint to Flamein's account.

5. On the likelihood that Voltaire's remains never actually made it to the Panthéon, see "Remains of Voltaire," n.p.

6. Cronk frames his superb *Very Short Introduction* to Voltaire around the way the latter created an image of himself as an author in a sort of theatrical performance (1–3).

7. *Dernier testament,* 17.

8. *Dernier testament,* 20–25.

9. Diderot, *Neveu de Rameau,* 109.

10. Deffand to Walpole, June 28, 1778, in *WDC,* 5:53.

11. The most invaluable of these is *Cher Voltaire.* See also *Lettres de Madame du Deffand à Voltaire.*

12. Voltaire to Deffand, November 26, 1775, in *CV,* 518–19. Letter 18631 in *VC,* 92:132.

13. Deffand to Voltaire, Paris, October 28, 1759, in *CV,* 56. As noted earlier, Deffand had a manuscript copy of the "Histoire d'un bon Bramin" in the personal papers she bequeathed to Walpole. *LWL,* MSS 11, Series 3, Box 10, Folder 19.

14. *CV,* 121.

15. Voltaire to Deffand, March 21, 1764, in *CV,* 136. Letter 10951 in *VC,* 54:212.

16. Voltaire to Deffand, March 21, 1764, in *CV,* 136–37. Letter 10951 in *VC,* 54:212.

17. Deffand to Walpole, Paris, April 12, 1779, in *WDC,* 5:130.

18. This phrase, quoted from Rousseau, underpins the classic essay by Paul de Man, "Criticism and Crisis," in which he observes that "The human mind will go through amazing feats to avoid facing 'the nothingness of human matters.'" See *Blindness and Insight,* 18.

19. Deffand to Voltaire, May 2, 1764, in *CV,* 138.

20. La Fontaine, *Fables,* 1:54.

21. *LWL,* MSS 11, Series 1, Box 1, Folder 34.

22. Voltaire to Deffand, aux Délices, May 9, 1764, in *CV,* 140. Letter 11028 in *VC,* 55:22.

23. Voltaire to Deffand, February 19, 1766, in *CV,* 202. Letter 12307 in *VC,* 60:120.

24. Voltaire to Deffand, February 19, 1766, in *CV,* 202. Letter 12307 in *VC,* 60:120.

25. Deffand to Voltaire, Paris, February 28, 1766, in *CV,* 204–5.

26. *LWL,* MSS 11, Series 3, Box 9, Folder 43. This manuscript is titled *Pensées et sentiment du Sieur Meslier Prêtre Curé d'Étrépigny en Champagne* (*Thoughts and Sentiment of Sir Meslier Parish Priest of Étrépigny en Champagne*).

27. Voltaire to d'Alembert, aux Délices, July 12, 1762, Letter 9772 in *VC,* 49:102.

28. Meslier, *Le testament de Jean Meslier,* 3:598. Emphasis in the original. This passage is tricky to translate, so I include the original French here: "Les

morts avec lesquels je suis sur le point d'aller, ne s'embarrassent plus de *rien* et ne se soucient plus de *rien*. Je finirai donc ceci par le *rien*, aussi ne suis-je guères plus que *rien*, et bientôt je ne serai *rien* etc."

29. Vovelle, *Mort et Occident*, 409.

30. Voltaire, *Testament de Meslier*, 159–60.

31. Voltaire, *Testament de Meslier*, 160.

32. Israel, *Democratic Enlightenment*, 650–75.

33. Voltaire, *Sophronime et Adélos*, 277.

34. Stéphane Pujol, "Sophronime et Adélos," in Goulemot et al., *Inventaire Voltaire*, 1261.

35. Voltaire, *Sophronime et Adélos*, 292.

36. Epictetus, *Discourses*, 43. The relevant passage appears in Book 3, Chapter 5, Sections 8–11. Special thanks to Brian Johnson of Fordham University for this reference, and more generally for guiding me on the Stoics.

37. Favre quotes the mystic Jeanne Guyon, accused of Quietism, writing of "the all of God and the nothingness of the creature," in *Mort dans la littérature*, 146. In his *Pensées*, the Jansenist Blaise Pascal, one of Voltaire's targets in the *Lettres philosophiques*, described man in nature as "nothing with regard to the infinite, everything with regard to nothingness, a middle ground between nothing and everything, infinitely removed from comprising the extremes." Pascal, "Pensées sur la religion."

38. Pomeau, *Religion de Voltaire*, 404. The date of "Le songe creux" is unknown. Vahlkamp makes an argument for 1773 in "Dates," 95, but Nablow has convincingly argued in his introduction to "Songe creux," 291–94, that it "was in all likelihood written in the last years of Voltaire's life" (294).

39. Nablow, introduction to "Songe creux" by Voltaire, 302.

40. Voltaire, "Songe creux: autograph manuscript," n.p. I have reproduced the text as it appears in the manuscript, restoring only missing apostrophes and spaces to ensure readability. For the critical edition of the poem, see Voltaire, "Songe-creux," 307–10.

41. Nablow, introduction to "Songe creux" by Voltaire, 300.

42. Nablow, introduction to "Songe creux" by Voltaire, 302.

43. Voltaire, *Contes en vers et en prose*, 2:520.

44. Vahlkamp, "Dates," 95. Favre presents a contrasting view in *Mort dans la littérature*, 203, strangely citing the poem as evidence that Voltaire "found a way . . . to make nothingness tolerable," but he neither justifies this interpretation nor acknowledges Deffand, who certainly did not find nothingness tolerable.

45. Nablow observes in his introduction to "Songe creux" that the cynicism of the ending "is unique among the *contes en vers*" (300).

46. Nablow, introduction to "Songe creux" by Voltaire, 300.

47. Voltaire, "Adieu: Autograph manuscript," n.p. I have reproduced the text as it appears in the manuscript, rather than standardizing capitalization, spelling, and punctuation as most editors do. Subsequent quotations from the poem will all refer to this manuscript. For the standard critical edition of the poem, see Voltaire, "Adieux à la vie," *OCV* 80C, 461–63.

48. In his entry on the poem in the *Inventaire Voltaire,* André Magnan characterizes "Adieux à la vie" as "perhaps the very last verses of the poet (1778?)—but the history of the text is poorly known" (25). For Simon Davies, editor of the poem in *OCV* 80C, the poem was "presumably written during Voltaire's stay in Paris in 1778" (461).

49. See Nablow, "Some Reflections."

50. Hume, *MOL,* 239.

51. See Lilti, *Invention of Celebrity.*

52. In his introduction to "Songe creux," Nablow suggests that "the butterfly imagery and the concept of nothingness remind us of Pope and the last book of *The Dunciad* (1743), with its concluding line: 'And universal darkness buries all' " (302).

53. Voltaire, *Notebooks II,* 508.

54. Deffand to Walpole, Paris, March 8, 1778, in *WDC,* 5:25. Emphasis in the original.

55. Deffand to Walpole, March 4, 1778, in *WDC,* 5:25.

56. Deffand to Walpole, Paris, March 22, 1778, in *WDC,* 5:34.

57. Historians of death have documented the reduction in traditional death rituals in Europe during this period, but from the contemporary perspective of Voltaire and Deffand, the religious trappings surrounding death remained formidable. See McManners, *Death and the Enlightenment,* 234–69.

58. See Madame du Deffand's Journal and "Madame du Deffand's Will" in *WDC,* 5:460, 6:5.

59. Wiart to Walpole, Paris, October 22, 1780, in *WDC,* 5:252.

5

Deffand's Nothingness

1. There are only a few scattered references to Deffand in Goodman's book and she appears neither in the bibliography of primary sources nor in the biographical sketches at the end of the book. See Goodman, *Republic of Letters,* 75–76, 78, and 139.

2. See Craveri, *Madame du Deffand,* 186.

3. Strachey, "Madame du Deffand," 64.

4. Lilti, *Monde des salons,* 9–14, 55–57, translated as *World of the Salons.* For two provocative critiques of Lilti's work, see Russo, review of *World of the Salons,* and Goodman, review of *World of the Salons.*

5. It may seem counterintuitive to use the term *soul* when referring to materialist thought. But the term was frequently used by staunch monist materialists such as Diderot to designate what we might refer to today as the mind or self. There were also many serious attempts to locate the organ of the soul in the human body. See Pangburn, "Bonnet's Theory."

6. Strictly speaking, Voltaire was a deist, but he certainly appears as a nonbeliever in his correspondence with Deffand.

7. In the early years of Deffand scholarship, notably in Mary Berry's 1810 edition of Deffand's letters, her birth date was believed to be 1697, but in his critical edition of the Deffand-Walpole correspondence, W. S. Lewis established that it was in fact 1696. See *WDC*, 5:368n23.

8. Horace Walpole to Thomas Walpole, Strawberry Hill, September 6, 1780, in *Walpole's Correspondence*, 36:171–72.

9. "Portrait of Madame du Deffand, by Walpole," in *WDC*, 6:56.

10. Sainte-Beuve, *Causeries*, 1:412.

11. Although Goodman does not discuss Deffand's correspondence, her approach in *Becoming a Woman* has been invaluable to me. See also Stewart, *Enlightenment of Age*, for an incisive reading that situates the Deffand-Walpole correspondence in the context of perceptions of aging women in the Enlightenment, and MacArthur, *Extravagant Narratives*, for a convincing account of the narrative emplotment of the relationship in the context of epistolary conventions and models.

12. Deffand to Walpole, Paris, May 4, 1780, in *WDC*, 5:227.

13. Deffand to Walpole, Paris, October 8, 1779, in *WDC*, 5:180.

14. Lilti, *Monde des salons*, 225.

15. "Madame du Deffand's Inventory," in *WDC*, 6:32.

16. Du Bos, *Réflexions critiques*, 3.

17. Louis de Jaucourt, "Ennui," in Diderot and d'Alembert, *Encyclopédie*, 5:694.

18. Jaucourt, "Ennui," 5:694.

19. It is difficult to determine whether Deffand was familiar with Jaucourt's article. The *Encyclopédie* does not appear in the inventory of books from her library included in her testament and she expressed hostility toward the encyclopedists following her break with Lespinasse and d'Alembert. Nonetheless, she occasionally commented on the *Encyclopédie* in her correspondence with Voltaire and Walpole, and given the way texts circulated in eighteenth-century salon culture it is certainly possible she could have read or at least heard of the article, especially given her interest in the topic.

20. Deffand to Walpole, March 22, 1780, in *WDC*, 5:216.

21. Jaucourt, "Ennui," 5:693; Deffand to Walpole, Paris, March 22, 1778, in *WDC*, 5:35.

22. Deffand to Walpole, Paris, May 17, 1767, in *WDC*, 1:293.

23. Deffand to Walpole, June 18, 1776, in *WDC*, 4:331. After Deffand's death, Wiart revealed in a letter to Walpole how much she had suffered from her increasing deafness at the end of her life: "Alas! Yes, Monsieur, her deafness was progressing greatly, and that gave her great sadness. When there were a lot of people in a room she could no longer hear anything." Wiart to Walpole, Paris, October 22, 1780, in *WDC*, 5:252.

24. See Deffand to Walpole, April 19, 1766; September 30, 1766; and February 3, 1767, in *WDC*, 1:2n1, 1:145, 1:224.

25. Deffand to Walpole, April 13, 1777, in *WDC*, 4:433.

26. Deffand to Walpole, Paris, March 17, 1776, in *WDC*, 4:285.

27. Deffand to Walpole, March 21, 1776, in *WDC*, 4:286–87.

28. See Silver, *Mind Is a Collection;* and Pasanek, *Metaphors of Mind.*

29. For example, Craveri speculates that Deffand was already hostile to Diderot before she broke with d'Alembert, because "She probably sensed a far more dangerous radicalism in Diderot than in her protégé." See her *Madame du Deffand*, 130. Craveri's account is generally weakened by her apparent hostility to her subject.

30. "Portrait de Madame la Marquise du Deffand, par M. de Forcalquier," in *WDC*, 6:51.

31. Craveri, *Madame du Deffand*, 7. The quotation is from Nicolas Chamfort's recounting of the anecdote.

32. Deffand to Walpole, December 20, 1778, in *WDC*, 5:94. Even Deffand's biographer Craveri, who frequently emphasizes Deffand's hostility to radical ideas, observes that "For a self-declared enemy of contemporary philosophy, Madame du Deffand revealed a determinist materialism as rigorous as any philosophy of Holbach or Helvétius." See her *Madame du Deffand*, 102.

33. Deffand to Walpole, May 22–26, 1776, in *WDC*, 4:318.

34. Deffand to Walpole, November 2, 1775, in *WDC*, 4:230.

35. Deffand to Walpole, Paris, May 23, 1767, in *WDC*, 1:296.

36. Strachey, "Madame du Deffand," 63.

37. Deffand to Walpole, Paris, April 1, 1769, in *WDC*, 2:219. For Sainte-Beuve's appreciation of the letter, see his *Causeries*, 1:424–25.

38. On the broader context for Deffand's philosophical musings on blindness, see Tunstall, *Blindness and Enlightenment.*

39. Sainte-Beuve, *Causeries*, 1:424.

40. Walpole to Deffand, April 6, 1769, in *WDC*, 2:220.

41. I have relied here on an eighteenth-century translation of the tragedy, Racine, *Athaliah*, 18.

42. Deffand to Walpole, May 3, 1779, in *WDC*, 5:137–38. See also Deffand to Walpole, Paris, February 3, 1780, in *WDC*, 5:202–3, where she describes *Athalie* as the most perfect work of literature.

43. Racine, *Athalie*, Act II scene 5, 1034.

44. Racine, *Athaliah,* Act II scene 5, 17.

45. Deffand to Louise Honorine Crozat, duchesse de Choiseul, Paris, January 19, 1774, in *Correspondance complète,* 3:68.

46. Deffand to Walpole, September 18, 1779, in *WDC,* 5:174.

47. See Toynbee, "Mme du Deffand and Hume." On the quarrel between Rousseau and Hume, see Scott and Zaretsky, *Philosophers' Quarrel.*

48. In *WDC,* see the inventory of Deffand's library, 6:32; Deffand to Walpole, Paris, August 9, 1767, 1:338; and Deffand to Walpole, Paris, May 2, 1773, 3:350. It should be noted that Deffand found many works boring, although she also expressed her veneration of a select number of authors and works.

49. Deffand to Walpole, Paris, September 7, 1776, in *WDC,* 4:355.

50. Hume, "Letter to Madame de Boufflers, 1776," *LWL,* MSS 11, Series 1, Box 7, Page 389.

51. Hume to the Comtesse de Boufflers, Edinburgh, August 20, 1776, Letter 539 in *Letters of David Hume,* 2:335. The letter is also found in *LWL,* MSS 11, Series 1, Box 7, Page 389.

52. For Rousseau, see Deffand to Walpole, July 5, 1778, in *WDC,* 5:57; for Geoffrin, see Deffand to Walpole, October 12, 1777, in *WDC,* 4:484.

53. Hume, *MOL,* 239. I have restored "I know that I had but few years to enjoy it" from Hume's manuscript, rather than "I knew that I could have but few years to enjoy it," as given in this edition. It seems to me that the temporal strangeness of this sentence may be intentional on Hume's part given the evident play with verb tenses in the following paragraph.

54. Deffand to Walpole, December 9–11, 1776, in *WDC,* 4:379.

55. Deffand to Walpole, March 27, 1777, in *WDC,* 4:425.

56. Hume, *La vie de David Hume,* manuscript, *LWL,* MSS 11, Series 3, Box 9, Folder 34. The translator commissioned by Deffand and the Comtesse de Boufflers was Jean Baptiste Antoine Suard, who later published his translation. There are a few very minor variations between the manuscript and published versions of the translation, but nothing I could detect of significance.

57. Adam Smith to William Strahan, August 23–26, 1776, *LWL,* MSS 11, Series 1, Box 3, Folder 22.

58. Duchesse de Choiseul to Deffand, April 19, 1777, *LWL,* MSS 11, Series 1, Box 1, Folder 11. This letter can also be found in Deffand, *Correspondance complète,* 3:260.

59. Deffand to Voltaire, Paris, May 9, 1775, in *CV,* 513.

60. Deffand to Walpole, September 25, 1777, in *WDC,* 4:479.

61. Voltaire to Deffand, March 30, 1775, in *CV,* 507. Letter 18277 in *VC,* 90:134.

62. Deffand to Walpole, June 18, 1776, in *WDC,* 4:331.

63. See, for example, the depiction of retreat at the end of Lafayette's novel, *La Princesse de Clèves,* 250–52.

64. Deffand to Walpole, November 19, 1777, in *WDC*, 4:494.

65. The 4th edition of the *Dictionnaire de l'Académie française*, published in 1762, defines *végéter* in the following terms: "To grow by an internal principle and through the roots. *Plants always vegetate until they die.* We say of a man who has almost no reason or sentiment, that he does nothing but vegetate." See *Dictionnaires d'autrefois*, ARTFL.

66. Deffand to Walpole, April 13, 1777, in *WDC*, 4:432.

67. Deffand to Walpole, Paris, April 20, 1777, in *WDC*, 4:436–37.

68. Genlis, *L'amant anonyme*, 165. Deffand refers to the same scene and identifies the author in a letter to the Duchesse de Choiseul. See Deffand to Choiseul, April 19, 1777, Deffand, *Correspondance complète*, 3:260–61.

69. Deffand to Walpole, May 18, 1777, in *WDC*, 4:442.

70. Crébillon, *Égarements*, 68.

71. Deffand to Walpole, April 8–12, 1776, in *WDC*, 4:300–301.

72. Voltaire to Deffand, Cirey par Vassy en Champagne, March 18, 1736, Letter 1002 in *VC*, 5:98. Quoted in Ozouf, *Mots des femmes*, 41.

73. Rousseau, *Confessions*, 202.

74. De Goncourt, *Femme*, 110.

75. Deffand to Walpole, June 30, 1780, in *WDC*, 5:235.

76. Russo, review of *World of the Salons*.

77. Deffand to Walpole, Paris, April 12, 1779, in *WDC*, 5:130.

78. Deffand to Walpole, May 22, 1776, in *WDC*, 4:319.

79. Deffand to Walpole, March 21–23, 1776, in *WDC*, 4:288.

80. Ozouf observes of Deffand's taste that "She is sure of her taste and of possessing the models of the beautiful, the good, and the true. Sainte-Beuve grants her that in this domain she was unrivaled. Posterity has ratified what she loved, has been grateful to her for having defended Montaigne against Walpole, and having had difficulty accepting that the latter could have loved both Sévigné and Crébillon." See her *Mots des femmes*, 36.

81. Deffand to Walpole, March 3, 1776, in *WDC*, 4:275.

82. Deffand to Walpole, March 3, 1776, in *WDC*, 4:275.

83. Deffand to Walpole, Paris, March 17, 1779, in *WDC*, 4:286.

84. Deffand to Walpole, June 28, 1778, in *WDC*, 5:54.

85. Deffand to Walpole, June 9, 1776, in *WDC*, 4:327.

86. Deffand to Walpole, November 5, 1779, in *WDC*, 5:186.

87. Wiart to Walpole, September 20, 1780, in *WDC*, 5:249.

88. Deffand, "Journal," n.p.; *WDC*, 5:460.

89. Wiart to Walpole, Paris, October 22, 1780, in *WDC*, 5:251.

90. Deffand to Walpole, Paris, August 17, 1780, in *WDC*, 5:242.

91. Deffand to Walpole, Paris, August 22, 1780, in *WDC*, 5:242.

92. Deffand to Walpole, Paris, August 22, 1780, in *WDC*, 5:243.

93. Deffand to Walpole, Paris, August 22, 1780, in *WDC*, 5:243.

94. Deffand to Walpole, Paris, August 22, 1780, in *WDC*, 5:243.

95. Horace Walpole to Thomas Walpole, Strawberry Hill, September 6, 1780, in *Walpole's Correspondence*, 36:171–72.

96. Wiart to Walpole, September 10, in *WDC*, 5:247.

97. Deffand to Walpole, February 8, 1778, in *WDC*, 5:15. Stewart analyzes Deffand's concurrent expressions of love and disdain for romance in her correspondence with Walpole, and her dislike for Crébillon, in the context of how aging women were viewed in the eighteenth century, in *Enlightenment of Age*, 121–71.

98. Sainte-Beuve, *Causeries*, 1:431.

99. Wiart to Walpole, September 17, 1780, in *WDC*, 5:248.

100. Deffand to Walpole, December 13, 1772, in *WDC*, 3:297.

101. Wiart to Walpole, September 20, 1780, in *WDC*, 5:249–50.

102. Deffand to Walpole, July 24, 1779, in *WDC*, 5:162.

103. Shakespeare, *King Lear*, Act I, Scene 4, 2509; Act I, Scene 1, 2496.

104. Sainte-Beuve, *Causeries*, 1:424.

Epilogue. Roland's Death

Epigraph: Roland, *Lettres*, 2:526.

1. Roland's last words are sometimes said to have been an invention of the Romantic poet Alphonse de Lamartine. They have also come down to us in another version: "Oh! liberty, how you've been played!"

2. Roland, *Mémoires*, 98.

3. Roland, *Mémoires*, 98–99.

4. Roland, *Mémoires*, 99.

5. Unlike Helvétius and Roland, Adam Smith was interested not in the killing of the spider, but rather in Lauzon's amusing himself with the spider as evidence of the human capacity to adjust to adverse circumstances. See his *Theory of Moral Sentiments*, 149. I am grateful to Lauren Kopajtik for this reference, and more generally for her insightful feedback on my work.

6. Helvétius, *De l'esprit*, 3:83–84.

7. Roland, *Mémoires*, 329. The thirteen years Roland refers to are 1780 to 1793.

8. Roland, *Mémoires*, 329n*.

9. Roland, *Mémoires*, 338.

10. Roland, *Mémoires*, 338–39.

11. Mercier, *Nouveau Paris*, 19.

12. Quoted by Paul de Roux in his Introduction to Roland, *Mémoires*, 29.

13. See Paul de Roux's note in Roland, *Mémoires*, 341n1.

14. Michelet, *Histoire*, 1:836. Quoted by Paul de Roux in Roland, *Mémoires*, 27n1.

15. Roland to Robespierre, October 14, 1793, from the infirmary at Sainte-Pélagie, in Roland, *Lettres,* 526.

16. Roland, *Mémoires,* 344.

17. Roland, *Mémoires,* 346.

18. Falconet to Diderot, December 1765, in *Pour et contre,* 6.

19. Necker, *Mélanges,* 3:287.

20. La Rochefoucauld, "Maxime 26," in *Maximes,* 13.

Bibliography

Primary Sources

Buffon, Georges Louis Leclerc, comte de. *Histoire naturelle, générale et particulière*. 36 vols. Paris: Imprimerie royale, 1749–89.

———. *Histoire naturelle, générale et particulière. Servant de suite à l'Histoire naturelle de l'homme, supplément, tome quatrième*. Vol. 41. Paris: Imprimerie royale, 1777.

———. *Histoire naturelle des minéraux*. 5 vols. Paris: Imprimerie royale,' 1783–88.

———. *De l'homme*. Edited by Michèle Duchet. Postface by Claude Blanckaert. 1971. Reprint, Histoire des sciences humaines. Paris: L'Harmattan, 2006.

———. *Œuvres*. Edited by Stéphane Schmitt with Cédric Crémière. Preface by Michel Delon. Bibliothèque de la Pléiade. Paris: Gallimard, 2007.

Buffon, Henri Nadault de, ed. *Correspondance inédite de Buffon*. 2 vols. Paris: Hachette, 1860.

Condillac, Étienne Bonnot de. *Traité des sensations*. Paris: Fayard, 1984.

Crébillon, Claude-Prosper Jolyot de. *Les égarements du cœur et de l'esprit*. Edited by René Etiemble. Paris: Armand Colin, 1961.

D'Alembert, Jean le Rond. *Œuvres de d'Alembert*. 5 vols. Paris: A. Belin, 1821–22.

Deffand, Marie de Vichy-Chamrond, marquise du. *Cher Voltaire: La correspondance de Madame du Deffand avec Voltaire*. Edited by Isabelle and Jean-Louis Vissière. Paris: Des femmes, 1987.

———. *Correspondance complète de Mme. du Deffand avec la duchesse de Choiseul, l'abbé Barthélemy et M. Craufurt*. 3 vols. Paris: Calmann Lévy, 1866–77.

———. *Horace Walpole's Correspondence with Madame du Deffand.* 6 vols. 1939. In *The Yale Edition of Horace Walpole's Correspondence,* edited by W. S. Lewis. 48 vols. New Haven: Yale University Press, 1937–83.

———. "Journal de Madame du Deffand, 1779 July 1–1780 September 10." W. S. Lewis Collection of Marie du Deffand, LWL MSS 11, Series 2, Box 8. The Lewis Walpole Library, Yale University.

———. *Lettres de Madame du Deffand à Voltaire 1759–1775.* Preface by Chantal Thomas. Paris: Payot & Rivages, 1994.

D'Épinay, Louise. *Les contre-confessions. Histoire de Madame de Montbrillant.* Preface by Elisabeth Badinter. Paris: Mercure de France, 1989.

Dernier testament de M. de Voltaire, Contenant ses sentiments à la fin de sa vie, & ses volontés après sa mort. Geneva: Frères Cramer, 1778.

D'Haussonville, Gabriel Paul Othenin de Cléron, comte. *Le salon de Madame Necker, d'après des documents tirés des archives de Coppet.* 2 vols. Paris: Calmann Lévy, 1882.

D'Holbach, Paul Henri Thiry, baron. *Lettres à Eugénie, ou Préservatif contre les préjugés.* 2 vols. London, 1768.

———. "Réflexions sur les craintes de la mort." In *Recueil philosophique ou mélange de pièces sur la religion & la morale. Par différents auteurs.* London, 1770.

Dictionnaires d'autrefois. University of Chicago: ARTFL. https://artfl-project .uchicago.edu/content/dictionnaires-dautrefois.

Diderot, Denis. *Correspondance.* Edited by George Roth and Jean Varloot. 16 vols. Paris: Minuit, 1955–70.

———. *Éléments de physiologie.* Edited by Jean Mayer. Société des textes français modernes. Paris: Marcel Didier, 1964.

———. *Éléments de physiologie.* Edited by Paolo Quintili. L'âge des lumières 27. Paris: Champion, 2004.

———. *Éléments de physiologie.* Edited by Jean Varloot with Michel Delon, Georges Dulac, and Jean Mayer. In Vol. 17 of *Œuvres complètes,* edited by Herbert Dieckmann, Jean Fabre, and Jacques Proust, with Jean Varloot. Paris: Hermann, 1986.

———. *Essai sur les règnes de Claude et de Néron.* Edited by Jean Deprun, Jean Ehrard, Annette Lorenceau, and Raymond Trousson. Vol. 25 of *Œuvres complètes,* edited by Herbert Dieckmann, Jean Fabre, and Jacques Proust, with Jean Varloot. Paris: Hermann, 1986.

———. *Lettres à Sophie Volland, 1759–1774.* Edited by Marc Buffat and Odile Richard-Pauchet. Paris: Non lieu, 2010.

———. *Le neveu de Rameau.* Edited by Jean Fabre. Geneva: Droz, 1977.

———. *Œuvres complètes.* Edited by Herbert Dieckmann, Jean Fabre, and Jacques Proust, with Jean Varloot. Paris: Hermann, 1975– .

———. *Le pour et le contre ou Lettres sur la postérité.* Edited by Emita Hill, Roland Mortier, and Raymond Trousson. Vol. 15 of *Œuvres complètes,* edited by Herbert Dieckmann, Jean Fabre, and Jacques Proust, with Jean Varloot. Paris: Hermann, 1986.

———. *Le rêve de d'Alembert.* Edited by Jean Varloot, with Michel Delon, Georges Dulac, and Jean Mayer. In Vol. 17 of *Œuvres complètes,* edited by Herbert Dieckmann, Jean Fabre, and Jacques Proust, with Jean Varloot. Paris: Hermann, 1987.

Diderot, Denis, and Jean le Rond d'Alembert, eds. *Encyclopédie, ou diction-naire raisonné des sciences, des arts et des métiers, etc.* University of Chicago: ARTFL Encyclopédie Project (Autumn 2022 ed.), edited by Robert Morrissey and Glenn Roe. http://encyclopedie.uchicago.edu.

Du Bos, Jean-Baptiste, abbé. *Réflexions critiques sur la poésie et sur la peinture.* Paris: École nationale supérieure des Beaux-Arts, 1993.

Epictetus. *Discourses, Books 3–4.* Translated by W. A. Oldfather. Loeb Classical Library. Cambridge: Harvard University Press, 1928.

Goncourt, Edmond and Jules de. *La femme au dix-huitième siècle.* Paris: Firmin Didot, 1862.

Graffigny, Françoise de. *Lettres d'une péruvienne.* Introduction by Joan DeJean and Nancy K. Miller. New York: Modern Language Association of America, 1993.

Helvétius, Claude Adrien. *De l'esprit.* 3 vols. La Haye: Pierre Motjens, 1759.

Hume, David. *Dialogues Concerning Natural Religion.* Edited by Norman Kemp Smith. New York: Macmillan and Library of Liberal Arts, 1947.

———. *An Enquiry Concerning Human Understanding.* Edited by Peter Millican. Oxford: Oxford University Press, 2007.

———. "Letter to Madame de Boufflers, 1776." W. S. Lewis Collection of Marie du Deffand, LWL MSS 11, Series 1, Box 7, Page 389. The Lewis Walpole Library, Yale University.

———. *The Letters of David Hume.* Edited by J. Y. T. Greig. 2 vols. 1932. Reprint, London: Clarendon Press, 1969.

———. *My Own Life.* In *Dialogues Concerning Natural Religion,* 229–48.

———. *A Treatise of Human Nature.* Edited by Ernest C. Mossner. London: Penguin Books, 1969.

———. *La vie de David Hume écrite par lui-même traduite de l'anglais.* W. S. Lewis Collection of Marie du Deffand, LWL MSS 11, Series 3, Box 9, Folder 34. The Lewis Walpole Library, Yale University.

Kant, Immanuel. "An Answer to the Question: 'What Is Enlightenment?'" In *Kant's Political Writings,* edited by Hans Reiss, translated by H. B. Nisbet, 54–60. Cambridge: Cambridge University Press, 1970.

Lafayette, Marie-Madeleine Pioche de La Vergne, Madame de. *La Princesse de Clèves.* Edited by Bernard Pingaud. Paris: Gallimard, 2000.

La Fontaine, Jean de. *Fables*. Vol. 1 of *Œuvres complètes*, edited by Jean-Pierre Collinet. Bibliothèque de la Pléiade. Paris: Gallimard, 1991.

La Rochefoucauld, François duc de. *Maximes: Suivies des réflexions diverses*. Paris: Garnier, 1967.

Lucretius. *On the Nature of Things. De rerum natura*. Edited and translated by Anthony M. Esolen. Baltimore: Johns Hopkins University Press, 1995.

Mercier, Louis Sébastien. *Le nouveau Paris*. Edited by Jean-Claude Bonnet. Paris: Mercure de France, 1994.

Meslier, Jean. *Le testament de Jean Meslier*. Edited by Rudolf Charles. 3 vols. Amsterdam: R. C. Meijer, 1864.

Michelet, Jules. *Histoire de la Révolution française*. Edited by Gérard Walter. 2 vols. Bibliothèque de la Pléiade. Paris: Gallimard, 1952.

Montaigne, Michel de. *The Complete Essays of Montaigne*. Translated by Donald M. Frame. Stanford: Stanford University Press, 1957.

———. *Les essais*. Edited by Jean Balsamo, Michel Magnien, and Catherine Magnien-Simonin. Bibliothèque de la Pléiade. Paris: Gallimard, 2007.

Necker, Suzanne Curchod. "Derniers moments et agonie de M. le comte de Buffon, décédé au Jardin du Roi dans la nuit du 15 au 16 avril 1788, à l'âge de quatre-vingt-un ans." In Buffon, *Correspondance inédite*, 2:612–14.

———. *Mélanges extraits des manuscrits de Mme. Necker*. 3 vols. Paris: Pougens, 1798.

Pascal, Blaise. "Pensées sur la religion." Français 9202, Département des manuscrits. Bibliothèque nationale de France, Paris. https://gallica.bnf.fr/ark:/12148/btv1b52504189f/f221.item.

Racine, Jean. *Athaliah. A Tragedy. Translated from the French of Monsieur Racine. By Mr. Duncombe*. London: J. Watts, 1746.

———. *Athalie*. In *Théâtre, poésies*, vol. 1 of *Œuvres complètes*, edited by Georges Forestier. Paris: Gallimard, 1999.

Roland de la Platière, Marie-Jeanne Phlipon. *Lettres de Madame Roland, publiées par Claude Perroud, 1780–1793*. Edited by Claude Perroud. 2 vols. Paris: Imprimerie nationale, 1900–1902.

———. *Mémoires de Madame Roland*. Edited by Paul de Roux. Rev. ed. Paris: Mercure de France, 1986.

Roucher, Jean-Antoine. *Les mois, poème en douze chants*. Paris: Froment, 1825.

Rousseau, Jean-Jacques. *Confessions*. In vol. 1 of *Œuvres complètes*, edited by Bernard Gagnebin, Marcel Raymond, and Robert Osmont. Bibliothèque de la Pléiade. Paris: Gallimard, 1959.

———. *Correspondance complète de Jean-Jacques Rousseau*. Edited by R. A. Leigh. 52 vols. Geneva: Institut et Musée Voltaire; Oxford: Voltaire Foundation, 1965–98.

———. *Émile.* In vol. 4 of *Œuvres complètes,* edited by Bernard Gagnebin and Marcel Raymond. Bibliothèque de la Pléiade. Paris: Gallimard, 1969.

———. *Œuvres complètes.* Edited by Bernard Gagnebin and Marcel Raymond. 5 vols. Bibliothèque de la Pléiade. Paris: Gallimard, 1959–95.

———. *Rêveries du promeneur solitaire.* In vol. 1 of *Œuvres complètes,* edited by Bernard Gagnebin, Marcel Raymond, and Robert Osmont. Bibliothèque de la Pléiade. Paris: Gallimard, 1959.

———. *Rousseau juge de Jean-Jaques* [sic]: *Dialogues.* In vol. 1 of *Œuvres complètes,* edited by Bernard Gagnebin, Marcel Raymond, and Robert Osmont. Bibliothèque de la Pléiade. Paris: Gallimard, 1959.

Saint Augustine. *Confessions.* Translated by Henry Chadwick. Oxford: Oxford University Press, 1992.

Sainte-Beuve, Charles-Augustin. *Causeries du lundi.* Vol. 1. 5th ed. Paris: Garnier frères, n.d.

Seneca. *Dialogues and Letters.* Translated by C. D. N. Costa. London: Penguin, 1997.

Shakespeare, William. *King Lear.* In *The Norton Shakespeare,* 3rd ed., edited by Stephen Greenblatt, with Walter Cohen, Suzanne Gossett, Jean E. Howard, Katharine Eisaman Maus, and Gordon McMullan. New York: W. W. Norton, 2016.

Smith, Adam. "Letter from Adam Smith, LL.D. to William Strahan, Esq." In Hume, *Dialogues,* 241–48.

———. *The Theory of Moral Sentiments.* Edited by D. D. Raphael and A. L. Macfie. Vol. 1 of *The Glasgow Edition of the Works and Correspondence of Adam Smith.* Oxford: Oxford University Press, 2014.

Staël, Germaine de. *Mémoires sur la vie privée de mon père, par Mme la Baronne de Staël-Holstein, suivis des Mélanges de M. Necker.* Paris: Colburn, 1818.

[Suard, Jean Baptiste Antoine]. *La vie de David Hume, ecrite par lui-même. Traduite de l'anglois.* London: n.p., 1777.

Vandeul, Marie-Angélique de. *Mémoires pour servir à l'histoire de la vie et des ouvrages de M. Diderot par Mme de Vandeul, sa fille.* Edited by Arthur M. Wilson and Blake T. Hanna. In vol. 1 of *Œuvres complètes,* by Denis Diderot, edited by Herbert Dieckmann, Jean Fabre, and Jacques Proust, with Jean Varloot. Paris: Hermann, 1975.

Voltaire. "Adieu je vais dans ce pays: Autograph manuscript, [1778]." Collection of letters and manuscripts of Voltaire, MA 638.87. Department of Literary and Historical Manuscripts, Morgan Library and Museum.

———. "Adieux à la vie." Edited by Simon Davies. In vol. 80C of *Les œuvres complètes de Voltaire,* edited by Nicholas Cronk. Oxford: Voltaire Foundation, 2009.

———. *Contes en vers et en prose.* Edited by Sylvain Menant. 2 vols. Paris: Classiques Garnier, 1992.

———. *Dialogue de Maxime de Madaure, entre Sophronime et Adélos*. Edited by Ute van Runset. In vol. 78A of *Les œuvres complètes de Voltaire*, edited by Nicholas Cronk. Oxford: Voltaire Foundation, 2010.

———. "Epître à Horace." Edited by Nicholas Cronk. In vol. 74B of *Les œuvres complètes de Voltaire*, edited by Nicholas Cronk. Oxford: Voltaire Foundation, 2006.

———. *Notebooks II*. Edited by Theodore Besterman. Vol. 82 of *Les œuvres complètes de Voltaire*, edited by Theodore Besterman. Geneva: Institut et Musée Voltaire and University of Toronto Press, 1968.

———. *Sentiment des citoyens*. Edited by Frédéric S. Eigeldinger. Paris: Honoré Champion, 1997.

———. "Le songe creux." Edited by Ralph A. Nablow. In vol. 77B of *Les œuvres complètes de Voltaire*, edited by Nicholas Cronk. Oxford: Voltaire Foundation, 2014.

———. "Le songe creux: Autograph manuscript, undated [17—?]." Collection of letters and manuscripts of Voltaire, MA 638.192. Department of Literary and Historical Manuscripts, Morgan Library and Museum.

———. *Voltaire's Correspondence*. Edited by Theodore Besterman. 107 vols. Geneva: Institut et Musée Voltaire, 1953–65.

Voltaire, ed. *Testament de Jean Meslier*. Edited by Roland Desné. Vol. 56A of *Les œuvres complètes de Voltaire*, edited by Haydn T. Mason and Nicholas Cronk. Oxford: Voltaire Foundation, 2001.

Walpole, Horace. *Walpole Family, 1725–1797*. Vol. 36 of *The Yale Edition of Horace Walpole's Correspondence*, edited by W. S. Lewis. New Haven: Yale University Press, 1973.

Woolf, Virginia. *Mrs. Dalloway*. 1925. Reprint, San Diego: Harcourt Brace Jovanovich, 1985.

Secondary Sources

Abele, Célia. "Rousseau's Herbaria: Leaves of Self, Books of Nature." *Eighteenth-Century Studies* 54, no. 2 (Winter 2021): 401–25.

Adam, Antoine. "Rousseau et Diderot." *Revue des sciences humaines* 53 (1949): 21–34.

Andrew, Edward. "The Senecan Moment: Patronage and Philosophy in the Eighteenth Century." *Journal of the History of Ideas* 65, no. 2 (April 2004): 277–99.

Ariès, Philippe. *L'homme devant la mort*. Paris: Seuil, 1977.

Aron, Paul, Sophie Basch, Manuel Couvreur, Jacques Marx, Éric Van der Schueren, and Valérie van Crugten-André, eds. *Vérité et littérature au XVIIIe siècle*. Paris: Honoré Champion, 2001.

Baecque, Antoine de. *La gloire et l'effroi: Sept morts sous la Terreur*. Paris: Bernard Grasset, 1997.

Baier, Annette C. *Death and Character: Further Reflections on Hume.* Cambridge: Harvard University Press, 2008.

Ballstadt, Kurt P. A. *Diderot: Natural Philosopher.* Studies on Voltaire and the Eighteenth Century 2008, no. 1. Oxford: Voltaire Foundation, 2008.

———. Review of *Éléments de physiologie,* by Denis Diderot, edited by Paolo Quintili. *French Studies: A Quarterly Review* 60, no. 3 (July 2006): 397–98.

Beaujour, Michel. *Miroirs d'encre: Rhétorique de l'autoportrait.* Paris: Seuil, 1980.

Becker, Carl L. *The Heavenly City of the Eighteenth-Century Philosophers.* New Haven: Yale University Press, 1932.

Bénichou, Paul. *Le sacre de l'écrivain, 1750–1830. Essai sur l'avènement d'un pouvoir spirituel laïque dans la France moderne.* Paris: Librairie José Corti, 1973.

Bonnet, Jean-Claude. *Naissance du Panthéon: Essai sur le culte des grands hommes.* Paris: Fayard, 1998.

Boon, Sonja. "Last Rites, Last Rights: Corporeal Abjection as Autobiographical Performance in Suzanne Curchod Necker's *Des inhumations précipitées* (1790)." *Eighteenth-Century Fiction* 21, no. 1 (Fall 2008): 89–107.

———. "Performing the Woman of Sensibility: Suzanne Curchod Necker and the Hospice de Charité." *Journal for Eighteenth-Century Studies* 32, no. 2 (2009): 235–54.

Bremner, Geoffrey. "Buffon and the Casting out of Fear." Studies on Voltaire and the Eighteenth Century vol. 205, 75–88. Geneva: Institut et Musée Voltaire, 1982.

———. "Les *Éléments de physiologie* et le sens de la vie." In France and Strugnell, *Diderot: Les dernières années,* 81–91.

Bringman, Gregory. *Artifacts for Diderot's* Elements of Physiology: *An Expanded, Hybrid Translation and Commentary.* Minneapolis: Les Ontœuvres, 2022.

Burgelin, Pierre. *La philosophie de l'existence de J.-J. Rousseau.* 1952. Reprint, Geneva: Slatkine, 1978.

Candaux, Jean-Daniel. "Un hommage à Jean-Jacques Rousseau dans la mouvance du Prince de Ligne." In Aron et al., *Vérité et littérature,* 57–65.

Chartier, Pierre, ed. Special issue, *Essai sur les règnes de Claude et de Néron. Recherches sur Diderot et sur l'Encyclopédie* 36 (2004).

Chaunu, Pierre. *La mort à Paris: XVIe, XVIIe et XVIIIe siècles.* Paris: Fayard, 1978.

Chouillet, Jacques. "Diderot et la retraite." In France and Strugnell, *Diderot: Les dernières années,* 19–29.

———. "La presence de J.-J. Rousseau après sa mort dans les écrits de Diderot." *Cahiers de Varsovie* 10 (1982): 177–88.

Clark, Andrew H. *Diderot's Part*. Aldershot, U.K.: Ashgate, 2008.

Clément, Pierre-Paul. *"Les rêveries du promeneur solitaire*: Dixième promenade." In *Rousseau et Voltaire en 1978, Actes du colloque international de Nice (Juin 1978)*, 366–80. Geneva: Éditions Slatkine, 1981.

Cobb, Richard. *Death in Paris, 1795–1801: The Records of the Basse-Geôle de la Seine, Vendémiaire Year IV–Fructidor Year IX*. Oxford: Oxford University Press, 1978.

Conroy, William Thomas, Jr. *Diderot's Essai sur Sénèque*. Studies on Voltaire and the Eighteenth Century 131. Oxford: Voltaire Foundation, 1975.

Cranston, Maurice. *The Solitary Self: Jean-Jacques Rousseau in Exile and Adversity*. Chicago: University of Chicago Press, 1997.

Craveri, Benedetta. *Madame du Deffand and Her World*. Translated by Teresa Waugh. 1982 (Italian ed.). Boston: David R. Godine, 1994.

Cronk, Nicholas. *Voltaire: A Very Short Introduction*. Oxford: Oxford University Press, 2017.

Curran, Andrew S. *Diderot and the Art of Thinking Freely*. New York: Other Press, 2019.

Daston, Lorraine. *Classical Probability in the Enlightenment*. Princeton: Princeton University Press, 1988.

Dawson, Virginia P. "The Limits of Observation and the Hypotheses of Georges Louis Buffon and Charles Bonnet." In *Beyond History of Science*, edited by Elizabeth Garber, 107–25. Bethlehem, Pa.: Lehigh University Press, 1990.

De Baere, Benoît. "L'écriture de la catastrophe dans l'*Histoire naturelle* de Buffon. Sciences de la terre, esthétique, anthropologie." *Les lettres romanes* 61, nos. 3–4 (2007): 185–203.

———. "Une histoire imaginée . . . mais vraie: Le problème du statut des *Époques de la nature* de Buffon." In *"Les songes de Clio": Fiction et histoire sous l'Ancien Régime*, edited by Sabrina Vervacke, Éric Van der Schueren, and Thierry Belleguic, Les collections de la République des Lettres, 247–61. Saint-Nicolas, Quebec: Les presses de l'Université Laval, 2006.

———. "La philosophie de l'homme de Buffon et son défi à l'égard de l'"inhumaine alliance des choses.'" In Studies on Voltaire and the Eighteenth Century 2005, no. 12, 179–204. Oxford: Voltaire Foundation, 2005.

Delon, Michel. Preface to *Œuvres* by Buffon, ix–xxxvii. Paris: Gallimard, 2007.

De Man, Paul. "Criticism and Crisis." In *Blindness and Insight: Essays in the Rhetoric of Contemporary Criticism*, 2nd ed., 3–19. Minneapolis: University of Minnesota Press, 1983.

Deutsch, Helen, and Mary Terrall, eds. *Vital Matters: Eighteenth-Century Views of Conception, Life, and Death*. Toronto: University of Toronto Press, 2012.

Dornier, Carole. "L'écriture de la citadelle intérieure ou la thérapeutique de l'âme du promeneur solitaire." *Annales de la Société Jean-Jacques Rousseau* 48 (2008): 105–24.

Duchet, Michèle. *Anthropologie et histoire au siècle des Lumières.* 2nd ed. Bibliothèque de l'évolution de l'humanité. Paris: Albin Michel, 1995.

Eddy, John H. "Buffon's *Histoire naturelle:* History? A Critique of Recent Interpretations." *Isis* 85, no. 4 (1994): 644–61.

Edelstein, Dan. *The Enlightenment: A Genealogy.* Chicago: University of Chicago Press, 2010.

Edelstein, Dan, ed. *The Super-Enlightenment: Daring to Know Too Much.* Studies on Voltaire and the Eighteenth Century 2010, no. 1. Oxford: Voltaire Foundation, 2010.

Ehrard, Jean. "Pourquoi Sénèque?" In Diderot, *Œuvres complètes,* 25:3–18.

Eigeldinger, Frédéric S. "Avatars du manuscrit des *Rêveries.*" In Aron et al., *Vérité et littérature au XVIIIe siècle,* 145–61.

Fabre, Jean. "Deux frères ennemis: Diderot et Jean-Jacques Rousseau." *Diderot Studies* 3 (1961): 155–213.

Favre, Robert. *La mort dans la littérature et la pensée françaises au siècle des Lumières.* Lyon: Presses universitaires de Lyon, 1978.

Fellows, Otis E. "Buffon and Rousseau: Aspects of a Relationship." *PMLA* 75, no. 3 (June 1960): 188.

Fellows, Otis E., and Stephen Milliken. *Buffon.* New York: Twayne, 1972.

Flamein, Richard. *Voltaire à Ferney: Adresse à la postérité moderne (1758– 2015).* Paris: Classiques Garnier, 2019.

Foucault, Michel. *L'herméneutique du sujet: Cours au Collège de France (1981– 1982).* Edited by François Ewald, Alessandro Fontan, and Frédéric Gros. Collection hautes études. Paris: Éditions EHESS/Seuil/Gallimard, 2001.

———. *Les mots et les choses: Une archéologie des sciences humaines.* Collection Tel. 1966. Reprint, Paris: Gallimard, 1990.

———. *Naissance de la clinique.* Quadrige. 7th ed. Paris: Presses universitaires de France, 2005.

———. Qu'est-ce que les Lumières?" In *1980–1988.* Vol. 4 of *Dits et écrits, 1954–1988,* edited by Daniel Defert, François Ewald, and Jacques Lagrange, 562–78. Paris: Gallimard, 1994.

Frame, Donald M. *Montaigne's Essais: A Study.* Englewood Cliffs, NJ: Prentice Hall, 1969.

France, Peter, and Anthony Strugnell, eds. *Diderot: Les dernières années, 1770–84.* Edinburgh: Edinburgh University Press, 1985.

Freedman, Jeffrey. "The Limits of Tolerance: Jews, the Enlightenment, and the Fear of Premature Burial." In *Into Print: Limits and Legacies of the Enlightenment. Essays in Honor of Robert Darnton,* edited by Charles Walton, 177–97. University Park: Pennsylvania State University Press, 2011.

Freedman, Jeffrey, ed. *A Cultural History of Death: In the Age of Enlightenment.* London: Bloomsbury Academic, 2024.

Garrard, Graeme. *Rousseau's Counter-Enlightenment: A Republican Critique of the Philosophes.* SUNY Series in Social and Political Thought. Albany: State University of New York Press, 2003.

Garréta, Anne. "Les *Dialogues* de Rousseau: Paradoxes d'une réception critique." In *Lectures de Rousseau: Rousseau juge de Jean-Jacques: Dialogues,* edited by Isabelle Brouard-Arends and Jean-François Perrin, 141–50. Rennes: Presses universitaires de Rennes, 2003.

Gatefin, Eric. *Diderot, Sénèque et Jean-Jacques: Un dialogue à trois voix.* Amsterdam: Rodopi, 2007.

Gay, Peter. Introduction to *The Question of Jean-Jacques Rousseau* by Ernst Cassirer, 3–30. 1954. Reprint, Bloomington: Indiana University Press, 1963.

Gayon, Jean, ed. *Buffon 88: Actes du colloque international pour le bicentenaire de la mort de Buffon.* Paris: J. Vrin; Lyon: Institut interdisciplinaire d'études épistémologiques, 1992.

Gohau, Gabriel. *Les sciences de la terre aux XVIIe et XVIIIe siècles: Naissance de la géologie.* Paris: Albin Michel, 1990.

Goldschmidt, Victor. *Anthropologie et politique: Les principes du système de Rousseau.* Paris: Librairie philosophique J. Vrin, 1974.

———. *Le système Stoïcien et l'idée du temps.* Bibliothèque d'histoire de la philosophie. Paris: J. Vrin, 1989.

González Fernández, Martín. "Voltaire y Montaigne." *Agora: Papeles de filosofía* 8 (1989): 79–91.

Goodman, Dena. *Becoming a Woman in the Age of Letters.* Ithaca: Cornell University Press, 2009.

———. *The Republic of Letters: A Cultural History of the French Enlightenment.* Ithaca: Cornell University Press, 1994.

———. Review of *The World of the Salons: Sociability and Worldliness in Eighteenth-Century Paris,* by Antoine Lilti, translated by Lydia G. Cochrane. *English Historical Review* 132, no. 555 (April 2017): 406–9.

Goulemot, Jean M. "La vieillesse des philosophes: le cas Diderot." *Diderot Studies* 32 (2012): 165–80.

Goulemot, Jean, André Magnan, and Didier Masseau, eds. *Inventaire Voltaire.* Paris: Gallimard, 1995.

Grmek, Mirko Drazen. *On Ageing and Old Age: Basic Problems and Historic Aspects of Gerontology and Geriatrics.* Monographiae biologicae 5, no. 2. The Hague: W. Junk, 1958.

———. "Les idées de Descartes sur le prolongement de la vie et le mécanisme du vieillissement." *Revue d'histoire des sciences et de leurs applications* 21, no. 4 (1968): 285–302.

Guéhenno, Jean. "La dernière confession de Jean-Jacques." *La nouvelle revue française* 35 (1955): 855–66.

Guyot, Charly. *Plaidoyer pour Thérèse Levasseur.* Neuchatel: Ides et Calendes, 1962.

Hadot, Pierre. *Philosophy as a Way of Life: Spiritual Exercises from Socrates to Foucault.* Edited with an introduction by Arnold I. Davidson. Translated by Michael Chase. Oxford: Blackwell, 1995.

Harris, James A. *Hume: An Intellectual Biography.* Cambridge: Cambridge University Press, 2015.

———. *Hume: A Very Short Introduction.* Oxford: Oxford University Press, 2021.

Hayes, Julie Candler. "Aspects du style tardif dans l'*Essai sur les règnes de Claude et de Néron.*" *Diderot Studies* 39 (2009): 37–44.

———. *Reading the French Enlightenment: System and Subversion.* Cambridge: Cambridge University Press, 1999.

Heller-Roazen, Daniel. *The Inner Touch: Archaeology of a Sensation.* New York: Zone, 2007.

Heymont, Paul. "Tomb of Rousseau at the Pantheon." Travel Gumbo (blog). September 20, 2023. https://www.travelgumbo.com/resource/tomb-of-rousseau-at-the-pantheon.

Hoffmann, Benjamin. *The Paradoxes of Posterity.* Translated by Alan Singerman. University Park: Pennsylvania State University Press, 2020.

Horkheimer, Max, and Theodor W. Adorno. *Dialectic of Enlightenment: Philosophical Fragments.* Edited by Gunzelin Schmid Noert. Translated by Edmund Jephcott. Stanford: Stanford University Press, 2002.

Hulliung, Mark. *The Autocritique of Enlightenment: Rousseau and the Philosophes.* Cambridge: Harvard University Press, 1994.

Israel, Jonathan. *Democratic Enlightenment: Philosophy, Revolution, and Human Rights, 1750–1790.* Oxford: Oxford University Press, 2011.

———. *Enlightenment Contested: Philosophy, Modernity, and the Emancipation of Man, 1670–1752.* Oxford: Oxford University Press, 2006.

———. "Rousseau, Diderot, and the 'Radical Enlightenment': A Reply to Helena Rosenblatt and Joanna Stalnaker." *Journal of the History of Ideas* 77, no. 4 (October 2014): 649–77.

Jardine, N., J. A. Secord, and E. C. Spary, eds. *Cultures of Natural History.* Cambridge: Cambridge University Press, 1996.

Kelly, Christopher. *Rousseau as Author: Consecrating One's Life to the Truth.* Chicago: University of Chicago Press, 2003.

Ker, James. *The Deaths of Seneca.* Oxford: Oxford University Press, 2009.

Kermode, Frank. *The Sense of an Ending: Studies in the Theory of Fiction.* Oxford: Oxford University Press, 1966.

Knee, Philip. "Diderot et Montaigne: Morale et scepticisme dans *Le neveu de Rameau.*" *Diderot Studies* 29 (2003): 35–51.

———. *La parole incertaine: Montaigne en dialogue.* Saint-Nicolas, Quebec City: Presses universitaires de Laval, 2003.

Knee, Philip, and Gérald Allard, eds. *Rousseau juge de Jean-Jacques: Études sur les Dialogues.* Paris: Honoré Champion, 2003.

Koselleck, Reinhart. *Futures Past: On the Semantics of Historical Time.* Translated by Keith Tribe. New York: Columbia University Press, 2004.

Kramnick, Jonathan. *Criticism and Truth: On Method in Literary Studies.* Chicago: University of Chicago Press, 2023.

———. "Living with Lucretius." In Deutsch and Terrall, *Vital Matters,* 13–38.

Kuhn, Bernhard. *Autobiography and Natural Science in the Age of Romanticism: Rousseau, Goethe, Thoreau.* Aldershot, U.K.: Ashgate, 2009.

Laissus, Yves. "L'histoire naturelle." In *Buffon, 1788–1988,* edited by Paul-Marie Grinevald, 73–89. Paris: Imprimerie nationale, 1988.

Laplassotte, François. "Quelques étapes de la physiologie du cerveau du XVIIe au XIXe siècle." *Annales: Histoire, sciences sociales* 25, no. 3 (May–June 1970): 599–613.

Laqueur, Thomas W. *The Work of the Dead: A Cultural History of Mortal Remains.* Princeton: Princeton University Press, 2015.

Leigh, R. A. "La mort de Rousseau: Images d'Épinal et roman policier." *Revue d'histoire littéraire de la France* 79 (1979): 187–98.

Le Roy Ladurie, Emmanuel. "Chaunu, Lebrun, Vovelle: La nouvelle histoire de la mort." In *Le territoire de l'historien,* 393–403. Paris: Gallimard, 1973.

Lewis, Wilmarth Sheldon. *Rescuing Horace Walpole.* New Haven: Yale University Press, 1978.

Lilti, Antoine. *The Invention of Celebrity: 1750–1850.* Translated by Lynn Jeffress. Cambridge: Polity Press, 2017.

———. *Le monde des salons: Sociabilité et mondanité à Paris au XVIIIe siècle.* Paris: Fayard, 2005.

———. *The World of the Salons: Sociability and Worldliness in Eighteenth-Century Paris.* Translated by Lydia G. Cochrane. Oxford: Oxford University Press, 2015.

———. "The Writing of Paranoia: Jean-Jacques Rousseau and the Paradoxes of Celebrity." Translated by David Bell and Jeremy Caradonna. *Representations* 103 (2008): 53–83.

Loveland, Jeff. *Rhetoric and Natural History: Buffon in Polemical and Literary Context.* Studies on Voltaire and the Eighteenth Century 2001, no. 3. Oxford: Voltaire Foundation, 2001.

Lynch, Deidre. *The Economy of Character: Novels, Market Culture, and the Business of Inner Meaning.* Chicago: University of Chicago Press, 1998.

———. *Loving Literature: A Cultural History.* Chicago: University of Chicago Press, 2015.

Manent, Pierre. "Montaigne and Rousseau: Some Reflections." Translated by
    Christopher Kelly and Eve Grace. In *The Challenge of Rousseau,* edited
    by Eve Grace and Christopher Kelly, 312–23. Cambridge: Cambridge
    University Press, 2012.
Mankin, Robert. "La maladie comme triomphe de la nature? *My Own Life* de
    David Hume." *Dix-huitième siècle* 47 (2015): 197–213.
Mason, John Hope. "Portrait de l'auteur, accompagné d'un fantôme: *l'Essai
    sur les règnes de Claude et de Néron.*" In France and Strugnell, *Diderot: Les
    dernières années,* 43–62.
Masters, Roger D. *The Political Philosophy of Rousseau.* Princeton: Princeton
    University Press, 1968.
Masters, Roger D., and Christopher Kelly, eds. Introduction to *Rousseau Judge
    of Jean-Jacques: Dialogues* by Jean-Jacques Rousseau, xiii–xxvii. Trans-
    lated by Judith R. Bush, Christopher Kelly, and Roger D. Masters. Hano-
    ver, N.H.: University Press of New England, 1990.
May, Gita. *Madame Roland and the Age of Revolution.* New York: Columbia
    University Press, 1970.
Mayer, Jean. *Diderot homme de science.* Rennes: Imprimerie Bretonne, 1959.
McManners, John. *Death and the Enlightenment: Changing Attitudes to Death
    Among Christians and Unbelievers in Eighteenth-Century France.* Oxford:
    Oxford University Press, 1981.
Melzer, Arthur M. *The Natural Goodness of Man: On the System of Rousseau's
    Thought.* Chicago: University of Chicago Press, 1990.
Metcalf, Peter, and Richard Huntington. *Celebrations of Death: The Anthropol-
    ogy of Mortuary Ritual.* 2nd ed., revised with a new introduction by Peter
    Metcalf. Cambridge: Cambridge University Press, 1991.
Milanesi, Claudio. "La mort-instant et la mort-processus dans la médecine
    de la seconde moitié du siècle." *Dix-huitième siècle* 23 (1991): 171–90.
Miller, Franklin G. "Two Philosophical Deaths: Hume and Hitchens." *Perspec-
    tives in Biology and Medicine* 56, no. 2 (Spring 2013): 251–58.
Miller, Stephen. *Three Deaths and Enlightenment Thought: Hume, Johnson,
    Marat.* Lewisburg, Pa.: Bucknell University Press, 2001.
Morford, Mark. *The Roman Philosophers, From the Time of Cato the Censor
    to the Death of Marcus Aurelius.* London: Routledge, 2002.
———. *Stoics and Neostoics: Rubens and the Circle of Lipsius.* Princeton:
    Princeton University Press, 1991.
Mornet, Daniel. *Les sciences de la nature en France au XVIIIe siècle.* 1911.
    Reprint, New York: Lenox Hell-Burt Franklin, 1971.
Moser, Walter. "Buffon: Exégète entre théologie et géologie." *Strumenti criti-
    ci* 53 (1987): 17–42.
Nablow, Ralph. "Some Reflections on Voltaire's Poetic Imagery." *Romanic
    Review* 74 (1983): 16–33.

Norton, David Fate, ed. *The Cambridge Companion to Hume*. Cambridge: Cambridge University Press, 1993.

Nouis, Lucien. "L'emploi du temps: Diderot et Rousseau lecteurs de Sénèque." *French Studies* 64, no. 2 (April 2010): 150–63.

Outram, Dorinda. "The Enlightenment Our Contemporary." In *The Sciences in Enlightened Europe*, edited by William Clark, Jan Golinski, and Simon Schaffer, 32–40. Chicago: University of Chicago Press, 1999.

———. *Georges Cuvier: Vocation, Science and Authority in Post-Revolutionary France*. Manchester: Manchester University Press, 1984.

Ozouf, Mona. *Les mots des femmes: Essai sur la singularité française*. Paris: Fayard, 1995.

Pangburn, Kris. "Bonnet's Theory of Palingenesis: An 'Enlightened' Account of Personal Resurrection?" In Edelstein, *Super-Enlightenment*, 191–214.

Pasanek, Brad. *Metaphors of Mind: An Eighteenth-Century Dictionary*. Baltimore: Johns Hopkins University Press, 2015.

Pearson, Roger. *Voltaire Almighty: A Life in Pursuit of Freedom*. New York: Bloomsbury, 2005.

Perrin, Jean-François. *Politique du renonçant: Le dernier Rousseau: Des Dialogues aux Rêveries*. Paris: Kimé, 2011.

Pomeau, René. *La religion de Voltaire*. Paris: Nizet, 1956.

Porter, Roy. *Flesh in the Age of Reason*. Foreword by Simon Schama. London: Allen Lane, 2003.

———. "Le stoïcisme révolutionnaire de Diderot dans l'*Essai sur Sénèque* par rapport à la *Contribution à l'Histoire des deux Indes*." *Recherches sur Diderot et sur l'"Encyclopédie"* 36 (April 2004): 29–42.

Rasmussen, Dennis C., ed. *Adam Smith and the Death of David Hume: The Letter to Strahan and Related Texts*. Lanham, Md.: Lexington Books/ Fortress Academic, 2018.

Reill, Peter Hanns. "Death, Dying and Resurrection in Late Enlightenment Science and Culture." In *Wissenschaft als kulturelle Praxis, 1750–1900*, edited by Hans Erich Bödeker, Peter Hanns Reill, and Jürgen Schlumbohm, 255–74. Veröffentlichungen des Max-Planck-Instituts für Geschichte 154. Göttingen: Vandenhoeck & Ruprecht, 1999.

———. *Vitalizing Nature in the Enlightenment*. Berkeley: University of California Press, 2005.

"Remains of Voltaire." *The Athenaeum*, no. 2157 (February 27, 1969).

Rey, Roselyne. "Buffon et le vitalisme." In Gayon, *Buffon 88*, 399–414.

Ridelhalgh, Anna. "Preromantic Attitudes and the Birth of a Legend: French Pilgrimages to Ermenonville, 1778–1789." In Studies on Voltaire and the Eighteenth Century 215, edited by Haydn Mason, 231–52. Oxford: Voltaire Foundation, 1982.

———. "Rousseau as God? The Ermenonville Pilgrimages in the Revolution."
    In Studies on Voltaire and the Eighteenth Century 278, edited by Haydn
    Mason, 287–308. Oxford: Voltaire Foundation, 1990.
Riskin, Jessica. "Mr. Machine and the Imperial Me." In Edelstein, *Super-
    Enlightenment*, 75–94.
———. *Science in the Age of Sensibility: The Sentimental Empiricists
    of the French Enlightenment.* Chicago: University of Chicago Press,
    2002.
Roger, Jacques. *Buffon: A Life in Natural History.* Edited by L. Pearce Williams.
    Translated by Sarah Lucile Bonnefoi. Ithaca: Cornell University Press,
    1997.
———. *Buffon: Un philosophe au Jardin du Roi.* Paris: Fayard, 1989.
———. Introduction to *Un autre Buffon,* edited by Jacques Roger and Jacques-
    Louis Binet, 21–22. Paris: Hermann, 1977.
Roman, Hanna. *The Language of Nature in Buffon's Histoire naturelle.* Oxford
    University Studies in the Enlightenment 2018, no. 10. Oxford: Liverpool
    University Press, on behalf of Voltaire Foundation, 2018.
Rosenblatt, Helena. "Rousseau, the 'Traditionalist.'" *Journal of the History of
    Ideas* 77, no. 4 (October 2014): 627–35.
Rousseau, G. S. *Enlightenment Borders: Pre- and Post-Modern Discourses:
    Medical, Scientific.* Manchester: Manchester University Press, 1991.
———. *Enlightenment Crossings: Pre- and Post-Modern Discourses: Anthropo-
    logical.* Manchester: Manchester University Press, 1991.
Rudwick, Martin J. S. *Bursting the Limits of Time: The Reconstruction of
    Geohistory in the Age of Revolution.* Chicago: University of Chicago Press,
    2005.
———. *The Meaning of Fossils: Episodes in the History of Palaeontology.* 2nd
    ed. 1976. Reprint, Chicago: University of Chicago Press, 1985.
Russo, Elena. Review of *The World of the Salons: Sociability and Worldliness
    in Eighteenth-Century Paris,* by Antoine Lilti, translated by Lydia G.
    Cochrane. *Reviews in History,* no. 2041 (January 2017): https://reviews
    .history.ac.uk/review/2041/.
———. "Slander and Glory in the Republic of Letters: Diderot and Seneca
    Confront Rousseau." *Republics of Letters: A Journal for the Study of Knowl-
    edge, Politics, and the Arts* 1, no. 1 (May 1, 2009): http://rofl.stanford.edu
    /node/40.
———. *Styles of Enlightenment: Taste, Politics and Authorship in Eighteenth-
    Century France.* Baltimore: Johns Hopkins University Press, 2007.
Saban, Robert. "Le testament de Buffon." In Gayon, *Buffon 88,* 97–115.
Said, Edward. *On Late Style: Music and Literature Against the Grain.* New
    York: Vintage, 2006.
Sandbach, F. H. *The Stoics.* 1975. Reprint, Indianapolis: Hackett, 1994.

Schmitt, Stéphane. Introduction to *Œuvres* by Buffon, xil–lviii. Paris: Gallimard, 2007.

Schwartz, Jerome. "Diderot and Montaigne: The Essais and the Shaping of Diderot's Humanism." Ph.D. diss., Columbia University, 1965.

Scott, John T., and Robert Zaretsky. *The Philosophers' Quarrel: Rousseau, Hume, and the Limits of Human Understanding.* New Haven: Yale University Press, 2009.

Sharples, R. W. *Stoics, Epicureans, and Sceptics.* London: Routledge, 1996.

Sheehan, Jonathan, and Dror Wahrman. *Invisible Hands: Self-Organization and the Eighteenth Century.* Chicago: University of Chicago Press, 2015.

Shomrat, Tal, and Michael Levin. "An Automated Training Paradigm Reveals Long-Term Memory in Planaria and Its Persistence Through Head Regeneration." *Journal of Experimental Biology* 217, no. 20 (October 2013): http://jeb.biologists.org/content/early/2013/06/27/jeb.087809.

Sider Jost, Jacob. *Prose Immortality, 1711–1819.* Charlottesville: University of Virginia Press, 2015.

Silver, Sean. *The Mind Is a Collection: Case Studies in Eighteenth-Century Thought.* Philadelphia: University of Pennsylvania Press, 2015.

Sloan, Phillip R. "The Buffon-Linnaeus Controversy." *Isis* 67 (1976): 356–75.

Spary, E. C. *Utopia's Garden: French Natural History from Old Regime to Revolution.* Chicago: University of Chicago Press, 2000.

Stalnaker, Joanna. "Emotions, Mortality, and Vitality: Two *Salonnières-Philosophes* Facing Death." In *A Cultural History of Death: In the Age of Enlightenment,* edited by Jeffrey Freedman, 67–88. London: Bloomsbury Academic, 2024.

———. "Jonathan Israel in Dialogue." *Journal of the History of Ideas* 77, no. 4 (October 2016): 637–48.

Standish, Frank Hall. *The Life of Voltaire: With Interesting Particulars Respecting His Death, and Anecdotes and Characters of His Contemporaries.* London: John Andrews, 1821.

Stanley, Liz. "The Writing of David Hume's *My Own Life:* The Persona of the Philosopher and the Philosopher Manqué." *Auto/Biography* 14 (2006): 320–38.

Starobinski, Jean. "Diderot et la parole des autres." *Critique* 296 (January 1972): 3–22.

———. *Diderot, un diable de ramage.* Paris: Gallimard, 2012.

———. *Jean-Jacques Rousseau, La transparence et l'obstacle. Suivi de sept essais sur Rousseau.* Paris: Gallimard, 1971.

Stewart, Joan Hinde. *The Enlightenment of Age: Women, Letters, and Growing Old in Eighteenth-Century France.* Foreword by Joan Dejean. Studies on Voltaire and the Eighteenth Century 2010, no. 9. Oxford: Voltaire Foundation, 2010.

Strachey, Lytton. "Madame du Deffand." *Edinburgh Review* (1913): 61–80.

Strugnell, Anthony. *Diderot's Politics: A Study of the Evolution of Diderot's Political Thought after the* Encyclopédie. The Hague: Nijhoff, 1973.

Toynbee, Paget. "Mme du Deffand and Hume." *Modern Language Review* 24 (January 1929): 447–51.

Trousson, Raymond. "Rousseau, sa mort et son œuvre dans la littérature périodique en 1778." *Revue internationale de philosophie* 32 (1978): 177–96.

Troyansky, David G. *Entitlement and Complaint: Ending Careers and Reviewing Lives in Post-Revolutionary France.* Oxford: Oxford University Press, 2023.

Tunstall, Kate E. *Blindness and Enlightenment: An Essay.* New York: Continuum, 2011.

———. "The Early Modern Embodied Mind and the Entomological Imaginary." In *Mind, Body, Motion, Matter: Eighteenth-Century British and French Literary Perspectives,* edited by Mary Helen McMurran and Alison Conway, 202–29. Toronto: University of Toronto Press, 2016.

———. "Paradoxe sur le portrait: Autoportrait de Diderot en Montaigne." *Diderot Studies* 30 (2007): 195–207.

Vartanian, Aram. "The Enigma of Diderot's "Eléments de physiologie." *Diderot Studies* 10 (1968): 285–301.

Vendler, Helen. *Last Looks, Last Books: Stevens, Plath, Lowell, Bishop, Merrill.* Princeton: Princeton University Press, 2010.

Venturi, Franco. "La vieillesse de Diderot." *Recherches sur Diderot et sur l'Encyclopédie* 13 (1992): 9–30.

Vovelle, Michel. *La mort et l'Occident de 1300 à nos jours.* 1983. New ed., Paris: Gallimard, 2000.

———. *Mourir autrefois: Attitudes collectives devant la mort aux XVIIe et XVIIIe siècles.* Paris: Gallimard, 1974.

Warman, Caroline. *The Atheist's Bible: Diderot and the* Éléments de physiologie. Cambridge: Open Book, 2020.

Williams, Elizabeth A. *A Cultural History of Medical Vitalism in Enlightenment Montpellier.* The History of Medicine in Context. Aldershot, U.K.: Ashgate, 2003.

———. *The Physical and the Moral: Anthropology, Physiology, and Philosophical Medicine in France, 1750–1850.* Cambridge History of Medicine. Cambridge: Cambridge University Press, 1994.

Wilson, Arthur M. *Diderot.* New York: Oxford University Press, 1972.

Wilson, Stephen. "Death and the Social Historians: Some Recent Books in French and English." *Social History* 5, no. 3 (October 1980): 435–51.

Wolfe, Charles T. *Materialism: A Historico-Philosophical Introduction.* SpringerBriefs in Philosophy. Heidelberg: Springer Cham, 2016.

Wolin, Richard. "Introduction to the Symposium on Jonathan Israel's *Democratic Enlightenment.*" *Journal of the History of Ideas* 77, no. 4 (October 2016): 615–26.

Index